PEARSON EDEXCEL INTERNATIONAL GCSE (9–1)
ACCOUNTING
Student Book

James Haigh
Sheila Robinson with Frank Wood

Published by Pearson Education Limited, 80 Strand, London, WC2R 0RL.

www.pearsonglobalschools.com

Copies of official specifications for all Edexcel qualifications may be found on the website: https://qualifications.pearson.com

Text © Pearson Education Limited 2018
Edited by Lucy Stratton, Andrew Lowe, Jenny Hunt and Stephen Cunningham
Designed by Cobalt id
Typeset by Tech-Set Ltd, Gateshead, UK
Original illustrations © Pearson Education Limited 2018
Illustrated by © Cobalt id
Cover design by Pearson Education Limited
Cover photo/illustration Blend Images / Alamy Stock Photo
Inside front cover: **shutterstock.com:** Dmitry Lobanov

The rights of James Haigh, Sheila Robinson and Frank Wood to be identified as the authors of this work have been asserted in accordance with the Copyright, Designs and Patents Act 1988.

First published 2018

21 20 19 18
10 9 8 7 6 5 4 3 2 1

British Library Cataloguing in Publication Data
A catalogue record for this book is available from the British Library

ISBN 978 0 435189 65 5

Copyright notice
All rights reserved. No part of this publication may be reproduced in any form or by any means (including photocopying or storing it in any medium by electronic means and whether or not transiently or incidentally to some other use of this publication) without the written permission of the copyright owner, except in accordance with the provisions of the Copyright, Designs and Patents Act 1988 or under the terms of a licence issued by the Copyright Licensing Agency, Barnard's Inn, 86 Fetter Lane, London EC4A 1EN (www.cla.co.uk). Applications for the copyright owner's written permission should be addressed to the publisher.

Acknowledgements
The authors and publisher would like to thank the following individuals and organisations for permission to reproduce photographs:
(Key: b-bottom; c-centre; l-left; r-right; t-top)
123RF.com: convisum 36tl, gjee 4bl, michaeljung 4tl; **Alamy Stock Photo:** Bruce MCGowan 183tl, Cultura Creative (RF) 147cl, Image Source Plus 146tl, Jacopo de' Barbari Portrait of Fra Luca Pacioli and an Unknown Young Man WGA1269 / Art Collection 3 61cl, Jordi Boixareu / The Passenger 80bl, Jose Luis Pelaez Inc / Blend Images 100tl, Peter Forsberg / Shopping 117t, PhotosIndia.com RM 14 223cr, STOCK4B GmbH / Alamy 206tl, Supernova / Gallo Images 221tc, Tim Gainey 148l, View Stock 18tr; **Getty Images:** Bill Bachmann / age photostock 7tl, Bloomberg 234cr, Peter Stuckings / Lonely Planet Images 203tc, Stuart Kinlough / IKON Images 2, 26, 98, 144, VikramRaghuvanshi / Vetta 155l; Shutterstock.com: Andrii Koval 217tl, arnet117 60tl, Cenz07 228bl, create jobs 51 152tl, Digital Storm 28tl, imtmphoto 11tl, Jambals 228b, Karashaev 193c, kurhan 5b, Lisa S. 132tl, Marco Richter 184bc, Maridav 147bc, Monkey Business Images 20tl, nd3000 31cl, 158tl, Popovic Dragan 154bc, PORTRAIT IMAGES ASIA BY NONWARIT 169tl, Pressmaster 16tr, SasinTipchai 228tl, Speedkingz 190tl, Syda Productions 147cr, Vlad Teodor 228cl, wavebreakmedia 108tl, wrangler 86tl, 121tl, wxin 149bc, ymgerman 9tr, Yorkman 138t
All other images © Pearson Education

We are grateful to the following for permission to reproduce copyright material:

Figures
Figure on page 20 adapted from https://www.app.college.police.uk/app-content/national-decision-model/the-national-decision-model/, The National Decision Model is © College of Policing licensed under the Open Government Licence v3.0.

Select glossary terms have been taken from *The Longman Dictionary of Contemporary English Online*.

Endorsement Statement
In order to ensure that this resource offers high-quality support for the associated Pearson qualification, it has been through a review process by the awarding body. This process confirms that this resource fully covers the teaching and learning content of the specification or part of a specification at which it is aimed. It also confirms that it demonstrates an appropriate balance between the development of subject skills, knowledge and understanding, in addition to preparation for assessment.

Endorsement does not cover any guidance on assessment activities or processes (e.g. practice questions or advice on how to answer assessment questions), included in the resource nor does it prescribe any particular approach to the teaching or delivery of a related course.

While the publishers have made every attempt to ensure that advice on the qualification and its assessment is accurate, the official specification and associated assessment guidance materials are the only authoritative source of information and should always be referred to for definitive guidance.

Pearson examiners have not contributed to any sections in this resource relevant to examination papers for which they have responsibility.

Examiners will not use endorsed resources as a source of material for any assessment set by Pearson. Endorsement of a resource does not mean that the resource is required to achieve this Pearson qualification, nor does it mean that it is the only suitable material available to support the qualification, and any resource lists produced by the awarding body shall include this and other appropriate resources.

CONTENTS

COURSE STRUCTURE	IV
ABOUT THIS BOOK	VI
ASSESSMENT OVERVIEW	VIII
1 THE ACCOUNTING ENVIRONMENT	2
2 INTRODUCTION TO BOOKKEEPING	26
3 INTRODUCTION TO CONTROL PROCESSES	98
4 THE PREPARATION OF FINANCIAL STATEMENTS AND END OF PERIOD ADJUSTMENTS	144
GLOSSARY	236
ACCOUNTING STANDARDS TERMINOLOGY	238
INDEX	239

COURSE STRUCTURE

UNIT 1 THE ACCOUNTING ENVIRONMENT

1 TYPES OF BUSINESS ORGANISATION   4
1.1 SOLE TRADER
1.2 PARTNERSHIP
1.3 PRIVATE SECTOR ORGANISATIONS
1.4 PUBLIC SECTOR ORGANISATIONS

2 USE OF TECHNOLOGY IN ACCOUNTING   11
2.1 INTRODUCTION TO TECHNOLOGY IN ACCOUNTING
2.2 FUNCTIONS OF ACCOUNTING SOFTWARE
2.3. ADVANTAGES AND DISADVANTAGES OF ACCOUNTING SOFTWARE
2.4 DATA LOSS
2.5 SECURITY

3 PROFESSIONAL ETHICS AND INTRODUCTION TO ACCOUNTING CONCEPTS   20
3.1 THE PRINCIPLES OF PROFESSIONAL ETHICS
3.2 ACCOUNTING ROLES AND FUNCTIONS
3.3 PUBLIC INTEREST
3.4 INTRODUCTION TO ACCOUNTING CONCEPTS

UNIT 2 INTRODUCTION TO BOOKKEEPING

4 BUSINESS DOCUMENTATION   28
4.1 INTRODUCTION TO BUSINESS DOCUMENTATION
4.2 PURCHASE ORDER
4.3 INVOICE
4.4 CREDIT NOTE
4.5 STATEMENT OF ACCOUNT
4.6 REMITTANCE ADVICE
4.7 RECEIPTS

5 BOOKS OF ORIGINAL ENTRY   36
5.1 BOOKS OF ORIGINAL ENTRY
5.2 THE LEDGERS
5.3 CLASSIFICATION OF ACCOUNTS
5.4 PURCHASE INVOICES
5.5 CASH AND CREDIT REVENUE
5.6 PURCHASE RETURNS (RETURNS OUTWARDS) AND PURCHASE CREDIT NOTES
5.7 SALES RETURNS (RETURNS INWARDS) AND PURCHASE RETURNS (RETURNS OUTWARDS)
5.8 SALES RETURNS (RETURNS INWARDS) AND CREDIT NOTES
5.9 CASH DISCOUNTS
5.10 BANK OVERDRAFTS AND THE CASH BOOK
5.11 THE JOURNAL
5.12 WRITING UP JOURNAL ENTRIES

6 LEDGER ACCOUNTING AND DOUBLE ENTRY BOOKKEEPING   60
6.1 THE LEDGERS
6.2 INTRODUCTION AND HISTORY OF THE DOUBLE ENTRY SYSTEM OF ACCOUNTING
6.3 THE DOUBLE ENTRY SYSTEM
6.4 RULES FOR DOUBLE ENTRY
6.5 THE IN AND OUT APPROACH
6.6 T ACCOUNTS
6.7 WORKED EXAMPLES: CASH TRANSACTIONS
6.8 INTRODUCTION TO CREDIT TRANSACTIONS
6.9 PURCHASE OF INVENTORY ON CREDIT
6.10 REVENUE OF INVENTORY ON CREDIT
6.11 RETURNS
6.12 EXPENSES ON CREDIT
6.13 WORKED EXAMPLE
6.14 REVENUE AND PURCHASES
6.15 COMPARISON OF CASH AND CREDIT TRANSACTIONS FOR PURCHASES AND REVENUE
6.16 BALANCING THE ACCOUNTS
6.17 THREE-COLUMN ACCOUNTS
6.18 WORKED EXAMPLE
6.19 ERRORS NOT REVEALED BY THE DOUBLE ENTRY SYSTEM

7 DEPRECIATION   86
7.1 CAUSES OF DEPRECIATION
7.2 METHODS OF CALCULATING DEPRECIATION CHARGES
7.3 RECORDING DEPRECIATION
7.4 THE DISPOSAL OF A NON-CURRENT ASSET

UNIT 3 INTRODUCTION TO CONTROL PROCESSES

8 TRIAL BALANCE   100
8.1 BALANCING OFF
8.2 THE TRIAL BALANCE
8.3 WORKED EXAMPLE
8.4 STEPS TO TAKE IF THE TRIAL BALANCE DOES NOT BALANCE

9 CORRECTION OF ERRORS   108
9.1 ERRORS NOT REVEALED BY A TRIAL BALANCE
9.2 ERRORS NOT AFFECTING TRIAL BALANCE AGREEMENT
9.3 ERRORS AFFECTING TRIAL BALANCE AGREEMENT

10 CONTROL ACCOUNTS   121
10.1 THE PRINCIPLE OF CONTROL ACCOUNTS

COURSE STRUCTURE

10.2 EXAMPLE: A TRADE RECEIVABLES LEDGER CONTROL ACCOUNT
10.3 INFORMATION FOR CONTROL ACCOUNTS
10.4 FURTHER EXAMPLES
10.5 OTHER TRANSFERS
10.6 CONTROL ACCOUNTS AND COMPUTERISED ACCOUNTING SYSTEMS
10.7 ADVANTAGES OF CONTROL ACCOUNTS
10.8 DISADVANTAGES OF CONTROL ACCOUNTS

11 BANK RECONCILIATION STATEMENTS 132
11.1 INTRODUCTION TO RECORDING TRANSACTIONS
11.2 REASONS FOR DIFFERENT BALANCES
11.3 UPDATING THE CASH BOOK BEFORE ATTEMPTING A RECONCILIATION
11.4 BANK OVERDRAFTS
11.5 DISHONOURED CHEQUES
11.6 OTHER REASONS FOR DIFFERENCES IN THE BALANCES

UNIT 4 THE PREPARATION OF FINANCIAL STATEMENTS AND END OF PERIOD ADJUSTMENTS

12 CAPITAL AND REVENUE EXPENDITURE 146
12.1 CAPITAL EXPENDITURE
12.2 REVENUE EXPENDITURE
12.3 DIFFERENCE BETWEEN EQUITY AND REVENUE EXPENDITURE
12.4 INCORRECT TREATMENT OF EXPENDITURE

13 ACCOUNTING CONCEPTS 152
13.1 DEFINITION OF ACCOUNTING CONCEPTS
13.2 FUNDAMENTAL ACCOUNTING CONCEPTS

14 FINANCIAL STATEMENTS OF A SOLE TRADER 158
14.1 INTRODUCTION TO THE INCOME STATEMENT
14.2 USES OF THE INCOME STATEMENT
14.3 PREPARATION OF AN INCOME STATEMENT
14.4 DEFINITION AND CONTENT OF A STATEMENT OF FINANCIAL POSITION
14.5 LAYOUT OF THE STATEMENT OF FINANCIAL POSITION LAYOUT

15 OTHER RECEIVABLES AND PAYABLES 169
15.1 ADJUSTMENTS NEEDED FOR EXPENSES OWING AND EXPENSES PAID IN ADVANCE
15.2 OTHER PAYABLES
15.3 OTHER RECEIVABLES
15.4 ADJUSTMENT FOR INVENTORY OF STATIONERY ETC. CARRIED FORWARD
15.5 REVENUE OWING AT THE END OF PERIOD
15.6 EXPENSES AND REVENUE ACCOUNT BALANCES AND THE STATEMENT OF FINANCIAL POSITION
15.7 WORKED EXAMPLE: FINANCIAL STATEMENTS FOR A SOLE TRADER
15.8 STEP-BY-STEP GUIDE: DEALING WITH FURTHER ADJUSTMENTS TO FINANCIAL STATEMENTS

16 IRRECOVERABLE DEBTS 183
16.1 IRRECOVERABLE DEBTS
16.2 ALLOWANCE FOR IRRECOVERABLE DEBT

17 INCOMPLETE RECORDS 190
17.1 PREPARING FINANCIAL STATEMENTS FROM INCOMPLETE RECORDS
17.2 STEP-BY-STEP GUIDE: INCOMPLETE RECORDS
17.3 INCOMPLETE RECORDS AND MISSING FIGURES

18 THE CALCULATION AND INTERPRETATION OF ACCOUNTING RATIOS 206
18.1 PROFITABILITY AND LIQUIDITY
18.2 PROFITABILITY RATIOS
18.3 LIQUIDITY RATIOS
18.4 DEFINITION OF WORKING CAPITAL
18.5 WORKED EXAMPLE: CALCULATING RATIOS
18.6 LIMITATIONS OF RATIOS

19 FINANCIAL STATEMENTS OF A PARTNERSHIP 217
19.1 THE NEED FOR PARTNERSHIPS
19.2 LIMITED PARTNERS
19.3 NATURE OF A PARTNERSHIP
19.4 WHERE NO PARTNERSHIP AGREEMENT EXISTS
19.5 THE FINANCIAL STATEMENTS
19.6 WORKED EXAMPLE: APPROPRIATION ACCOUNT
19.7 CURRENT ACCOUNTS

20 FINANCIAL STATEMENTS OF A MANUFACTURER 228
20.1 DIRECT AND INDIRECT COSTS
20.2 FORMAT OF FINANCIAL STATEMENTS
20.3 WORKED EXAMPLE: A MANUFACTURING ACCOUNT

ABOUT THIS BOOK

This book is written for students following the Pearson Edexcel International GCSE (9–1) Accounting specification.

The course has been structured to support logical progression in teaching and learning, both in the classroom and in independent learning, as well as to support the exam specification. The book contains four units that cover all areas of content in the specification. The introductory text at the beginning of each unit details how students will need to apply their learning for the different parts of the exam.

Each unit is split into multiple chapters to break down content into manageable chunks and to ensure full coverage of the specification. Each chapter features a mix of learning and activities. Global case studies are embedded throughout and require students to practise a range of techniques presented in the chapter. Summary questions at the end of each chapter help to put learning into practice.

There are also exam-style questions at the end of each chapter.

A comparison of the International Finance Reporting Standards (IFRS) terminology and the UK GAAP (Generally Accepted Accounting Practice in the UK) terminology is included in the back of the book. IFRS terminology is used in the Pearson Edexcel International GCSE (9–1) Accounting qualification. Centres should be aware that these terms are also referred to as International Accounting Standards (IAS) in certain contexts within the industry. However, the definitions and meaning remain the same.

Learning objectives
These chapter-by-chapter objectives are carefully tailored to address key assessment objectives central to the course.

Getting started
An introduction to the chapter, letting you think about the concepts you will be introduced to. Activities are designed to stimulate discussion and prior knowledge. These can be tackled as individuals, pairs, groups or the whole class.

Key points
Core information is made easy to understand.

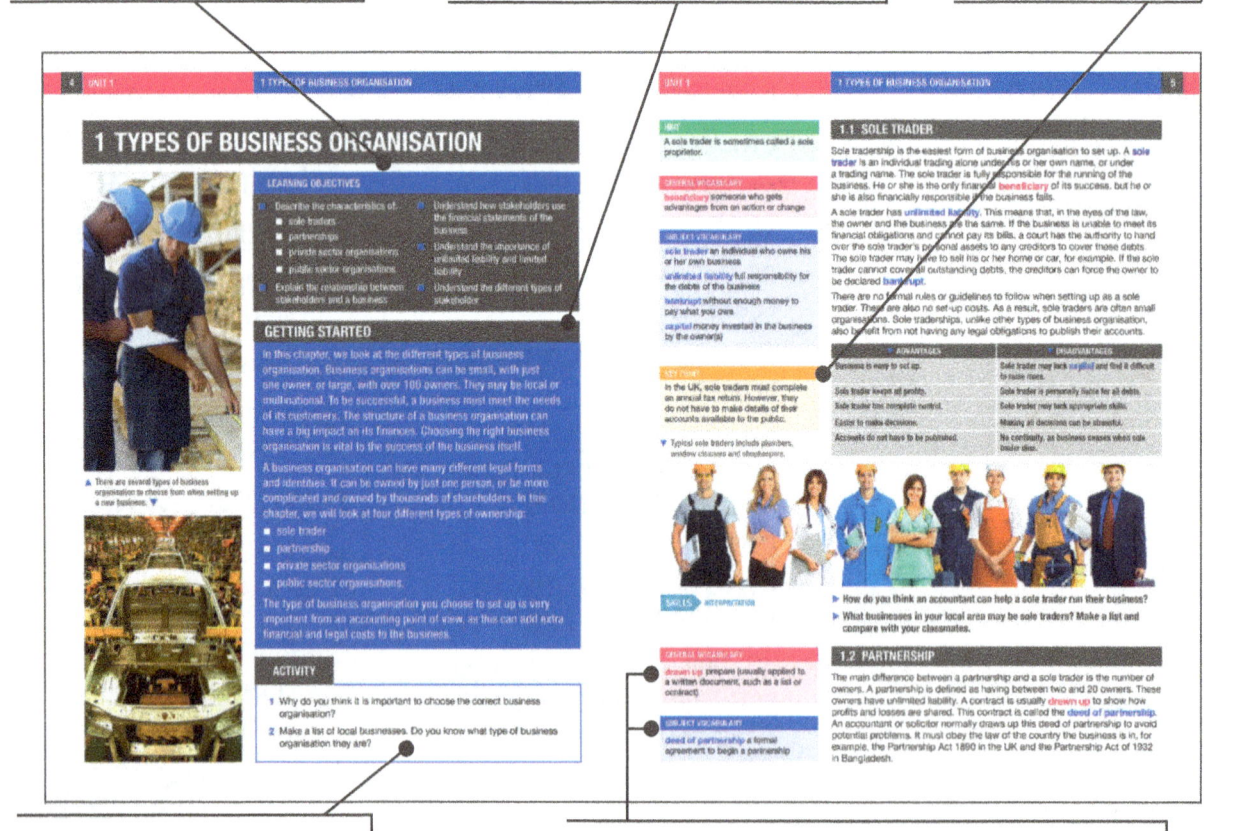

Activities
Each chapter includes activities to embed understanding through case studies and questions.

Subject vocabulary and General vocabulary
Useful words and phrases are colour coded within the main text and picked out in the margin with concise and simple definitions. These help understanding of key subject terms and support students whose first language is not English.

ABOUT THIS BOOK

Case studies
Case studies drawn from a range of large and small businesses from around the world will help you to apply your learning to real-world contexts.

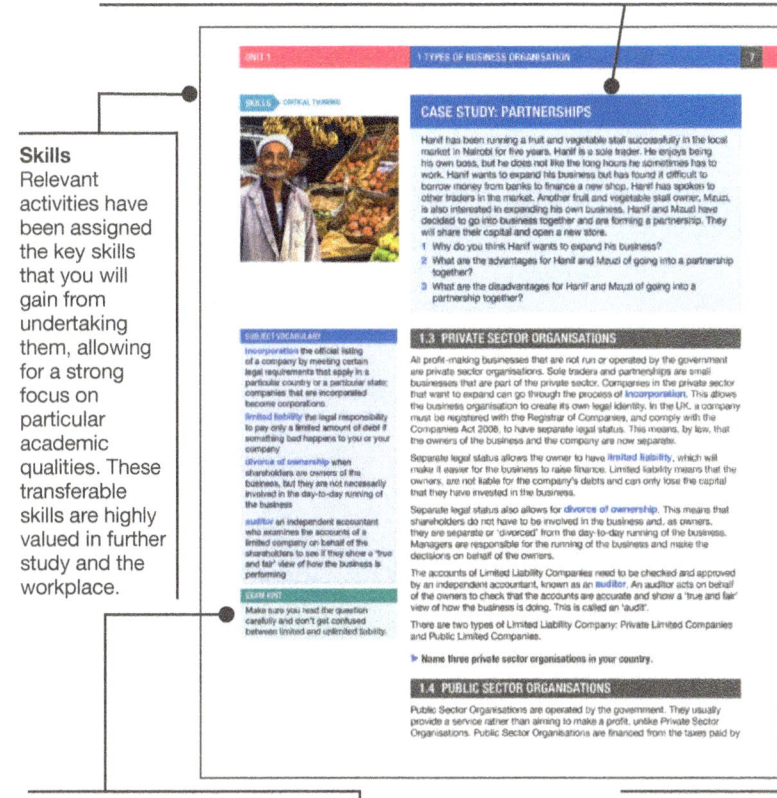

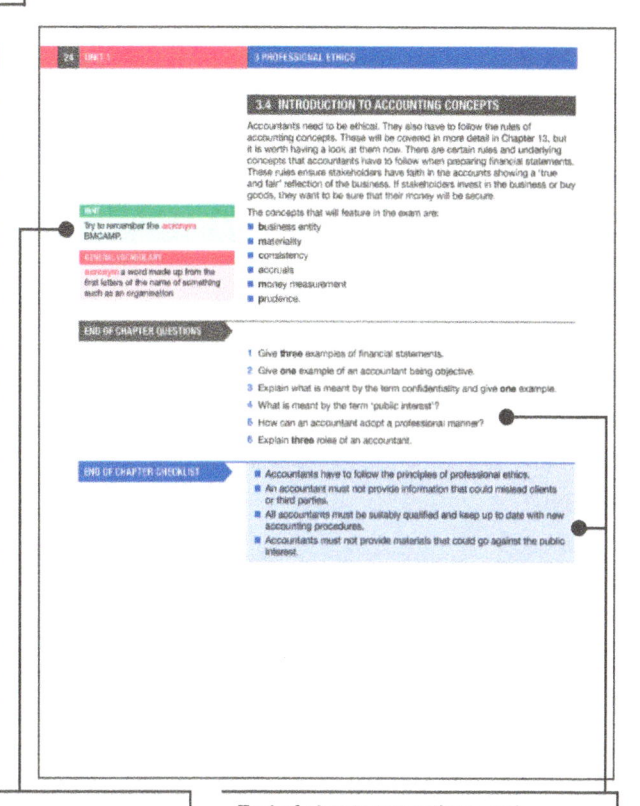

Skills
Relevant activities have been assigned the key skills that you will gain from undertaking them, allowing for a strong focus on particular academic qualities. These transferable skills are highly valued in further study and the workplace.

Exam hints
These boxes give you tips on importantn points to remember in your examination.

Hints
These provide aids for learning and also give notes about differences in terminology or variations in accounting standards.

End of chapter questions and checklist
Revision questions and a summary of the chapter's key points help to consolidate learning.

Assessment objectives
Questions are tagged with the relevant assessment objectives that are being examined.

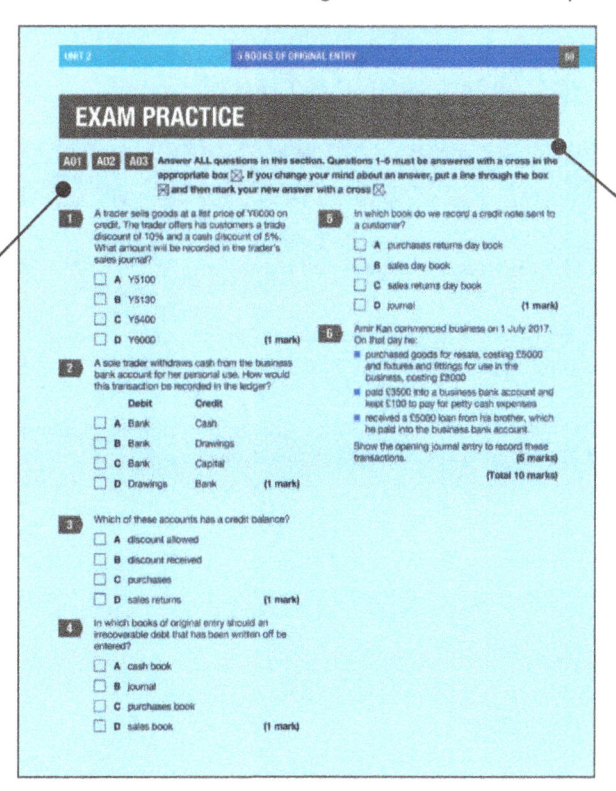

Exam practice
These exam-style questions are found at the end of each chapter. They are tailored to the Pearson Edexcel (9–1) specification to allow for practice and development of exam technique.

ASSESSMENT OVERVIEW

The following tables give an overview of the assessment for this course. You should study this information closely to help ensure that you are fully prepared for this course and know exactly what to expect in each part of the assessment.

PAPER 1	PERCENTAGE	MARK	TIME	AVAILABILITY
INTRODUCTION TO BOOKKEEPING AND ACCOUNTING Written exam paper Paper code 4AC1/01 Externally set and assessed by Pearson Edexcel Single tier of entry	60%	100	2 hours	June exam series First assessment June 2019

PAPER 2	PERCENTAGE	MARK	TIME	AVAILABILITY
FINANCIAL STATEMENTS Written exam paper Paper code 4AC1/02 Externally set and assessed by Pearson Edexcel Single tier of entry	40%	50	1 hour 15 minutes	June exam series First assessment June 2019

ASSESSMENT OBJECTIVES AND WEIGHTINGS

ASSESSMENT OBJECTIVE	DESCRIPTION	% IN INTERNATIONAL GCSE
AO1	Demonstrate a knowledge and understanding of accounting terminology, principles, procedures and techniques	35–40%
AO2	Select and apply their knowledge and understanding of accounting procedures to a variety of accounting problems	41–47%
AO3	Analyse, evaluate and present information in appropriate accounting formats and communicate reasoned explanations	17–20%

ASSESSMENT OVERVIEW

RELATIONSHIP OF ASSESSMENT OBJECTIVES TO UNITS

UNIT NUMBER	ASSESSMENT OBJECTIVE		
	AO1	AO2	AO3
PAPER 1	25–28%	23–25%	9–10%
PAPER 2	11–12%	19–21%	8–9%
TOTAL FOR INTERNATIONAL GCSE	36–40%	42–46%	17–19%

ASSESSMENT SUMMARY

PAPER 1	DESCRIPTION	MARKS	ASSESSMENT OBJECTIVES
INTRODUCTION TO BOOKKEEPING AND ACCOUNTING PAPER CODE 4AC1/01	**Structure** Paper 1 assesses 60 % of the total Accounting qualification. The examination comprises a mixture of multiple-choice, short- and long-answer questions, and is presented in two sections. Students must answer all questions. **Section A** comprises 10 1-mark multiple-choice questions and three short-answer questions worth 5 marks each. **Section B** comprises five multi-part questions worth 15 marks each. **Content summary** Students must study **all** of the following topics: Topic 1: The accounting environment Topic 2: Introduction to bookkeeping Topic 3: Introduction to control processes. **Assessment** This is a single-tier exam paper and all questions cover the full ranges of grades from 9–1. The assessment duration is 2 hours Calculators may be used in the examination.	The total number of marks available is 100	Questions will test the following Assessment Objectives: AO1 – 25–28% AO2 – 23–25% AO3 – 9–10%

PAPER 2	DESCRIPTION	MARKS	ASSESSMENT OBJECTIVES
FINANCIAL STATEMENTS PAPER CODE 4AC1/02	**Structure** Paper 2 assesses 40 % of the total Accounting qualification. Students must answer all questions. The examination comprises two multi-part questions focusing on the preparation, analysis or evaluation of financial statements. **Content summary** Students must study **both** of the following topics: Topic 4: The preparation of financial statements Topic 5: Accounting for end of period adjustments. **Assessment** This is a single-tier exam paper and all questions cover the full ranges of grades from 9–1. The assessment duration is 1 hour 30 minutes. Calculators may be used in the examination.	The total number of marks available is 50	Questions will test the following Assessment Objectives: AO1 – 11–12% AO2 – 19–21% AO3 – 8–9%

EDEXCEL INTERNATIONAL GCSE (9–1)
GEOGRAPHY
Student Book: Teacher Resource Pack

- Resources follow the teaching order of the Student Book and provide answers to the chapter questions.

- Easy-to-follow **lesson plans** save you valuable planning time.

- **Worksheets** give you additional ready-to-use activities.

- Guidance on the **Fieldwork** requirement of the course with exemplars.

- Sample questions and model answers in **exam practice Powerpoints** teach you and your students how to succeed in the exam.

- Prepare for exam success with **practice exam papers** and mark schemes.

P Pearson

CONTENTS

STUDENT BOOK ANSWERS .... PAGE 1

LESSON PLANS .... PAGE 1

WORKSHEETS .... PAGE 1

FIELDWORK PRACTICALS .... PAGE 2

PRACTICE EXAM PAPERS .... PAGE 2

EXAM PRACTICE POWERPOINTS ... PAGE 2

SCHEME OF WORK.................. PAGE 2

STUDENT BOOK TEACHER RESOURCE PACK

STUDENT BOOK ANSWERS

LESSON PLANS

Chapter 1: River environments

Chapter 2: Coastal environments

Chapter 3: Hazardous environments

Chapter 4: Economic activity and energy

Chapter 5: Rural environments

Chapter 6: Urban environments

Chapter 7: Fragile environments and climate change

Chapter 8: Globalisation and migration

Chapter 9: Development and human welfare

WORKSHEETS

River environments

Coastal environments

Hazardous environments

Economic activity and energy

Rural environments

Urban environments

Fragile environments and climate change

Globalisation and migration

Development and human welfare

FIELDWORK PRACTICALS

Rural environments

Economic activity and energy

Hazardous environments

Urban environments

Coastal environments

River environments

PRACTICE EXAM PAPERS

Paper 1: Physical geography paper

Physical geography paper resource booklet

Physical geography paper mark scheme

Paper 2: Human geography paper

Human geography paper resource booklet

Human geography paper mark scheme

EXAM PRACTICE POWERPOINTS

SCHEME OF WORK

STUDENT BOOK TEACHER RESOURCE PACK

Published by Pearson Education Limited, 80 Strand, London, WC2R 0RL.

www.pearsonglobalschools.com

Copies of official specifications for all Edexcel qualifications may be found on the website: qualifications.pearson.com

Text © Pearson Education Limited 2017
Cover design by Pearson Education Ltd
Cover photo © Getty images: wiratgasem

The rights of Michael Chiles and Alison Barraclough to be identified as authors of this work have been asserted by them in accordance with the Copyright, Designs and Patents Act 1988.

The publisher would like to thank the following for their kind permission to reproduce their photographs:

Key: b-bottom; c-centre; l-left; r-right; t-top)

Alamy Stock Photo: Adam Burton FW 5.1-pg3, Derek Croucher MP 1-2b, geogphotos 1-1b, Juice Images FW 6.2-pg2, keith morris FW 4.1-pg2, Michael Pearcy FW 6.1-pg2, Nigel Sawtell WK 8-Fig2, Paul Wood RB 1- Fig 3cl, Phil Hill Geo Pics FW 5.1-pg2, Rob Rayworth WK 23-Fig 1, ton koene WK 27-Fig 2, US Navy Photo RB 1-Fig 1cl, RB 1-Fig 3cr, VIEW Pictures Ltd WK 10-Fig 1; Getty Images: Jodi Cobb / National Geographic WK 17-Fig 2; Pearson Education Ltd: RB 2-Fig 2c, RB 2-Fig 7a, Oxford Designers & Illustrators Ltd. Pearson Education Ltd RB 2-Fig 7c, Arvind Singh Negi/Red Reef Design Studio. Pearson India Education Services Pvt. Ltd RB 2-Fig 9c; Shutterstock.com: CHULKOVA NINA RB2-Fig9a, creativeoneuk RB 2-Fig 3a, Doctor Jools RB 2-Fig 3c, ES_SO WK 18-Fig 1, DAK RB 2-Fig 2a, iQoncept RB 2-Fig 8c, vectorlib.com RB 2-Fig1a, zeber RB 2- Fig 8a

All other images © Pearson Education

First published 2017

ISBN 978 0 435 19122 1

Copyright notice

All rights reserved. The material in this publication is copyright. Activity sheets may be freely photocopied for classroom use in the purchasing institution. However, this material is copyright and under no circumstances may copies be offered for sale. If you wish to use the material in any way other than that specified you must apply in writing to the publishers.

The resource contains editable Word files. Pearson Education Limited cannot accept responsibility for the quality, accuracy or fitness for purpose of the materials contained in the Word files once edited. To revert to the original Word files, re-load from the resource.

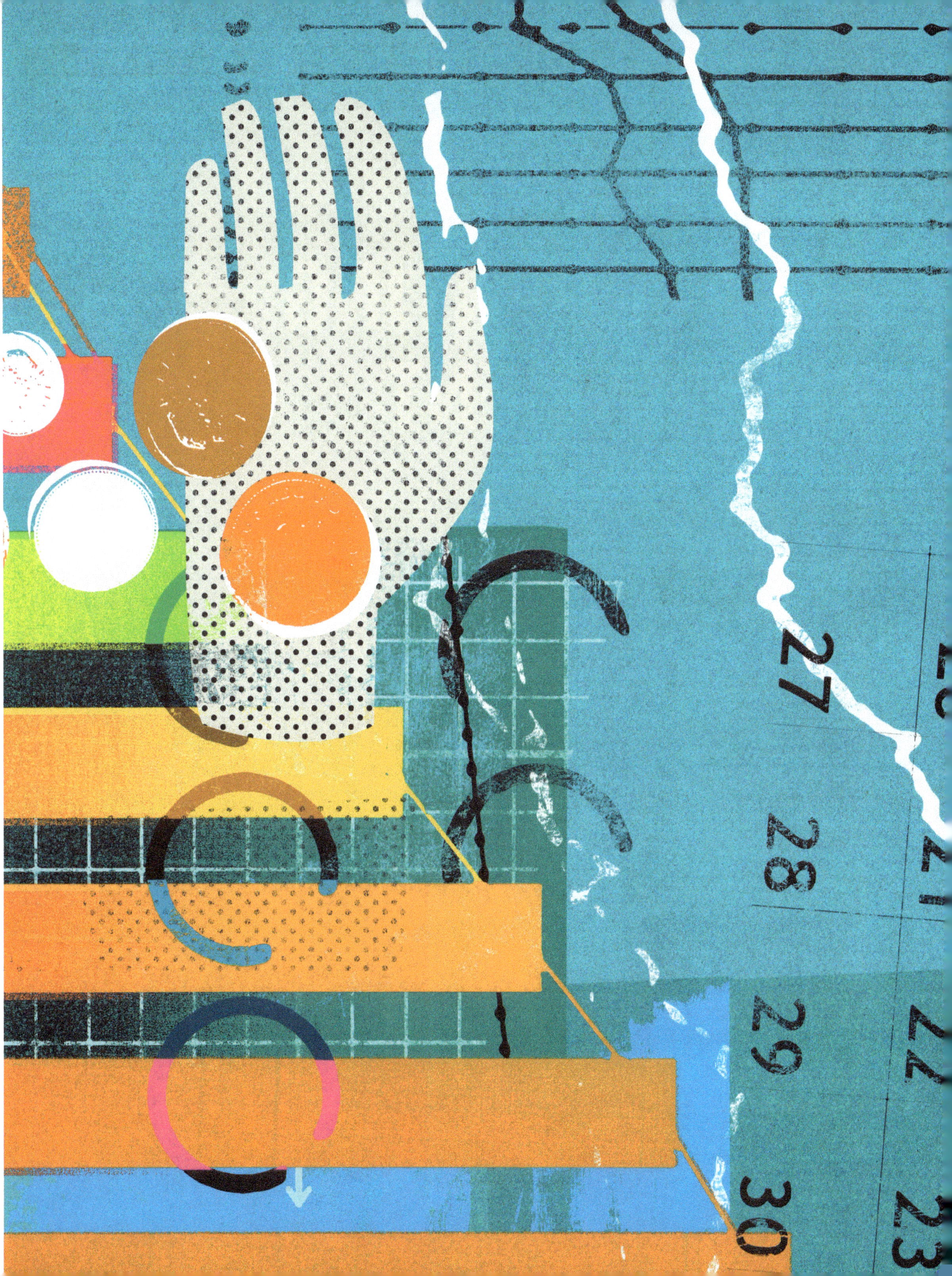
27
28
29
30
22
23

1 TYPES OF BUSINESS ORGANISATION | 4   2 USE OF TECHNOLOGY IN ACCOUNTING | 11   3 PROFESSIONAL ETHICS | 20

UNIT 1
THE ACCOUNTING ENVIRONMENT

Assessment Objective AO1

Demonstrate a knowledge and understanding of accounting terminology, principles, procedures and techniques

Assessment Objective AO2

Select and apply their knowledge and understanding of accounting procedures to a variety of accounting problems

Assessment Objective AO3

Analyse, evaluate and present information in appropriate accounting formats and communicate reasoned explanations

Unit 1 explains the different types of organisation a business can have and covers some key concepts you need to understand to work in the accounting environment. Technology is increasingly important in the field of accounting and this unit covers the benefits of technology as well as some of the main difficulties, such as data security and confidentiality.

The unit also explains the concept of professional ethics, which is vital on both an individual level and a company level.

This unit will be examined in Paper 1 of the examination, 'Introduction to Bookkeeping and Accounting'. You will need to answer a mixture of multiple choice and short- and long-answer questions. These questions will test your ability to meet the Assessment Objectives for this unit. You will also need to have a good understanding of this unit to be able to answer the questions in Paper 2.

1 TYPES OF BUSINESS ORGANISATION

LEARNING OBJECTIVES

- Describe the characteristics of:
  - sole traders
  - partnerships
  - private sector organisations
  - public sector organisations
- Explain the relationship between stakeholders and a business
- Understand how stakeholders use the financial statements of the business
- Understand the importance of unlimited liability and limited liability
- Understand the different types of stakeholder

GETTING STARTED

In this chapter, we look at the different types of business organisation. Business organisations can be small, with just one owner, or large, with over 100 owners. They may be local or multinational. To be successful, a business must meet the needs of its customers. The structure of a business organisation can have a big impact on its finances. Choosing the right business organisation is vital to the success of the business itself.

A business organisation can have many different legal forms and identities. It can be owned by just one person, or be more complicated and owned by thousands of owners. In this chapter, we will look at four different types of ownership:

- sole trader
- partnership
- private sector organisations
- public sector organisations.

The type of business organisation you choose to set up is very important from an accounting point of view, as this can add extra financial and legal costs to the business.

▲ There are several types of business organisation to choose from when setting up a new business. ▼

ACTIVITY

1 Why do you think it is important to choose the correct business organisation?

2 Make a list of local businesses. Do you know what type of business organisation they are?

UNIT 1 — 1 TYPES OF BUSINESS ORGANISATION

HINT
A sole trader is sometimes called a sole proprietor.

GENERAL VOCABULARY
beneficiary someone who gets advantages from an action or change

SUBJECT VOCABULARY
sole trader an individual who owns his or her own business

unlimited liability full responsibility for the debts of the business

bankruptcy when someone is judged to be unable to pay their liabilities by a court of law

capital or equity money invested in the business by the owner(s)

KEY POINT
In the UK, sole traders must complete an annual tax return. However, they do not have to make details of their accounts available to the public.

1.1 SOLE TRADER

Sole tradership is the easiest form of business organisation to set up. A **sole trader** is an individual trading alone under his or her own name, or under a trading name. The sole trader is fully responsible for the running of the business. He or she is the only financial **beneficiary** of its success, but he or she is also financially responsible if the business fails.

A sole trader has **unlimited liability**. This means that, in the eyes of the law, the owner and the business are the same. If the business is unable to meet its financial obligations and cannot pay its bills, a court has the authority to hand over the sole trader's personal assets to cover these debts. The sole trader may have to sell his or her home or car, for example. If the sole trader cannot cover all outstanding debts, the sole trader may be forced to declare him or herself **bankrupt**.

There are no formal rules or guidelines to follow when setting up as a sole trader. There are also no set-up costs. As a result, sole traders are often small organisations. Sole tradships, unlike other types of business organisation, also benefit from not having any legal obligations to publish their accounts.

▼ ADVANTAGES	▼ DISADVANTAGES
Business is easy to set up.	Sole trader may lack **capital or equity** and find it difficult to raise more.
Sole trader keeps all profits.	Sole trader is personally liable for all debts.
Sole trader has complete control.	Sole trader may lack appropriate skills.
Easier to make decisions.	Making all decisions can be stressful.
Accounts do not have to be published.	No continuity, as business ceases when sole trader dies.

▶ Typical sole traders include plumbers, window cleaners and shopkeepers.

SKILLS INTERPRETATION

▶ How do you think an accountant can help a sole trader run their business?

▶ What businesses in your local area may be sole traders? Make a list and compare with your classmates.

1.2 PARTNERSHIP

GENERAL VOCABULARY
drawn up prepare (usually applied to a written document, such as a list or contract)

SUBJECT VOCABULARY
deed of partnership a formal agreement to begin a partnership

The main difference between a partnership and a sole trader is the number of owners. A partnership is defined as having between two and 20 owners. These owners have unlimited liability. A contract is usually **drawn up** to show how profits and losses are shared. This contract is called the **deed of partnership**. An accountant or solicitor normally draws up this deed of partnership to avoid potential problems. It must obey the law of the country the business is in, for example, the Partnership Act 1890 in the UK and the Partnership Act of 1932 in Bangladesh.

SUBJECT VOCABULARY

limited partnership a type of partnership where partners are responsible for the partnership's debts only up to the amount they originally invested

▼ ADVANTAGES	▼ DISADVANTAGES
More capital or equity can be raised through additional partners.	The partners have unlimited liability. This means they will have to cover the debts of each partner. For example, if one of the partners steals money from the business, the other partners will have to cover these debts and may have to sell their personal assets to do so (note: this excludes **limited partners**, see below).
Losses can be shared between partners.	A partnership is dissolved on the death of a partner.
Additional partners may bring more skills and expertise to the business.	It is difficult to liquidate or transfer partnerships.
The responsibility of management can be shared between the partners.	A partnership may still find it difficult to raise capital or equity for expansion, as increased unlimited liability could act as a deterrent.
Partnerships are ideal organisations for professional practices such as medicine, law and accounting.	Profits have to be shared between the partners.
Profits from a partnership are taxed as the personal income of the partnership.	There could be conflict between the partners.
Financial information is not published.	

SKILLS COMMUNICATION

▶ Give examples of businesses in your local area that are partnerships. Why do you think they are partnerships?

LIMITED PARTNERS

A partnership may be unlimited or limited. In a limited partnership, there must be at least one partner who is not limited. Limited partners are not liable for the debts of the business. They can only lose the capital or equity they have invested in the business. All limited partners must be registered with the Registrar of Companies.

DEED OF PARTNERSHIP

A Deed of Partnership is a contract between partners that can be either written or verbal. A Deed of Partnership has no specific requirements by law, so it can contain as much or as little as the partners wish. In fact, by law you do not need a Deed of Partnership, but it can help to solve any arguments later. It normally includes:

- the capital or equity contributed by each partner
- the ratio at which profits and losses are to be shared
- salaries to be paid to partners
- interest, if any, to be paid on capital or equity
- interest, if any, to be charged on partners' **drawings**.

SUBJECT VOCABULARY

drawings money taken (withdrawn) from the business by the owner(s)

UNIT 1   1 TYPES OF BUSINESS ORGANISATION   7

SKILLS CRITICAL THINKING

CASE STUDY: PARTNERSHIPS

Hanif has been running a fruit and vegetable stall successfully in the local market in Nairobi for five years. Hanif is a sole trader. He enjoys being his own boss, but he does not like the long hours he sometimes has to work. Hanif wants to expand his business but has found it difficult to borrow money from banks to finance a new shop. Hanif has spoken to other traders in the market. Another fruit and vegetable stall owner, Mzuzi, is also interested in expanding his own business. Hanif and Mzuzi have decided to go into business together and are forming a partnership. They will share their capital or equity and open a new store.

1. Why do you think Hanif wants to expand his business?
2. What are the advantages for Hanif and Mzuzi of going into a partnership together?
3. What are the disadvantages for Hanif and Mzuzi of going into a partnership together?

SUBJECT VOCABULARY

incorporation the official listing of a company by meeting certain legal requirements that apply in a particular country or a particular state; companies that are incorporated become corporations

limited liability the legal responsibility to pay only a limited amount of debt if something bad happens to you or your company

divorce of ownership when shareholders are owners of the business, but they are not necessarily involved in the day-to-day running of the business

auditor an independent accountant who examines the accounts of a limited company on behalf of the owners to see if they show a 'true and fair' view of how the business is performing

EXAM HINT

Make sure you read the question carefully and don't get confused between limited and unlimited liability.

1.3 PRIVATE SECTOR ORGANISATIONS

All profit-making businesses that are not run or operated by the government are private sector organisations. Sole traders and partnerships are small businesses that are part of the private sector. Companies in the private sector that want to expand can go through the process of **incorporation**. This allows the business organisation to create its own legal identity. In the UK, a company must be registered with the Registrar of Companies, and comply with the Companies Act 2006, to have separate legal status. This means, by law, that the owners of the business and the company are now separate.

Separate legal status allows the owner to have **limited liability**, which will make it easier for the business to raise finance. Limited liability means that the owners, are not liable for the company's debts and can only lose the capital or equity that they have invested in the business.

Separate legal status also allows for **divorce of ownership**. This means that owners do not have to be involved in the business and, as owners, they are separate or 'divorced' from the day-to-day running of the business. Managers are responsible for the running of the business and make the decisions on behalf of the owners.

The accounts of Limited Liability Companies need to be checked and approved by an independent accountant, known as an **auditor**. An auditor acts on behalf of the owners to check that the accounts are accurate and show a 'true and fair' view of how the business is doing. This is called an 'audit'.

There are two types of Limited Liability Company: Private Limited Companies and Public Limited Companies.

▶ Name three private sector organisations in your country.

1.4 PUBLIC SECTOR ORGANISATIONS

Public Sector Organisations are operated by the government. They usually provide a service rather than aiming to make a profit, unlike Private Sector Organisations. Public Sector Organisations are financed from the taxes paid by companies and individuals. Some of the services provided by the government in the UK are free, including hospitals, libraries and education up to the age of 18. Other public services, such as travelling by bus, are paid services.

▶ Name three public sector organisations in your country.

THE CONNECTION BETWEEN STAKEHOLDERS AND A BUSINESS

A stakeholder is any person or business who is affected by the actions of that business. These include: owners, managers, employees, customers, suppliers, competitors, providers of external finance and the government.

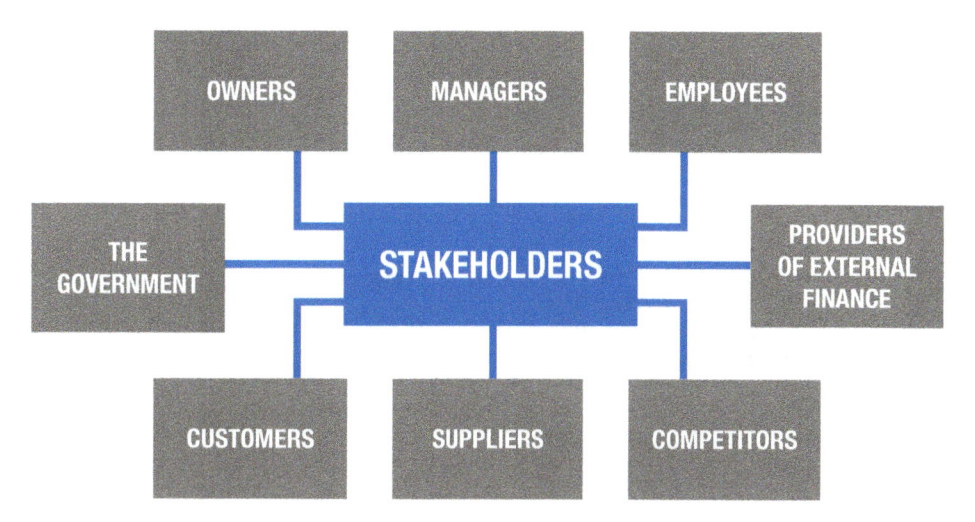

▲ Figure 1.1 Different types of stakeholder

SUBJECT VOCABULARY

Income Statement a statement of all income and expenses recognised during a specified period

The **owners** look at the overall profitability of the business. They monitor how the business traded over the previous financial year. They compare the business performance with the previous year to judge how safe their capital or equity is and whether they would get a return on their investment. The owners look at the Income Statement to assess if they will receive any share of profit.

Managers run the business on behalf of the owners. They monitor the accounts to see how the business is performing. They make decisions based on the financial data available.

Employees may want to look at the accounts to see how well the business is performing and whether they have job security. The employees would look at the Income Statement to assess the overall profitability of the business. They could also use the accounts to try to secure a pay rise.

Customers may want to see how financially stable the company is. They can then assess whether the supply of goods and services is secure, and whether they should trade with the company.

GENERAL VOCABULARY

liquidity the ability of a business to pay its debts

Suppliers look at the company accounts to see how stable the business is. The supplier can then assess what credit terms to give and how much interest to charge.

SUBJECT VOCABULARY

Statement of Financial Position shows the value of a business on a specific date, including the assets, liabilities and capital or equity

Providers of external finance assess the company's ability to pay back any money that they lend the business, such as loans. They would look at the Statement of Financial Position to assess the liquidity of the business.

The **government** looks at the profits of the business to monitor whether the business is paying enough tax.

UNIT 1
1 TYPES OF BUSINESS ORGANISATION

SKILLS CRITICAL THINKING

CASE STUDY: DYSON LTD

Dyson Ltd was founded in 1991 by Sir James Dyson. His most famous invention is the dual-cyclone vacuum cleaner, also known as the 'bagless' vacuum cleaner. Dyson Ltd also manufactures the bladeless fan, hand dryers and hairdryers. It employs more than 9000 people and sells products in more than 65 countries.

1. What are the advantages for Dyson Ltd of being a private sector organisation?
2. Why do you think Dyson Ltd is not a public sector organisation?
3. Which is the most important stakeholder in a company like Dyson Ltd?

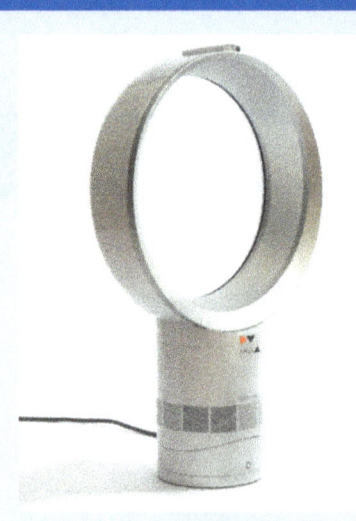

▲ The Dyson Ltd range of fans is called Dyson Cool™.

HINT
If a company name is followed by 'Ltd', this means that it is a Private Limited Company. This is not to be confused with a Public Limited Company (plc). Plcs are known as incorporations in the US (Inc). Public and Private limited companies are both types of limited liability private sector organisation.

END OF CHAPTER QUESTIONS

1. Explain the meaning of the term 'unlimited liability'.
2. Explain briefly what is meant by the phrase 'divorce of ownership'.
3. Give **two** examples of businesses that would typically be sole traders.
4. What are the **two** types of partnership?
5. Explain the role of an auditor in producing financial statements.
6. Briefly explain what is meant by a Public Sector Organisation.
7. Identify **five** stakeholders and explain how they are affected by the business.
8. State **two** differences between sole trader business and partnership business.
9. Two partners decide to form a Limited Liability Company. Evaluate their decision.

END OF CHAPTER CHECKLIST

- A sole trader is set up to make a profit and has only one owner. The owner has unlimited liability and is personally responsible for the debts of that business.
- A partnership is made up of between two and 20 partners. The partners have unlimited liability and are responsible for the actions of the other partners.
- Limited companies have a separate legal identity to the owner and can **sue** or be sued in their own name.
- Limited companies have limited liability. This means the owners can only lose the capital or equity they have invested in the business.
- In the UK, limited companies have to publish their accounts at Companies House.
- A stakeholder is anybody who has an interest in, or is affected by, a company.

GENERAL VOCABULARY
sue make a legal claim against someone, especially for money, because they have harmed you in some way

EXAM PRACTICE

A01 Answer ALL questions in this section. Questions 1–10 must be answered with a cross in the box ☒. If you change your mind about an answer, put a line through the box ☒ and then mark your new answer with a cross ☒.

1 Which of the following is not a stakeholder for a business?
- A doctor
- B competitor
- C supplier
- D government (1 mark)

2 Which of the following is a disadvantage of becoming a sole trader?
- A you keep all the profit
- B you have unlimited liability
- C you have full control over your business
- D the business is easy to set up (1 mark)

3 Which of these is most likely to be a Public Sector Organisation?
- A a car manufacturer
- B a biscuit factory
- C the Police
- D a restaurant (1 mark)

4 What does the word 'limited' after a business name indicate?
- A the number of owners is limited
- B there is a limit to the number of loans that can be issued
- C the owners' liability for the debts of the business is limited
- D there is a limit to the number of businesses of this type (1 mark)

5 A limited company must have which of the following?
- A unlimited liability
- B the ability to sell shares to friends and family
- C an auditor check on its financial statements
- D a government-run business (1 mark)

6 Which of the following is the best definition of a stakeholder?
- A someone who is affected by a business
- B someone who has control over a business
- C someone who is paid by a business
- D someone who sponsors a business (1 mark)

7 Why should a sole trader record all the financial information about her business?
- A because she is required to do so by law
- B so that she knows how much to pay her suppliers
- C so that she can prepare financial statements
- D so that she knows how much her customers owe her (1 mark)

8 Which best describes the term 'limited liability'?
- A the owner is responsible for all the debts of the business
- B the owner is only responsible for the assets of the business
- C the owner is only liable for the money they have invested in the business
- D the owner is only liable for the taxes that are paid by the business (1 mark)

9 Which of the following is a disadvantage of a partnership?
- A increased capital or equity
- B increased workload
- C increased knowledge
- D increased arguments (1 mark)

10 Why might a government department be interested in the financial statements of a company?
- A to check that the company is paying the correct amount of tax
- B to decide whether to invest in the company
- C to ensure that the company continues to receive supplies
- D to see if the company could repay a loan (1 mark)

(Total 10 marks)

2 USE OF TECHNOLOGY IN ACCOUNTING

▲ IT is now an essential part of the accounting environment.

LEARNING OBJECTIVES

- Explain the benefits of using the following technology in the accounting environment:
  - accounting software
  - spreadsheets
- Explain the issues regarding the security of data in terms of:
  - data loss
  - access
  - confidentiality
- Explain the methods of protecting data through:
  - hardware
  - software

GETTING STARTED

Information technology (IT) has become an integral part of business and accounting. There are many different types of specialist equipment you can use. Relying on technology can lead to other issues, however, such as the safety and security of important and confidential data. In this chapter, we look at the ways businesses use IT in the accounting environment.

ACTIVITY

Find information on the internet about specific IT software packages for accounting. Make notes on the types of services they offer and the types of accounts they can help you with.

2.1 INTRODUCTION TO TECHNOLOGY IN ACCOUNTING

Today, computers are very widely used to operate accounting systems. Sophisticated technology is now available at a reasonable cost. Large to medium-sized businesses have used specially written IT software for many years, working with IT companies such as Adobe and Sage to tailor IT software to their individual needs. Most large companies also have IT departments who monitor their financial systems 24 hours a day, 7 days a week. Until recently, most smaller enterprises did not set up their own systems because of the cost of such software. Now, however, even small businesses can afford to use computerised systems with **off-the-shelf** packages such as Sage or QuickBooks. These packages carry out the same **double entry** functions of data processing and recording financial information as manual systems, and also offer other features such as management information.

GENERAL VOCABULARY

off-the-shelf already made and available in shops rather than being designed for a specific customer

SUBJECT VOCABULARY

double entry the accounting system in which each transaction is recorded twice, as a debit in one account and as a credit in another

INTERNET ACCESS

Internet access enables such things as online banking, and the payment of suppliers and employees. An organisation that has its own website can advertise its products and services and offer online ordering systems. In addition, the internet is a useful source of information and data that an organisation may need to access. It also allows customers to deal directly with businesses, with more and more transactions carried out online. Some businesses have become internet only in their business plans, for example Amazon, Alibaba and eBay.

Today, so much accounting information is sent via the internet, and so many transactions are processed online, that businesses without computer facilities may struggle to succeed.

> **KEY POINT**
> Accurate inputting of data ensures reliable output.

COMPUTER HARDWARE AND SOFTWARE

Computer hardware is the physical aspects of the computer. These include the monitor, keyboard, mouse, data storage area (hard drive), graphics card, sound card and mother board. These can be password protected to stop access.

Computer software is the data and instructions that are sent to the hardware that allows the computer to act in the way you want it to. This includes the operating system and the computer programs that you want to use. These can be password protected to restrict access to only certain members of staff.

2.2 FUNCTIONS OF ACCOUNTING SOFTWARE

A computerised accounting system offers similar functions as a manual system. However, it also provides useful reports and management information. The system is integrated, so basic data that is entered is processed and automatically posted to supplier and customer accounts. The nominal (general) ledger, and the inventory records, are also automatically updated. In some instances, automatic re-ordering systems are in place. The main functions of a computerised accounting package are described below.

Accounting software allows financial statements to be produced more quickly than traditional hand-written methods. The use of pre-programmed formulae and layouts means that financial data only needs to be entered once. The software can then make various uses of this information, and can store it in different ways. The software can use data provided to complete all aspects of a transaction, such as generating documentation (once programmed by the user) and providing reporting functions.

REVENUE

This involves preparation and printing of revenue invoices, credit notes and month end statements. Data from these documents is entered, processed and recorded:

- in the customer accounts in the receivables ledger
- by automatic update of the inventory records.

PURCHASES

> **SUBJECT VOCABULARY**
> **remittance** an amount of money that you send to pay for something

Data from purchase invoices and credit notes is entered, processed and recorded:

- in the supplier accounts in the payables ledger
- by automatic update of the inventory records
- via a print-out of **remittance**.

ONLINE BANK ACCOUNT AND APPS

Accounting systems record data such as customer receipts, supplier payments, other payments and receipts.

Many banks offer online banking facilities. These mean the organisation's bank account is always up to date.

All receipts and payments are linked to the personal accounts of the trade receivables and trade payables. The system allows for such transactions to automatically update these accounts.

Many banks now offer apps (applications) that you can download for your phone. They allow you to access your account anywhere, as long as you have internet access. This is known as mobile banking.

Accounting systems automatically update the ledger.

SUBJECT VOCABULARY

payroll packages a software package that allows a firm to organise its staff wages and income tax

WAGES/SALARIES

EXAM HINT
Questions on payroll will not be asked in the exam.

Organisations have the option of using a combined computerised accounting and wages/salary package. Alternatively, they may use a separate **payroll package**. Such packages perform all the necessary payroll functions.

INVENTORY CONTROL

HINT
An inventory check is when you physically count all your inventory in your business. This is usually carried out monthly, but will depend on the size of the business. This is sometimes known as an 'stock-take'.

Inventory control includes raw materials and ordinary goods purchased for resale. This means that inventory records are automatically updated after each revenue invoice or purchase invoice is entered into the system. This ensures an accurate figure of inventory is held in the system at all times.

At the end of the financial year when an organisation undertakes an inventory check, it is crucial to have an up-to-date inventory list. A computerised accounting system ensures this list is available. Inventory lists are used in the physical inventory check and allow variances to be identified and amended.

MANAGEMENT REPORTS

HINT
The receivables ledger contains all sales of goods and/or raw materials on credit. The receivables ledger used to be called the receivables ledger. The payables ledger contains all purchases of goods and/or raw materials on credit.

One of the main features of a computerised accounting system is the facility to provide the owners and/or managers of the business with useful financial data and reports. At the end of each month or specific accounting period, certain 'month end/year end' functions are carried out to provide the following information:

- day books for customers and suppliers
- general (nominal) ledger and bank account transactions
- activity reports on all ledger transactions
- an audit trail
- analysis reports for aged trade receivables and trade payables
- financial statements including the trial balance, income statement, statement of financial position
- ratio analysis
- reports (such as on staff attendance etc.) for human resources and payroll.

The functions are summarised in **Figure 2.1**.

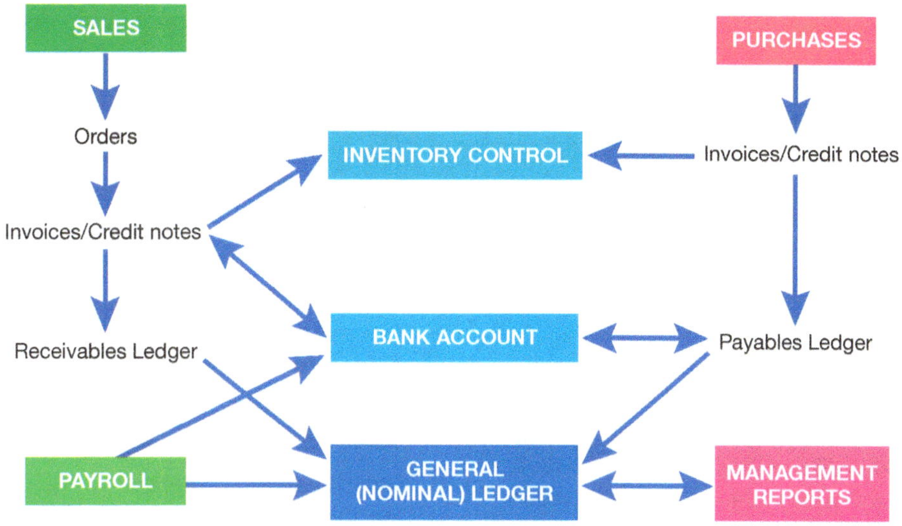

DID YOU KNOW?
VisiCalc was the first accounting program. It was launched in 1979. It was the first program to automatically update cells on a spreadsheet.

▲ Figure 2.1 Functions of accounting software.

SPREADSHEETS

GENERAL VOCABULARY

cell an individual box on a spreadsheet that holds information
formula a calculation that allows two or more cells to be calculated together.

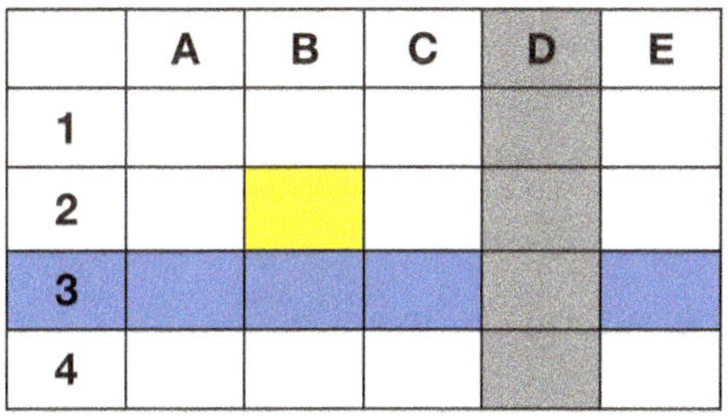

▲ Figure 2.2 Getting to know your spreadsheet

Spreadsheets are used to provide financial budgets or cash-flow budgets, and non-current asset registers. They are also used to calculate loan interest payments, and many other sums.

A computer software spreadsheet allows data to be presented in a tabular format. The electronic document can be saved and updated when necessary. Examples of spreadsheet programs include Microsoft® Excel®, Apple® Numbers®[1] from Apple Office Suite and Google® Sheets™[2].

A spreadsheet is a series of cells presented in rows and columns. Numerical data or words can be entered into the sheet. For example, row 3, column D and **cell** B2 are highlighted in **Figure 2.2** (left).

When the details have been input into the spreadsheet, users can add calculations using set **formulae**. This speeds up the process of inputting data as the spreadsheet can automatically total columns or rows as needed, for example. It can also be used as a planning tool for different scenarios such as increases or decreases in revenue and how this impacts profit.

For example, cell C4 could have a formula inserted so it automatically subtracts cell C3 from cell C2.

Spreadsheets have speeded up the accounting process as they allow data to be presented in a number of different ways and can be easily adapted and changed.

2.3 ADVANTAGES AND DISADVANTAGES OF ACCOUNTING SOFTWARE

There are many advantages and disadvantages of using accounting packages. The following are particularly important.

Accounting software allows financial statements to be produced more quickly than traditional hand-written methods The use of pre-programmed formulae and layouts means that financial data only needs to be entered once. The

[1] NUMBERS® IS A TRADEMARK OF APPLE INC., REGISTERED IN THE U.S. AND OTHER COUNTRIES
[2] © 2015 GOOGLE INC. ALL RIGHTS RESERVED. GOOGLE® SHEETS™ IS A TRADEMARK OF GOOGLE INC

	A	B	C
1			£
2		Revenue	2000
3		Costs	600
4		Profit or Loss	
5			

This can be automatically calculated by the spreadsheet software

▲ **Figure 2.3** Spreadsheet software can be programmed to make calculations

SUBJECT VOCABULARY

back up to make a copy of information stored on a computer

DID YOU KNOW?

Data must be **backed up** regularly based on the needs of the business.

software can then make various uses of this information, and can store it in different ways. The software can use data provided to complete all aspects of a transaction, such as generating documentation (once programmed by the user) and providing reporting functions.

ADVANTAGES

- Data is entered and processed very rapidly, much faster than in a manual system.
- Accuracy is improved since data is only entered once and documents are updated automatically. In a manual system, data may have to be entered twice or more.
- Documents such as invoices, credit notes, statements and remittance advices can be produced easily and quickly.
- Accounting records are updated in real time, so they accurately reflect customers' accounts. This enables remedial action to be taken if necessary.
- Management information can quickly be made available in report form, for example, aged trade receivables and trade payables analysis reports.
- A system connected to the internet can make financial transactions electronically.
- Resources can be used more efficiently, for example, by needing fewer accounting staff.
- Documents can be shared online, or scanned and saved, reducing filing space.

DISADVANTAGES

- Installation can be expensive. Ongoing maintenance and updating costs can also be high.
- The introduction of the system will affect most other areas of the business, which may lead to considerable disruption. Staff may also be resentful of a new system.
- Staff will need to be trained to use the system. There will be training costs.
- System downtime can be very disruptive.
- Data back-up at regular intervals is essential.
- Fraudulent access can seriously affect the business's operation and its profitability.
- Security measures are vital. For example, passwords for staff and protection against viruses and hacking.
- There are health risks associated with the use of computer keyboards and screens. These include eyestrain, back problems due to poor posture, and muscular fatigue in the arms and wrists from keyboard use. Regular rest intervals away from workstations are essential.

SKILLS PROBLEM SOLVING

CASE STUDY: MONITORING INVENTORY USING IT

▲ This business imports motorcycle components to make up and sell as motorcycles.

Ahmed owns a small manufacturing business in Colombo, Sri Lanka. The business imports motorcycle components from all over China and India. Ahmed then manufactures the motorcycles to sell in Sri Lanka. Ahmed sometimes struggles to keep up to date with all his inventory as he can receive up to 10 deliveries a day and the boxes aren't clearly labelled. Ahmed doesn't employ a lot of staff so these boxes of components may not be opened for days and are not organised in a specific order. Ahmed needs to monitor his inventory levels as he sometimes encounters problems when he runs out of parts or cannot locate the components he needs. Produce a presentation to show Ahmed why he should introduce an IT inventory system to monitor his inventory levels.

2.4 DATA LOSS

Protection of data is vitally important to any business for reasons of record maintenance as well as access and security.

It is important that data held on a computer is saved regularly, and protected against data loss. Electronic data can be stored by different methods; for example, on a hard drive or a memory stick. Both of these types of storage devices can be encrypted or password protected. This would stop access to the data if the devices were lost or stolen.

It is also vital to back up data held on the system. Most operating systems offer an option to automatically back up material at regular intervals. This means that a temporary copy of your document is held, for example on the hard drive. If you do lose material, or forget to save it, a back up means that you can recover the information. Operating systems also include the option to 'restore' data, either to the last saved version, or to a specified back-up version. If you don't back up your data, and make sure that you have activated the 'restore' functionality, you risk having to start your accounts from scratch.

2.5 SECURITY

All organisations regard their financial information as sensitive. Most want their financial information to remain confidential, except when legislation demands that certain information is made available to external bodies. Preventing unauthorised access to electronic accounting data is vital.

KEY POINT

When a system uses internet connections, there is the constant threat of fraudulent access and corruption.

Staff working on computerised accounting systems are allocated passwords that restrict access to their area of work. Passwords should be changed regularly to help prevent the possibility of non-authorised persons accessing the system. Most computer systems have packages to resist viruses and attack by hacking. These systems must be constantly reviewed and updated.

Most medium-sized or large organisations will use computer networks rather than standalone computers. This calls for extra security measures, such as ensuring that the network is not public.

To protect your hardware and software it is worth taking the following actions.

ACTION	BENEFIT
Install a firewall	This helps to control the information that goes to and from your computer. It can block internet traffic based on the security features you select.
Install antivirus software	This will search for, detect and remove any possible viruses on your computer and prevent new viruses from damaging your files.
Install anti-spyware software	This stops programs such as malware from being installed on your computer. Malware allows other users to look at your work and may allow someone else to take control of your computer.
Use complex and secure passwords	Always make sure your password contains upper and lowercase letters, numbers and symbols. Never write down your passwords. You must change your password regularly.
Check the security settings on your internet browsers	You can set your internet zone security to high or medium.

CASE STUDY: ACCOUNTING SOFTWARE

▲ Chefs don't only cook, they also need to organise their accounts.

Anson Lau owns several restaurants in Macau. Each restaurant runs its own paper-based accounting system.

It is therefore difficult for Mr Lau to manage his business. He visits each restaurant at least once a week, and has to file accounts for each outlet separately. This is both expensive and time-consuming.

Explain the benefits to Mr Lau of using (an) accounting software (package).

SKILLS REASONING

EXAM HINT

Always relate your answers on IT to accounting. If you don't you will lose important marks as you haven't applied your knowledge.

END OF CHAPTER QUESTIONS

1. Explain the different ways in which you can protect your financial information on a computer.
2. Explain **two** ways that you may be able to send financial data electronically.
3. Give **three** advantages of using ICT in accounting.
4. Give **three** disadvantages of using ICT in accounting.

END OF CHAPTER CHECKLIST

- Computers are widely used in organisations for operating accounting systems.
- Most computerised accounting software packages are integrated systems and communicate with each other.
- It is essential that users of computerised systems regularly back up their data to stop potential catastrophic loss of data.
- There are many advantages to using computer accounting software. These include speed, accuracy, cost effectiveness and the ease of producing financial reports.
- The disadvantages include the cost of software and hardware, the training of staff and potential security concerns.

EXAM PRACTICE

A01 Answer ALL questions in this section. Questions 1–4 must be answered with a cross in the appropriate box ☒. If you change your mind about an answer, put a line through the box ☒ and then mark your new answer with a cross ☒.

1 Which software is an accountant most likely to use for recording customers' addresses?

☐ **A** spreadsheets
☐ **B** databases
☐ **C** word processing programs
☐ **D** internet **(1 mark)**

2 What is electronic mail used for?

☐ **A** to send and receive messages over a network
☐ **B** to send and receive messages via the internet
☐ **C** to send and receive messages via radio waves
☐ **D** all of the above **(1 mark)**

3 In spreadsheets, what are values, formulae and labels stored in?

☐ **A** ranges
☐ **B** functions
☐ **C** labels
☐ **D** cells **(1 mark)**

4 What is computer hardware?

☐ **A** a medium for data communications
☐ **B** a physical device driven by data
☐ **C** a physical device driven by software
☐ **D** all of the above **(1 mark)**

(Total 4 marks)

3.4 PROFESSIONAL ETHICS

▲ Certain standards of behaviour are expected in corporate life.

SKILLS ▶ INTERPRETATION

LEARNING OBJECTIVES

- Describe the principles of professional ethics
- Apply the principles of professional ethics to accounting roles and functions
- Explain the concept of public interest and how it is applied to accounting roles and functions

GETTING STARTED

In this chapter, we will explore the importance of ethics in accounting and learn about some of the different roles in accounting. We will also look at what is meant by the term 'public interest'.

ACTIVITY

Why do you think accountants have to have a code of ethics? Use the internet to research some news stories about accounting fraud and see how many examples you can find of accountants being unethical.

3.1 THE PRINCIPLES OF PROFESSIONAL ETHICS

Professional ethics are the personal and corporate rules that govern behaviour within a particular organisation or profession. They are professionally accepted standards of personal and business behaviour. Sometimes they are called codes of practice. Professionals use these rules as a guide to perform their jobs based on sound and consistent ethical principles.

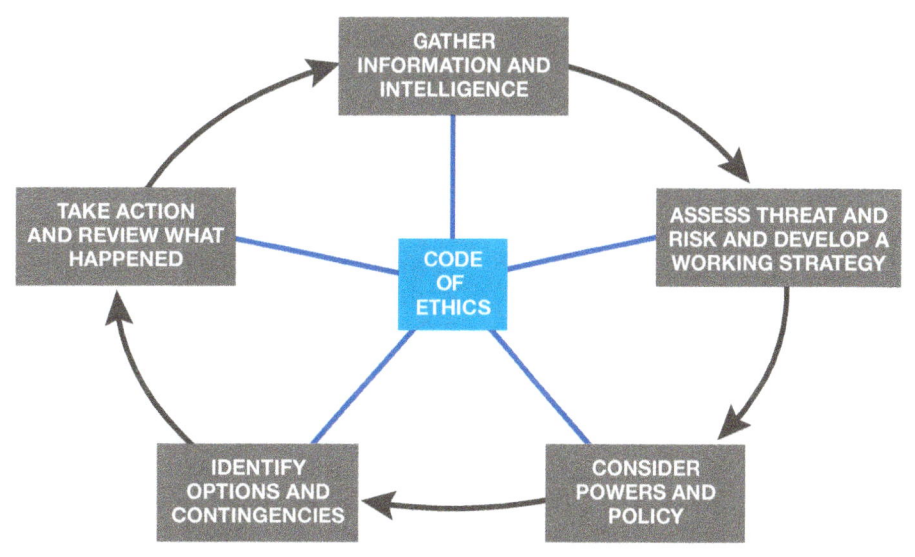

▲ Figure 3.1 Code of ethics

Professional ethics in accounting has five main aspects:

1 INTEGRITY

This refers to fair dealing and trustworthiness. An accountant must be straightforward and honest in all professional and business relationships. An accountant must not knowingly produce financial statements or financial reports that contain false or misleading information. In addition, they must not produce financial statements or financial reports that deliberately omit any data that could lead to misunderstandings. Behaving with integrity also includes not taking bribes to change the data they are presenting.

Example 1 A business must not overstate its profits by implying that its costs are lower than they are. For example, underestimating the depreciation figure for non-current assets is comparable to stating that these assets will last longer than they will. If depreciation is entered as £4,000 instead of £10,000, profit and the net assets of the business will be inflated by £6,000.

Example 2 A business must not overstate the value of its assets. If closing inventories are valued at £20,000, rather than the correct figure of £16,000, profit will increase by £4,000 and the net assets will also increase by £4,000.

2 OBJECTIVITY

All accountants must make their own judgements on the accounts. Accountants must be free from bias or conflict of interest and must not be under the influence of others. Behaving with integrity includes not preparing the accounts of a family member or for a company that they have shares in.

Example 1 A business owner's personal expenses should not be put through the books of the business. These expenses should be recorded as 'drawings' instead. If a business owner put his or her personal motor expenses through the business, this would be an example of not being objective. It would mislead stakeholders of the business and would lower the business' overall profit.

Example 2 If you prepare accounts of a family member you may not be objective or unbiased when valuing assets or calculating profit, and therefore may show the business to be in a better financial position than it actually is.

3 PROFESSIONAL COMPETENCE AND DUE CARE

This rule requires all accountants to keep up to date with any changes in accounting policies and regulations. Accountants' knowledge and skills must be relevant so their clients receive a professional service. This includes becoming qualified to the appropriate level and maintaining the standard expected of a professional accountant.

Example 1 Accountants must keep up to date with all the latest terminology and regulatory framework.

Example 2 Accounting firm managers should carry out skills analysis of the work force and make sure that only competent and fully qualified staff are producing the financial documents. Staff must also act in a professional manner at all times and produce work in a timely manner.

4 CONFIDENTIALITY

Accountants have a legal obligation to maintain the confidentiality of materials they have been given. This includes not giving key information to third parties such as competitors or investors, as this could break confidentiality agreements. However, there are some cases where accountants may have to

---

DID YOU KNOW?
The International Federation of Accountants represents over 3 million accountants in over 130 countries: www.ifac.org

SUBJECT VOCABULARY

money laundering hiding illegally obtained money in a business, e.g. exchanging good money (notes and coins) for stolen money through normal day-to-day business transactions

break confidentiality to be able to comply with the law. One example of this would be a client trying to deceive the government by paying less tax. Another example would be when an accountant finds evidence of **money laundering**.

Example 1 An accountant should not give out financial information to third parties without the permission of the business. If a competitor is given access to a company's revenue and costs, this would give them an advantage, for example regarding pricing.

Example 2 If an investor is given access to confidential financial information, they might decide not to invest and could prevent the expansion of that business.

5 ADOPT PROFESSIONAL BEHAVIOUR

This imposes an obligation on all accountants to comply with all relevant laws and regulations so as not to bring the accounting profession into disrepute. An example would be exaggerating your accounting skills or making unprofessional comments about colleagues or other accounting professionals.

Example 1 An accountant should never overestimate their accounting skills when trying to attract new clients. For example, it is unprofessional to claim that you are a specialist in tax accounting when this is not the case.

6 PUBLIC INTEREST

Accountants need to behave in the public interest, i.e. in a manner so that the public can have confidence that profits stated are true and fair. They must not mislead the public with overstated figures when producing accounts for a firm.

Example 1 If the public believe that financial accounts are biased they may start to lose faith in all financial reports and will stop investing their money. This would mean that firms wouldn't grow and expand.

CASE STUDY: THE SATYAM SCANDAL

Satyam Computer Services was an Indian IT services company. In 2009, they were charged with falsifying their books of accounts. B. Ramalinga Raju, the company's former chairman, admitted that 95% of the cash in the business was false. Due to this acknowledgement, investors in Satyam lost around Rs14 000 crore ($2.2 billion) as Satyam's shares fell. B. Ramalinga Raju was arrested and sentenced to seven years in jail.

Why must companies behave in an ethical manner?

3.2 ACCOUNTING ROLES AND FUNCTIONS

There are many different roles within an accounting department. Departments are organised in different ways and the way they operate can vary greatly. However, most accounting roles usually cover the same five areas:

1 **Accounts payable.** This role is responsible for keeping a check on the money that goes out of the business to pay for bills and expenses. Payments have to go out on time. The role also involves maintaining good relationships with trade payables and checking the business is getting the best deals, for example by seeing if any discounts are available. In this role, it is important to ensure no costs are incurred for late payments and no interest is incurred.

2. **Accounts receivable.** This role involves checking that the business has received all the money it is entitled to. This includes tracking invoices to make sure they are paid on time. A 'friendly' reminder service can be set up for customers to make sure no irrecoverable debts occur.

3. **Payroll.** This is a critical part of an accountancy department, ensuring that all staff are paid on time and the government receives the correct amount of tax.

4. **Reporting and financial statements.** This role involves preparing financial reports for internal and external use. This could include budgets and forecasting to check the viability of a new product or store. The Income Statement, Statement of Financial Position and Statement of Cash Flow for the company's Annual Report, may also need to be provided, as well as information for possible investors, banks and other professionals who are involved in the development of the company.

5. **Checking the accounts.** This role is responsible for controlling the finances of the business, for example, ensuring that the correct procedures are followed and the correct accounting standards are adhered to. This role also involves putting systems in place to show compliance and to protect against fraud and theft. This is sometimes called the internal audit.

3.3 PUBLIC INTEREST

To understand the term **public interest**, it is easier to look at what is meant by the term 'public' and what is meant by the term 'interest'.

For accountants, the term 'public' includes the following.

- **Investors, owners and business owners of public sector and private sector organisations.** These parties require good financial information that is free from bias. They need to base their actions and decisions on the most reliable data.

- **Customers and competitors.** These parties rely on sound financial information as decisions based on this data could have significant impacts on the costs and benefits to them.

- **Taxpayers.** Any financial information that may have a detrimental impact on taxpayers is of significant interest to these parties.

The term 'interest' can be defined as all things that are valued by society. This includes economic wellbeing and certainty in the business environment. Sound financial information must be given to stakeholders so that they are not misled. Comparing the financial information from two different companies allows investors to make the best decisions. Sound financial data can improve the efficiency and lower the costs of government and private organisations. The term 'interest' also includes financial information that leads to the protection of the environment and reduces the depletion of natural resources.

To act in the 'public interest', accountants must work towards the highest levels of ethical and professional standards. Accountants are required to produce high quality financial statements that are audited to ensure accuracy. There is an international code of conduct for all accountants across the globe. They also need to guarantee that there are rigorous checking systems. Accountants who behave in an unethical manner are dealt with through strict structures of disciplinary measures and sanctions.

DID YOU KNOW?
The International Ethics Standards Board for Accountants® (IESBA®) is an independent standard-setting body that serves the public interest by setting robust, internationally appropriate ethics standards, including auditor independence requirements, for professional accountants worldwide: www.ethicsboard.org

INTRODUCTION TO ACCOUNTING CONCEPTS

At the end of a financial year organisations prepare their financial statements, i.e. Income Statement and Statement of Financial Position. There are, however, other issues to consider with the preparation of the financial statements which are known as 'accounting concepts' or 'rules of accounting'. These concepts or rules have evolved over the years for practical as much as theoretical reasons. As a consequence, this has made the preparation of the financial statements more standardised enabling the information to be more easily understood and reliable, and to enable clearer comparisons between different businesses. Accountants need to be ethical. They also have to follow the rules of accounting concepts. These will be covered in more detail in Chapter 13, but it is worth having a look at them now. There are certain rules and underlying concepts that accountants have to follow when preparing financial statements. These rules ensure stakeholders have faith in the accounts showing a 'true and fair' reflection of the business. If stakeholders invest in the business or buy goods, they want to be sure that their money will be secure.

The concepts that will feature in the exam are:

- **b**usiness entity
- **m**ateriality
- **c**onsistency
- **a**ccruals
- **m**oney measurement
- **p**rudence.

> **HINT**
> Try to remember the **acronym** BMCAMP.

> **GENERAL VOCABULARY**
> **acronym** a word made up from the first letters of the name of something such as an organisation

END OF CHAPTER QUESTIONS

1. Give **three** examples of financial statements.
2. Give **one** example of an accountant being objective.
3. Explain what is meant by the term confidentiality and give **one** example.
4. What is meant by the term 'public interest'?
5. How can an accountant adopt a professional manner?
6. Explain **three** roles of an accountant.

END OF CHAPTER CHECKLIST

- Accountants have to follow the principles of professional ethics.
- An accountant must not provide information that could mislead clients or third parties.
- All accountants must be suitably qualified and keep up to date with new accounting procedures.
- Accountants must not provide materials that could go against the public interest.

EXAM PRACTICE

A01 Answer ALL questions in this section. Questions 1–5 must be answered with a cross in the box ☒. If you change your mind about an answer, put a line through the box ☒ and then mark your new answer with a cross ☒.

1 Which accounting objective states that the information in financial statements must be free from error and bias?
- ☐ **A** comparability
- ☐ **B** relevance
- ☐ **C** reliability
- ☐ **D** confidentiality   **(1 mark)**

2 What are accounts produced to show?
- ☐ **A** an accurate and fair view of the business
- ☐ **B** a true and fair view of the business
- ☐ **C** a true and honest view of the business
- ☐ **D** a fair and honest view of the business   **(1 mark)**

3 Who does the term 'public' refer to when used in accountancy?
- ☐ **A** owners
- ☐ **B** employees
- ☐ **C** customers
- ☐ **D** suppliers   **(1 mark)**

4 Which of the following is not an accounting concept?
- ☐ **A** materiality
- ☐ **B** auditory
- ☐ **C** objectivity
- ☐ **D** consistency   **(1 mark)**

5 Which of the following is not one of the main aspects of professional ethics?
- ☐ **A** identity
- ☐ **B** integrity
- ☐ **C** objectivity
- ☐ **D** confidentiality   **(1 mark)**

(Total 5 marks)

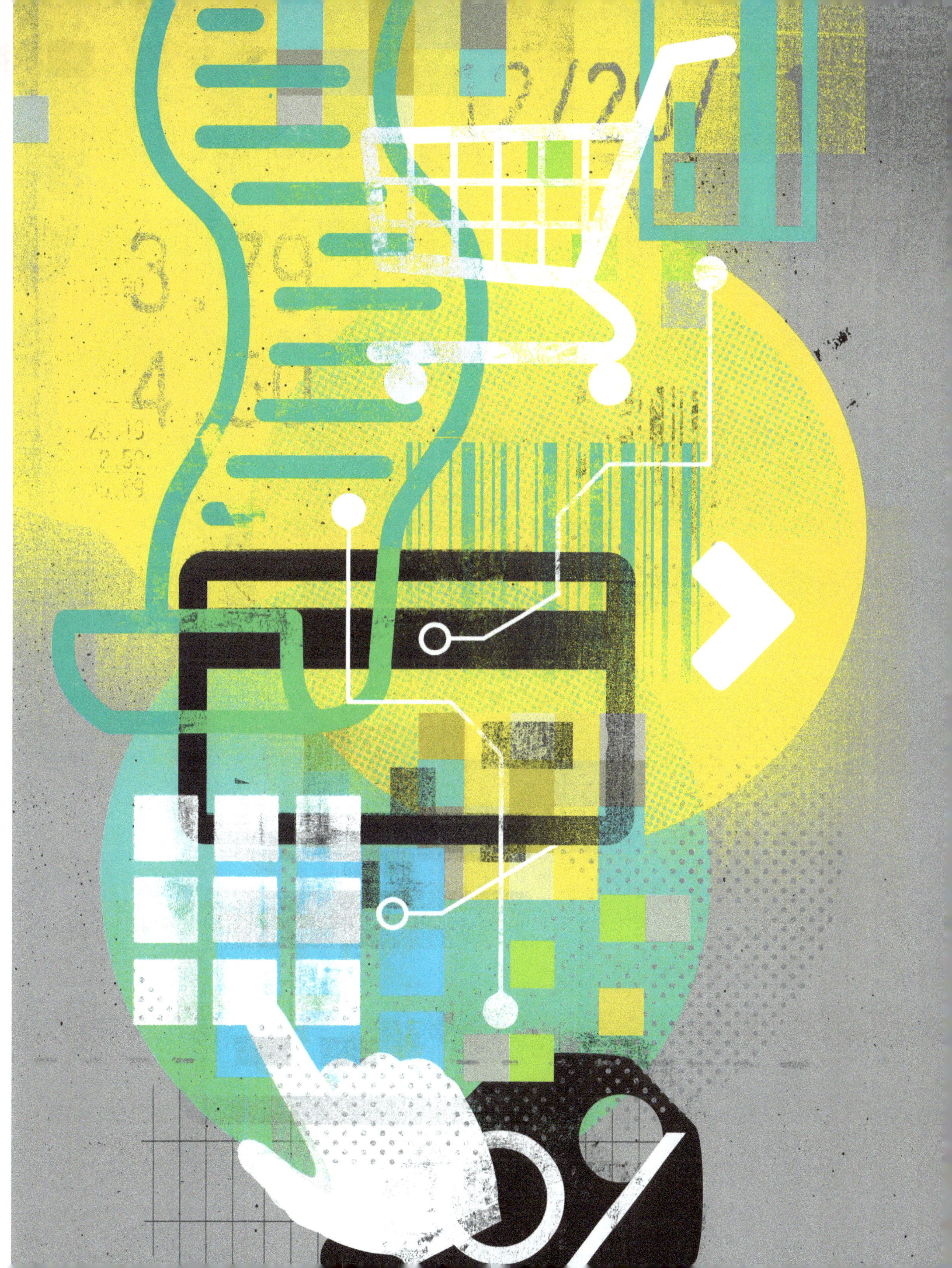

| 4 BUSINESS DOCUMENTATION | 28 | 5 BOOKS OF ORIGINAL ENTRY | 36 |
| 6 LEDGER ACCOUNTING AND DOUBLE ENTRY BOOKKEEPING | 60 | 7 DEPRECIATION | 86 |

UNIT 2
INTRODUCTION TO BOOKKEEPING

Assessment Objective AO1
Demonstrate a knowledge and understanding of accounting terminology, principles, procedures and techniques

Assessment Objective AO2
Select and apply their knowledge and understanding of accounting procedures to a variety of accounting problems

Assessment Objective AO3
Analyse, evaluate and present information in appropriate accounting formats and communicate reasoned explanations

All businesses and organisations are involved in the buying and selling of goods and/or services. Every time a business purchases or sells inventory, it completes several documents. These are kept to show proof of purchase/sale. Imagine how many documents a company like McDonald's or Alibaba has for all its customers and suppliers – millions! Luckily, computers can track all the relevant documentation. However, in accounting it is very important that you understand the documents as they are frequently examined. We will look at them in the course of this unit.

4 BUSINESS DOCUMENTATION

▲ It is vital to have a thorough understanding of the different types of accounting documentation.

LEARNING OBJECTIVES

- Explain the purpose of business documents
- Prepare the following business documents:
  - purchase order
  - purchase invoice
  - sales invoice
  - credit note
  - statement of account
  - remittance advice
  - petty cash voucher
  - cash receipt

GETTING STARTED

In this chapter, we will learn about the business documents that are filled in when you buy or sell items. It is very important that you keep these documents. You are required to keep them, by law, for your company's audit. You will also need these documents to check that you receive all the monies you are due, and to make sure you pay all your suppliers on time.

ACTIVITY

When you go shopping, do you keep your receipts? What do you do with them? Have a look at the information on them. Have you ever bought anything with a bank card? Do you keep that receipt and check it off against your bank statement to see if there are any mistakes? This is what you should do and this is why businesses have to look after their business documents. How many receipts do you have each day? How many receipts do you think a company like McDonald's issues each day?

4.1 INTRODUCTION TO BUSINESS DOCUMENTATION

All businesses and organisations are involved in trading. Trading is the buying and selling of goods and/or services so that you can make a profit. The financial transaction of buying and selling involves some very important documents, including: source/business documents; journals and daybooks; ledgers; trial balances; and financial statements, as shown in **Figure 4.1**. Both the buyer and the seller need these documents.

These documents have been in general use for many years. They are part of an established procedure. If the documents are used properly, they help trading to proceed smoothly. They can also be used to quickly solve any disputes between a buyer and a seller. Both parties use the same documents, and they follow a standard sequence. **Figure 4.2** shows the normal trading documentation sequence.

▲ **Figure 4.1** Business documentation

SUBJECT VOCABULARY

financial statements documents produced by an organisation to show the financial status of a business at a particular time, including the income Statement and Statement of Financial Position

Flow of source documents

Purchase Order — Sent by buyer to order goods from supplier

↓

Invoice — Sent by supplier to buyer when goods are delivered, advising of amount owed

↓

Credit Note — Sent by supplier to buyer to credit buyer for the return of goods

↓

Statement — Sent by supplier to buyer showing transactions to month end and amount due

↓

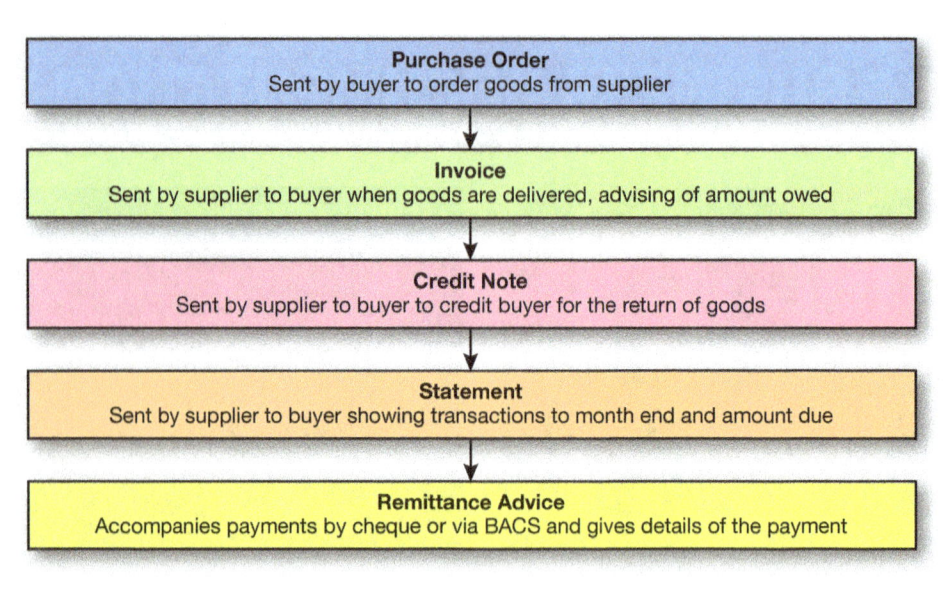

Remittance Advice — Accompanies payments by cheque or via BACS and gives details of the payment

▲ Figure 4.2 Flow of source documents

4.2 PURCHASE ORDER

When a business or organisation decides to buy goods or use the services of another company, it usually issues a **purchase order**. This document contains the following information:

- name and address of supplier
- purchase order number
- date of order
- details of the goods or services ordered including part numbers or catalogue references.
- quantity required
- delivery date
- authorised signature of a senior member of the company, such as the buyer

KEY POINT

A purchase order is normally raised by the customer's purchasing office and then sent to the supplier. Once it has been accepted by the supplier, a formal contract exists between the two parties. An example of a purchase order is shown in **Figure 4.3**.

KEY POINT

A formal contract is a contract that is bound by law as it has been signed by both parties.

PURCHASE ORDER

Gramson's Sports
School Lane,
Lincoln, LN1 1PP

Tel: 0131 874428
Rivett Rugby & Football Club
Jacks Lane
Ipswich
IP1 1AY

order number: 4355
date: 6 April 2017

Please supply

quantity	description	unit price £	£
20	Football Shirts	12.00	240.00
20	Football Shirts	8.00	160.00
			400.00

Delivery Required: Early May

C. Ventura
Purchasing Manager

▲ Figure 4.3 Purchase order

4 BUSINESS DOCUMENTATION

4.3 INVOICE

An invoice is a document prepared by the seller when he or she sells goods or provides services on credit. The invoice is usually numbered for easy identification and for filing in a suitable storage system. An invoice contains the following information:

- seller's name and address
- purchaser's name and address
- description of goods and services supplied
- quantity
- price per item
- total amount due.

Details of the transaction need to be entered into the accounts books of both the seller and the buyer. **Figure 4.4** is an example of an invoice.

> **KEY POINT**
>
> An invoice is a document that a business issues to its customers, asking the customers to pay for the goods or services that the business has supplied to them. From a bookkeeper's point of view, the invoice is one of the most important accounting documents.

INVOICE
Rivett Rugby & Football Club
Jacks Lane, Ipswich, IP1 1AY
Tel: 0161 229 9229

Gramson's Sports
School Lane
Lincoln
LN1 1PP

invoice number: 3189
date: 4 May 2017

quantity	description	unit price £	£
20	Football Shirts	12.00	240.00
20	Football Shirts	8.00	160.00
			400.00

Terms: 30 days

▲ Figure 4.4 An example of an invoice.

4.4 CREDIT NOTE

When the supplier has decided to give credit, he or she raises a **credit note**. The credit note is for the value of the returned goods. The note will then be sent to the customer.

A credit note is usually printed in red to distinguish it from an invoice and while it contains similar information to that found in an invoice, some details will differ.

For instance, often a customer will return only a part of a consignment. The credit note needs to show this clearly.

Credit notes are important documents. They are entered into the accounts books because the amount owed by the buyer is reduced by the amount of the credit note.

Sometimes a supplier does not allow a customer to return the full amount of goods. For example, a customer may return goods worth $30 accompanied by a debit note, but the supplier may only accept goods worth $25 and issue a credit note for $25.

> **KEY POINT**
>
> A credit note is effectively a negative invoice. It is a way of showing a customer that they do not have to pay the full amount of an invoice. A credit note might cancel an invoice out completely (if it is for the same amount as the invoice) or it might be for less than the invoice.

UNIT 2
4 BUSINESS DOCUMENTATION

Figure 4.5 shows a credit note.

CREDIT NOTE
Rivett Rugby & Football Club
Jacks Lane, Ipswich, IP1 1AY
Tel: 0161 229 9229

Gramson's Sports
School Lane
Lincoln
LN1 1PP

credit note number: 118
date: 15 May 2017

quantity	description	unit price £	£
2	Football Shirts	12.00	24.00
			24.00

Reason for credit: Faulty stitching

▲ Figure 4.5 An example of a credit note.

SKILLS   CRITICAL THINKING

CASE STUDY: SOURCE DOCUMENTS

Scott Leung has been in business for many years. He sells computer consoles and computer games in his shop. Scott doesn't always keep his source documents in an organised file and gets confused by them. He has found the following transactions, but is not sure what source document goes with them. Complete the table below to help him locate the correct source document for each transaction.

TRANSACTION	SOURCE DOCUMENT
Paid for stationery in cash	
Deposited takings into his own bank account	
Purchased inventory on credit from D. Chiu	
Received payment from a customer by credit transfer	
Returned inventory to a supplier that had previously been bought on credit	

▼ Scott's games consoles are very popular with both children and adults.

4.5 STATEMENT OF ACCOUNT

At the end of each month, businesses send out a document known as a **statement of account**. This statement contains details of all the customer's transactions during the previous month. The statement of account starts with the opening balance outstanding from the previous month. It then lists the amounts owing from the current month's invoices. Any amounts that have been paid are deducted. Credit notes are also included. This results in the total amount outstanding. This total amount is then due for payment at the end of the month.

When the customer receives the statement of account, they should check the details against their own records. This is to ensure they agree with the statement. If the invoices listed on the statement have been approved for

KEY POINT

A statement of account is a detailed report of the contents of an account. An example is a statement sent to a customer showing billings to and payments from the customer during a specific period, resulting in an ending balance.

payment, the customer arranges to pay the account. **Figure 4.6** shows an example of a statement of account.

STATEMENT

Rivett Rugby & Football Club
Jacks Lane, Ipswich, IP1 1AY

Tel: 0161 229 9229

Gramson's Sports
School Lane
Lincoln
LN1 1PP

Statement date: 31 May 2017
Account No: C 52
Page No: 1

Date	Reference	Debit	Credit	Balance
04/5/17	Invoice No 3189	400.00		400.00
14/5/17	Credit Note No 118		24.00	376.00
			Total outstanding	376.00

Terms: 30 days from date of invoice

▲ **Figure 4.6** An example of a statement of account.

4.6 REMITTANCE ADVICE

KEY POINT

A remittance advice is a note sent from a customer to their supplier, informing the supplier that they have paid their invoice.

KEY POINT

Bankers' Automated Clearing System (BACS) is a prepayment system to process electronic bank payments, rather than using cash or cheques.

When a buyer pays a supplier, it is important that the supplier has details of the payment so that the money is correctly allocated. Therefore, the buyer usually includes a **remittance advice**. A remittance advice is similar to a statement, as it shows details of the business's most recent transactions and final balance outstanding; it may be prepared at the same time as a statement. The remittance advice should be accompanied by a cheque to cover the final balance outstanding. If payment is made by the Bankers' Automated Clearing Service (BACS), then a record of this payment should be included with the remittance advice.

If an invoice is not paid for any reason, it will be left outstanding and can then be queried. **Figure 4.7** shows a remittance advice.

REMITTANCE ADVICE

Gramson's Sports
School Lane, Lincoln, LN1 1PP

Tel: 0131 874428

VAT Reg: 811 6571 56
Remittance Advice: 6/151
Date: 26 June 2017

Rivett Rugby & Football Club
Jacks Lane
Ipswich
IP1 1AY

Account Number: C 52

Date	Invoice or credit note no	Invoice	Credit note	Payment
04/5/2017	3189	400.00		400.00
14/5/2017	118		24.00	(24.00)
			Total Payment	376.00

▲ **Figure 4.7** An example of a remittance advice.

4.7 RECEIPTS

Occasionally, a member of staff may wish to purchase postage from the petty cashier or perhaps have some photocopying done for their own personal use. In these cases, the petty cashier will issue a receipt to the staff member for the amount received. **Figure 4.8** shows an example of a receipt.

RECEIPT

Received from: Luisa Moro		**Date:**	25 May 2017
The sum of: Six pounds only		**No.**	26

	£	p
Cheque	—	—
Cash	6	00
	6	00

Re: Postage

Ed Shankar
WITH THANKS

▲ Figure 4.8 An example of a petty cash voucher.

If a staff member wants to make a claim, he or she should complete a petty cash voucher. The petty cash voucher must show the date and details of the item(s) purchased or expenditure incurred, including VAT if applicable. The voucher must be signed by the **claimant** and **countersigned** by his or her manager (see **Figure 4.9**). If the claim exceeds the authority of the petty cashier, say £25, the claim will have to be referred to the senior cashier or accountant.

Petty Cash Voucher

No. 1
Date 2 May 2017

Description	Amount	
	£	p
Stationery	11	75

Signature   Helena Kazim
Authorised Natasha Allen

▲ Figure 4.9 An example of a petty cash voucher.

Only items of expenditure approved by the business will be reimbursed unless prior agreement has been received for a particular expense claim.

The **petty cash book** is a book of original entry from when items are first entered, i.e. petty cash vouchers.

SUBJECT VOCABULARY

claimant someone who claims something, especially money, from the government, a court, etc., because they think they have a right to it

countersign sign a paper that has already been signed by someone else

HINT

Remember the order of the documents: purchase order, invoice, credit note, statement of account and remittance advice.

END OF CHAPTER QUESTIONS

1 Which business document contains the details of purchases, returns and payments occurring during a trading period?

2 Which business document is sent when goods are sold to another business on credit?

3 When will a business issue a credit note?

END OF CHAPTER CHECKLIST

- Organisations use many documents during their trading activities.
- When a buyer has agreed to buy goods, a purchase order is sent to the supplier. This records the quantity, size, colour etc. required.
- An invoice is sent by the supplier to the buyer, detailing the amount still owed.
- If goods are faulty or not fit for purpose, a credit note is normally issued. The amount is deducted from the original invoice.
- At the end of the month, a statement of account is sent detailing what has been purchased and returned during the previous month. It also lists any outstanding balance that still needs to be paid.

EXAM PRACTICE

A01 A02 A03 Answer ALL questions in this section. Questions 1–4 must be answered with a cross in the appropriate box ☒. If you change your mind about an answer, put a line through the box ☒ and then mark your new answer with a cross ☒.

Questions 1–4 must be answered with a cross in the appropriate box ☒. If you change your mind about an answer, put a line through the box ☒ and then mark your new answer with a cross ☒.

1 Which document from a supplier reduces the amount owed by a customer?

☐ A credit note
☐ B purchase order
☐ C invoice
☐ D statement **(1 mark)**

2 Hansi is a trader. She returns goods to her supplier.
Which document will Hansi send to her supplier?

☐ A credit note
☐ B purchase order
☐ C invoice
☐ D statement **(1 mark)**

3 Which task is carried out by a bookkeeper?

☐ A analysing information
☐ B assessing information
☐ C interpreting information
☐ D recording information **(1 mark)**

4 Paul had the following transactions with David, a new customer.

March 4: goods invoiced to David	$350
March 7: debit note received from David	$25
March 8: credit note issued to David	$20
March 19: cheque received from David	$300
March 28: goods invoiced to David	$470
April 1: cheque received from David	$30

Paul sent a statement of account to David on 31 March. What was shown as the balance due on that date?

☐ A $470
☐ B $475
☐ C $500
☐ D $52 **(1 mark)**

5 Anakin sells goods on credit to Caleb.
Four documents were issued during July. Copy and complete the table below, using a tick (✓) to show who would issue each document.

DOCUMENT	ANAKIN	CALEB
Invoice	✓	
Credit note		
Purchase order		
Statement of account		

(3 marks)

6 Sheva bought goods on credit from her supplier, Limpu Limited. The goods were faulty so she returned them. Name the business document that Limpu Limited issued to Sheva:

a when the goods were supplied
b when the goods were returned. **(2 marks)**

(Total 9 marks)

5 BOOKS OF ORIGINAL ENTRY

▲ Transactions are not generally recorded as they occur.

LEARNING OBJECTIVES

- Explain the purpose of the books of original entry
- Prepare the following books of original entry:
  - purchases day book/journal
  - sales day book/journal
  - purchases returns day book
  - sales return day book
  - three-column cash book
  - petty cash book
  - general journal

GETTING STARTED

The books of original entry provide a convenient way of entering transactions into the double entry system. Instead of entering the transactions as they occur, businesses tend to collect the business documents, such as sales invoices, over a period of time and then post them in bulk to the book of original entry. Waiting to collect the business documents together is more efficient and therefore more cost-effective.

Small businesses satisfactorily maintain their double entry accounts in one account book. This book is called the ledger. Larger businesses, however, need a better system because they have so much financial data to record. Consequently, several books are used to record the many different transactions.

ACTIVITY

Find examples of the documents described in Chapter 4: Business documentation. See if you can guess which books of original entry they should appear in. Tick them off as you go through this chapter.

SUBJECT VOCABULARY

book of original entry the accounting journals in which business transactions are initially recorded. The information in these books is then summarised and posted into a general ledger, from which financial statements are produced

business document documents used when processing the sale or purchase of goods and services

5.1 BOOKS OF ORIGINAL ENTRY

A **book of original entry** is where a transaction is first recorded. There are separate books for each different kind of transaction, for example, revenue is entered in one book, purchases in another book, cash in another book, and so on. All transactions that are entered into the bookkeeping system originate from a **business document** such as an invoice, credit note, cheque book stub, paying-in slip, and so on.

In Chapters 5–7 we will be looking at invoices and credit notes that are raised when goods or services are sold to customers. In Chapter 5 we will learn about cash books. Cash and cheques are recorded in cash books.

UNIT 2 — 5 BOOKS OF ORIGINAL ENTRY

TYPES OF BOOKS OF ORIGINAL ENTRY

There are several types of books of original entry that will be looked at in this chapter. These are:

- **Sales Day Book.** Used for credit revenue
- **Purchases Day Book.** Used for purchases
- **Sales Returns Day Book.** Used for sales returns from customers
- **Purchase Returns Day Book.** Used for goods returned to the supplier
- **Cash Book.** Used for receipts and payments of cash
- **Petty Cash Book.** Used for recording small items of expenditure
- **Journal.** Used for other items.

5.2 THE LEDGERS

Details of a transaction are first entered into a book of original entry. Then the information is entered into the ledgers through the double entry system. This procedure is often referred to as **posting**. Revenue transactions are posted to the receivables ledger, and purchase transactions are posted to the trade receivables ledger. Other items to the accounts are posted to the general or trade payables ledger (see below).

TYPES OF LEDGER

There are different types of ledger, as shown below (their alternative names are shown in brackets).

TYPES OF LEDGER		
Receivables ledger (Trade Receivables Ledger)	**Payables ledger** (Trade Payables Ledger)	**Nominal ledger** (General ledger)
Shows records of customers' personal accounts.	Shows records of suppliers' personal accounts.	Contains the remaining double entry accounts, such as assets, equity, expenses and income.

Figure 5.1 shows the various books that are used in accounting.

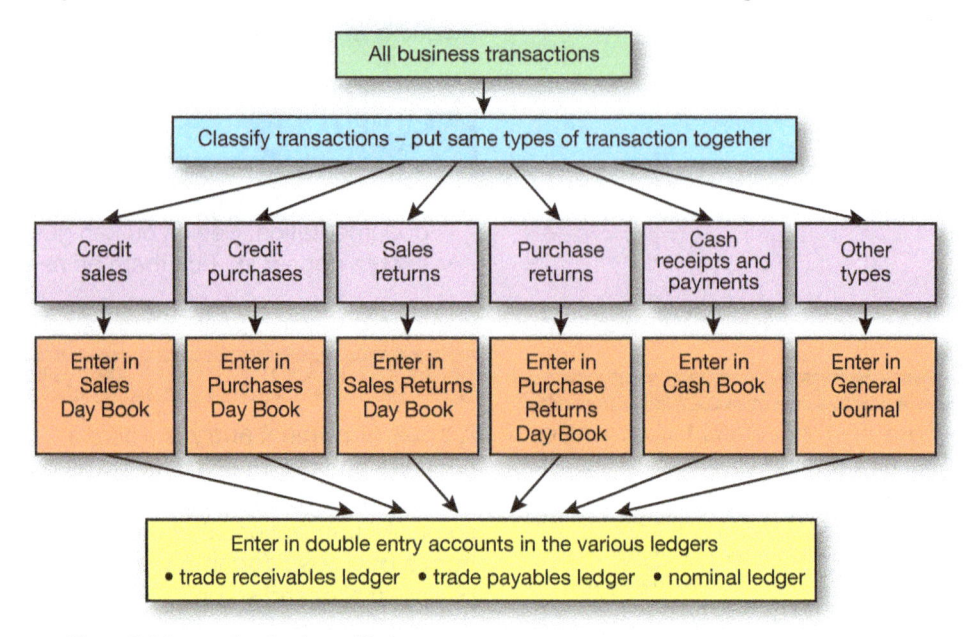

▲ Figure 5.1 Accounting books and ledgers.

5.3 CLASSIFICATION OF ACCOUNTS

Accounts are divided into **personal accounts** and **impersonal accounts** (see **Figure 5.2**).

- **Personal accounts.** These are accounts for people or businesses, i.e. the trade receivables and trade payables.
- **Impersonal accounts.** Includes all other accounts. Impersonal accounts are divided into:
  1. **real accounts.** These deal with the possessions of the business. For example, buildings, machinery, computer equipment, fixtures and fittings, inventory, etc.
  2. **nominal accounts.** Expenses and income are recorded here. For example, revenue, purchases, wages, electricity, commissions received, etc.

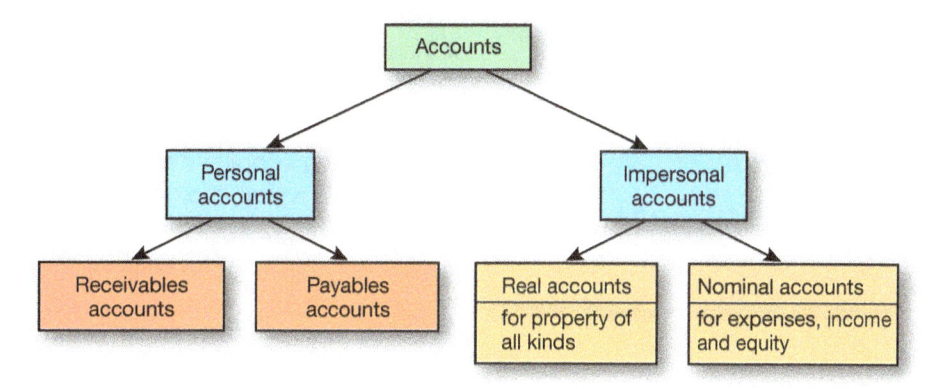

▲ **Figure 5.2** Types of account.

5.4 PURCHASE INVOICES

When a business purchases goods or services from a supplier on credit, they are sent a purchase invoice. The purchase invoice lists the goods or services supplied. It also lists the price of the goods or services. In the previous chapter we learned how revenue invoices are entered into the sales day book. Similarly, purchase invoices (source documents) are entered into the purchases day book. The following information is recorded:

- date of the invoice
- name of the supplier from whom the goods were purchased
- goods (net cost)
- total amount due.

The supplier and the customer both require an invoice. The invoice shown in **Figure 4.4** was prepared and sent by Rivett Rugby and Football Club to their customer, Gramson's Sports.

- In the accounting records of Rivett Rugby and Football Club it is a **revenue invoice**.
- In the accounting records of Gramson's Sports it is a **purchase invoice**.

Figure 5.3 shows a purchases day book. Several invoices have been entered

UNIT 2   5 BOOKS OF ORIGINAL ENTRY

HINT

In Accounts, *Dr* means Debit and *Cr* means Credit.

NOTE

The 'Total' column in **Figure 5.3** is posted to the trade payables control account. This is explained in Chapter 15.

for the month of December 2016.

Purchases Day Book *(page 38)*

Date	Details	Total
2016		£
Dec 8	Fuller & Sons	172.80
Dec 14	Cuenco Products	336.00
Dec 17	A Lewis	624.00
Dec 30	J Mita	86.40
		1219.20

▲ Figure 5.3 An example of a purchases day book.

POSTING CREDIT PURCHASES TO THE PAYABLES LEDGER

Invoices are first entered into the purchases day book. Next, each invoice is posted to the individual supplier's account in the payables ledger. At the end of the period, usually each month, the totals in the purchases day book are posted to the 'purchases account' in the nominal ledger. The double entry requirements are then to:

- **credit** each supplier's account in the payables ledger with the total of each individual invoice (the goods have come OUT of each supplier)
- **debit** the purchases account with the total of the 'net purchases' (the purchases have come IN to the purchases account).

EXAMPLE: POSTING CREDIT PURCHASES

Figure 5.4 shows how the invoices from purchases day book would be posted to the suppliers' accounts in the payables ledger, using the double entry procedures.

Trade Receivables Ledger

Fuller & Sons Account

Dr				Cr
IN			OUT	
		2016		£
		Dec 8 Purchases	PB 38	172.80

Cuenco Products Account

Dr				Cr
IN			OUT	
		2016		£
		Dec 14 Purchases	PB 38	336.00

A Lewis Account

Dr				Cr
IN			OUT	
		2016		£
		Dec 17 Purchases	PB 38	624.00

J Mita Account

Dr				Cr
IN			OUT	
		2016		£
		Dec 30 Purchases	PB 38	86.40

▲ Figure 5.4 Example entries in a receivables ledger.

The postings to the nominal ledger are shown in **Figure 5.5**.

Dr		Nominal Ledger Purchases Account				(page 43) Cr
	IN				OUT	
2016						
Dec 31	Credit purchases for the month	PB 38	£1219.20			

▲ **Figure 5.5** Entries in the nominal ledger.

The sequence of entries of purchase invoices is summarised in **Figure 5.6**.

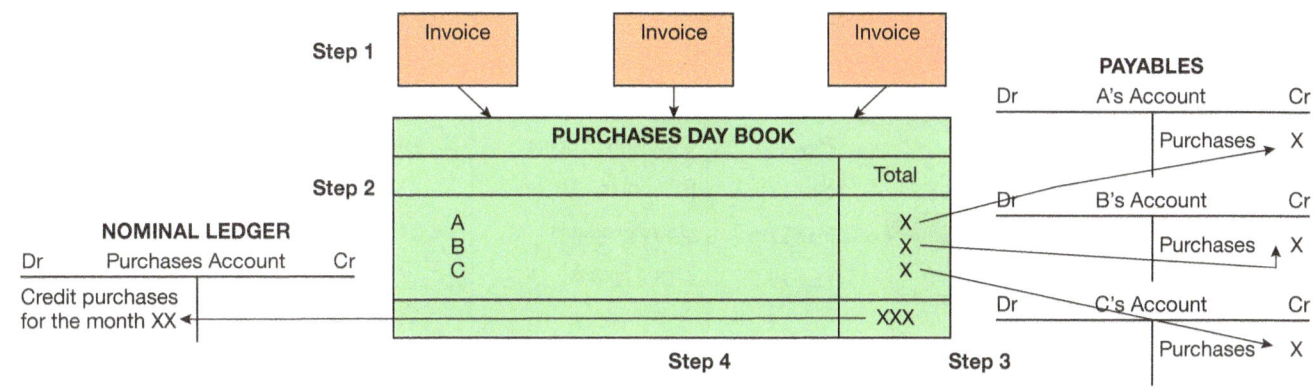

▲ **Figure 5.6** The sequence of entries of purchase invoices.

5.5 CASH AND CREDIT REVENUE

CASH REVENUE

When a customer purchases goods and pays for them immediately by cash, there is no need to enter the sale of these goods into the sales day book or the receivables ledger. This is because the customer is not in debt to the business, so there is no need to record the customer's name and address.

CREDIT REVENUE

In many businesses, most of the revenue will be made on credit rather than cash. In fact, some businesses and organisations earn revenue entirely from credit revenue.

For each credit sale, the supplier sends a document to the buyer showing details and prices of the goods sold. This document is known as a revenue invoice to the supplier, and a purchase invoice to the buyer. **Figure 4.4** showed an example of an invoice.

Most businesses have individually designed invoices, but inevitably they follow a generally accepted accounting format. All invoices are numbered and include the names and addresses of both the supplier and the customer. In **Figure 4.4** the supplier is Rivett Rugby and Football Club and the customer is Gramson's Sports.

REVENUE INVOICES

A **revenue invoice** is made out by the supplier when the supplier despatches the goods to the buyer. The top copy of the revenue invoice is sent to the buyer. Further copies are kept by the supplier for use within the organisation. For example, one copy will be sent to the accounts department so they can record the sale of goods on credit in the sales day book and receivables ledger. Another copy may be passed to the revenue department, and so on.

The accounts department will then enter all the revenue invoices into the sales day book, including:

- date of the invoice
- customer's name
- goods (net cost)
- total amount due.

Figure 5.7 shows a **sales day book**. It shows how the invoices are entered, starting with the entry of the invoice shown in **Figure 4.4**.

Sales Day Book		
Date	Details	Total
2017		£
May 4	Gramson's Sports	480.00
May 12	BY Sports	100.80
May 22	Delve Products	144.00
May 29	Zhang Sports	213.60
		938.40

▲ Figure 5.7 Example entries in a sales day book.

> **NOTE**
> The 'Total' column in the sales day book is posted to the Trade receivables control account but this will be dealt with in Chapter 10.

The sequence of entries of sales invoices is summarised in **Figure 5.8**.

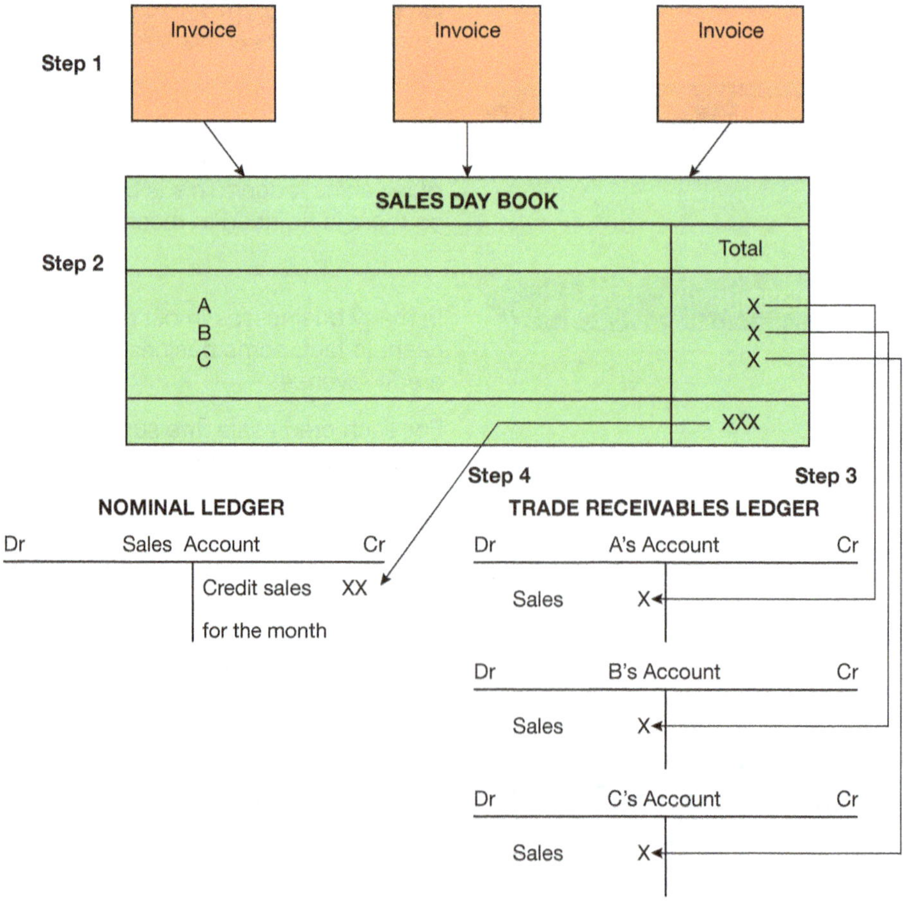

▲ Figure 5.8 The sequence of entries of sales invoices.

POSTING CREDIT REVENUE TO THE RECEIVABLES LEDGER

After the invoices have been entered into the sales day book, the next step is to post each invoice to the individual customer's account in the receivables ledger. At the end of the period, usually each month, the totals in the sales day book are posted to the revenue account in the nominal ledger. The double entry requirements are to:

- **debit** each customer's account in the receivables ledger with the total of each individual invoice (the goods go IN to their account)
- **credit** the revenue account with the total of the 'net revenue' (the revenue comes OUT from the supplier).

EXAMPLE: POSTING CREDIT REVENUE

Each of the invoices from the sales day book (**Figure 5.7**) is then posted to the customers' accounts in the receivables ledger, using the double entry procedures. This is shown in **Figure 5.9**.

Notice the folio columns show the sales day book reference in the ledger accounts and the ledger references in the day book.

	Trade Receivables Ledger		
Dr	Gramson's Sports Account		Cr
2017	Folio	£	
May 4 Revenue	SB 26	480.00	
Dr	BY Sports Account		Cr
2017	Folio	£	
May 12 Revenue	SB 26	100.80	
Dr	Delve Products Account		Cr
2017	Folio	£	
May 22 Revenue	SB 26	144.00	
Dr	Zhang Sports Account		Cr
2017	Folio	£	
May 29 Revenue	SB 26	213.60	

▲ Figure 5.9 Example entries in a receivables ledger.

The postings to the nominal ledger are shown in **Figure 5.10**.

	Nominal Ledger		(page 44)
Dr	Revenue Account		Cr
	2017	Folio	£
	May 31	SB 26	938.40

▲ Figure 5.10 Entries in the nominal ledger.

5.6 PURCHASE RETURNS (RETURNS OUTWARDS) AND PURCHASE CREDIT NOTES

Sometimes a business buys goods for resale but then has to return some of the goods. These returns are known as 'purchase returns' or 'returns outwards'. When the customer returns the goods to the supplier, the supplier issues a credit note. This credit note is sent to the customer.

BOOKKEEPING ENTRIES FOR PURCHASE CREDIT NOTES

The credit notes are listed in a **purchase returns day book**. This is also called the 'returns outwards day book'. In **Figure 5.3**, various invoices are entered into the purchases day book. Let us assume that some of the goods received from two of the business's suppliers were not satisfactory and were returned. The suppliers would then issue credit notes to rectify the situation. The credit notes will be entered into the purchase returns day book, as shown in **Figure 5.11**.

Purchase Returns Day Book		
Date	Details	Total
2017		£
Jan 15	Fuller & Sons	38.40
Jan 26	A Lewis	120.00
		158.40

▲ Figure 5.11 Entries in a purchase returns day book.

NOTE
The 'Total' column in the purchase returns day book is posted to the Purchases/trade payables' control account. We will learn about this in Chapter 15.

POSTING CREDIT NOTES TO THE PURCHASE AND NOMINAL LEDGER

After the credit notes have been entered into the purchase returns day book, the next step is to post each credit note to the individual suppliers' accounts. At the end of the month the total net goods returned are posted to the purchase returns in the nominal ledger. The bookkeeper will now:

- **debit** each individual suppliers' account in the payables ledger with the total of each credit note
- **credit** the purchase returns account with the total of the 'net goods returned'.

Using IN and OUT, the entries would be as follows: the goods returned to the supplier go IN to the suppliers' accounts and come OUT of the purchase returns account.

EXAMPLE: POSTING PURCHASE CREDIT NOTES

Using the purchases day book from **Figure 5.3** and the payables ledger accounts from the example in Chapter 5 (see pages 39–40), each of the credit notes is now posted to the suppliers' accounts in the Trade payables ledger (see **Figure 5.12**). The folio columns have been completed.

		Trade Payables Ledger			
Dr		Fuller & Sons Account			Cr
2017	Folio	£	2016	Folio	£
Jan 15 Purchase returns	PR 40	38.40	Dec 8 Purchases	PB 38	172.80
Dr		A Lewis Account			Cr
2017	Folio	£	2016	Folio	£
Jan 26 Purchase returns	PR 40	120.00	Dec 17 Purchases	PB 38	624.00
		Nominal Ledger			
Dr		Purchase Returns Account			Cr
	Folio	£	2017	Folio	£
			Jan 31 Total PRDB	PR 40	158.40

▲ Figure 5.12 Entries in the Trade payables ledger and the nominal ledger.

5 BOOKS OF ORIGINAL ENTRY

5.7 SALES RETURNS (RETURNS INWARDS) AND PURCHASE RETURNS (RETURNS OUTWARDS)

When goods are bought and sold, it is inevitable that some goods will be unsuitable. For example, they may be:

- faulty or damaged
- not suitable, for example, the wrong type, size, or colour
- part of an incomplete consignment
- subject to an overcharge on the invoice.

When this happens, the supplier must correct the situation.

> **HINT**
> Sales returns are also referred to as **returns inwards** while purchase returns are known as **returns outwards**.

5.8 SALES RETURNS (RETURNS INWARDS) AND CREDIT NOTES

If the goods supplied are unsuitable, the supplier will need to rectify the situation. The customer (trade receivable) was sent an invoice when the goods were delivered, so they are in debt to the supplier (trade receivable) for the value of the goods. Therefore, when the supplier makes an allowance for goods that have been returned, or a reduction in price is agreed, the supplier issues a **credit note** to the customer (trade receivable). The credit note shows the amount of the agreed reduction. **Figure 4.5** shows an example of a credit note.

BOOKKEEPING ENTRIES FOR REVENUE CREDIT NOTES

Credit notes are source documents. They are listed in a separate day book called the sales returns day book or the returns inwards day book.

Figure 5.7 shows some entries in a sales day book. If two of the customers had a problem with some of the goods invoiced and were each sent a credit note to rectify the situation, the credit notes will be entered into the sales returns day book, as shown in **Figure 5.13**.

Sales Returns Day Book		(page 11)
Date	Details	Total
2017		£
June 11	Gramson's Sports	86.40
June 24	Zhang Sports	67.20
		153.60

▲ Figure 5.13 Entries in a sales returns day book.

> **NOTE**
> The 'Total' column in **Figure 5.13** is posted to the Revenue/trade receivables' control account. We will learn about this in Chapter 15.

POSTING CREDIT NOTES TO THE REVENUE AND NOMINAL LEDGER (CREDIT NOTES ISSUED)

After the credit notes have been entered into the sales returns day book, each credit note must be posted to the individual customer's account. At the end of the month the total net goods returned are posted to the revenue returns in the nominal ledger. The bookkeeper will now:

- **credit** each customer's account in the receivables ledger with the total of each individual credit note
- **debit** the revenue returns account with the total of the net goods returned.

Again, you may find it easier to use IN and OUT. Goods returned to the seller are entered on the IN side of the revenue returns account because the goods are coming back IN. The goods returned are entered on the OUT side of the individual relevant customer's account as they are sending the goods back (OUT) to the supplier.

AN EXAMPLE OF POSTING REVENUE CREDIT NOTES

Using the sales returns day book from **Figure 5.13** and the receivables ledger accounts from **Figure 5.9**, each of the credit notes can be posted to the customers' accounts in the trade receivables ledger (see **Figure 5.14**). The folio references have also been completed.

Trade Receivables Ledger					
Dr		Gramson's Sports Account			Cr
2017	Folio	£	2017		£
			Folio		
May 4 Revenue	SB 26	480.00	June 11 Revenue returns	SR 11	86.40
Dr		Zhang Sports Account			Cr
2017	Folio	£	2017		£
May 29 Revenue	SB 26	213.60	June 24 Revenue returns	SR 11	67.20

▲ Figure 5.14 Entries in a trade receivables ledger.

The totals from the sales returns day book will then be posted to the revenue returns in the nominal ledger, as shown in **Figure 5.15**.

Nominal Ledger				
Dr		Revenue Returns Account		Cr
2017	Folio	£	Folio	£
June 30 Total SRB	SR 11	153.60		

▲ Figure 5.15 Entries in the nominal ledger.

5.9 CASH DISCOUNTS

Businesses prefer customers to pay their accounts quickly as it helps cash flow. A business may accept a smaller sum in full settlement if payment is made within a certain period of time. The reduction in the sum to be paid is known as a **cash discount**: the term 'cash discount' refers to the allowance given for quick payment. It is still called a cash discount even if the account is paid by cheque or by direct transfer into the bank account.

The rate of cash discount is usually stated as a percentage. Full details of the percentage allowed will be quoted on all revenue documents produced by the selling company. The revenue documents will also state the period within which payment is to be made. A typical period during which a discount may be allowed is one month from the date of the original transaction.

DISCOUNTS ALLOWED AND DISCOUNTS RECEIVED

A business may have two types of cash discount in its books. These are:
- **discounts allowed.** Cash discounts allowed by a business to its customers when they pay their accounts quickly
- **discounts received.** Cash discounts received by a business from its suppliers when they pay their accounts quickly.

We will consider the effect of discounts by looking at two examples.

Example 1:
C Chan owes us $100. On 2 September 2017, he pays by cash within the time limit and the business allows him 5% cash discount.

Therefore, Chan will pay $100 less $5 cash discount = $95 in full settlement of his account.

EFFECT	ACTION
1 Of cash:	
Cash is increased by $95.	**Debit:** Cash account, i.e. enter $95 in debit column of cash book.
Asset of trade receivables is decreased by $95.	**Credit:** C Chan $95.
2 Of discounts:	
Asset of trade receivables is decreased by $5. (After the cash is paid, there remains a balance of $5. As the account has been paid, this asset must now be cancelled.)	**Credit:** C Chan $5.
Expenses of discounts allowed increased by $5.	**Debit:** Discounts allowed account $5.

This means that C Chan's debt of $100 is shown as fully settled. The accounts also show exactly how the settlement took.

Example 2:

A business owed R Abbas $400. They paid him by cheque on 3 September 2017 – within the specified 30 days – so the business claimed $2\frac{1}{2}\%$ cash discount. The amount paid to R Abbas is $400 less $10 cash discount = $390 in full settlement of the account.

EFFECT	ACTION
1 Of cheque:	
Asset of bank is reduced by $390.	**Credit:** Bank, i.e. enter $390 credit bank column.
Liability of trade payables is reduced by $390.	**Debit:** R Abbas' account with $390.
2 Of discounts:	
Liability of trade payables is reduced by $10. (After the cheque is paid, the balance of $10 remains. As the account has been paid, the liability must now be cancelled.)	**Debit:** R Abbas' account $10.
Revenue of discounts received increased by $10.	**Credit:** Discounts received account $10.

The accounts in the business's books for C Chan and R Abbas are shown in **Figure 5.16**.

Dr			Cash Book					Cr
	Folio	Cash	Bank			Folio	Cash	Bank
2017		$	$	2017				$
Sept 2 C Chan	SL 12	95		Sept 3	R Abbas	PL 75		390

	Nominal Ledger			
Dr	Discounts Allowed Account			Cr
2017	Folio	$		
Sept 2 C Chan	SL 12	5		
Dr	Discounts Received Account			Cr
		2017	Folio	$
		Sept 3 R Abbas	PL 75	10

UNIT 2 — 5 BOOKS OF ORIGINAL ENTRY

Trade Receivables Ledger

Dr					C Chan Account				Cr
2017				$	2017		Folio		$
Sept 1	Balance			100	Sept 2	Cash	CB 32		95
					Sept 2	Discount	GL 17		5
				100					100

Trade Payables Ledger

Dr					R Abbas Account			Cr
2017		Folio		$				$
Sept 3	Bank	CB 32		390		Balance		400
Sept 3	Discount	GL 18		10				
				400				400

▲ **Figure 5.16** Account entries for C Chan and R Abbas.

It is an accounting custom to enter the word 'Discount' in the personal accounts, without stating whether it is a discount received or a discount allowed.

DISCOUNT COLUMNS IN THE CASH BOOK

The discounts allowed account and the discounts received account are in the nominal ledger, along with all the other revenue and expense accounts. However, you should try to avoid too much reference to the nominal ledger.

To record discounts, add an extra column on each side of the cash book and record discounts in this column. Enter discounts received in the discounts column on the credit side of the cash book, and enter discounts allowed in the discounts column on the debit side of the cash book.

The cash book for the two examples we have looked at so far would appear as shown in **Figure 5.17**.

Cash Book (page 32)

		Folio	Discount	Cash	Bank			Folio	Discount	Cash	Bank
2017			$	$	$	2017			$	$	$
Sept 2	C Chan	SL 12	5	95		Sept 3	R Abbas	PL 75	10		390

▲ **Figure 5.17** Example cash book entries, showing discounts.

You must also make entries in the discount accounts in the nominal ledger:

Total of discounts column on receipts side of cash book } Enter on debit side of discounts allowed account

Total of discounts column on payments side of cash book } Enter on credit side of discounts received account

5 BOOKS OF ORIGINAL ENTRY

WORKED EXAMPLE

Here is an example of a three-column cash book for the month of May. It shows the ultimate transfer of the totals of the discount columns to the discount accounts in the nominal ledger.

2017		€
May 1	Balances brought down from April:	
	Cash balance	29
	Bank balance	65
	Trade receivables' accounts:	
	B Schultz	120
	N Ritter	280
	D Bernard	40
	Trade payables' accounts:	
	U Singh	60
	A Mendez	440
	R Rossi	100
May 2	B Schultz pays us by cheque, having deducted $2\frac{1}{2}$% cash discount €3	117
May 8	We pay R Rossi his account by cheque, deducting 5% cash discount €5	95
May 11	We withdraw €100 cash from the bank for business use	100
May 16	N Ritter pays us his account by cheque, deducting $2\frac{1}{2}$% discount €7	273
May 25	We pay expenses in cash	92
May 28	D Bernard pays us in cash, deducting $2\frac{1}{2}$% cash discount €2	38
May 29	We pay U Singh by cheque less 5% cash discount €3	57
May 30	We pay A Mendez by cheque less $2\frac{1}{2}$% cash discount €11	429

The relevant sections of the accounts books are shown in **Figure 5.18**.

Cash Book

Dr											*Cr*
		Folio	Discount	Cash	Bank			*Folio*	Discount	Cash	Bank
2017			€	€	€	2017			€	€	€
May 1	Balances	b/d		29	654	May 8	R Rossi	PL 58	5		95
May 2	B Schultz	SL 13	3		117	May 11	Cash	C			100
May 11	Bank	C		100		May 25	Expenses	GL 77		92	
May 16	N Ritter	SL 84	7		273	May 29	U Singh	PL 15	3		57
May 28	D Bernard	SL 91	2	38		May 30	A Mendez	PL 98	11		429
						May 31	Balances	c/d		75	363
			12	167	1044				19	167	1044
Jun 1	Balances	b/d		75	363						

Trade Receivables Ledger

Dr				B Schultz Account				*Cr*
2017			*Folio*	€	2017		*Folio*	€
May 1	Balance		b/d	120	May 2	Bank	CB 64	117
					May 2	Discount	CB 64	3
				120				120

Dr				N Ritter Account				Cr
2017		Folio	€	2017		Folio		€
May 1	Balance	b/d	280	May 16	Bank	CB 64		273
				May 16	Discount	CB 64		7
			280					280

Dr				D Bernard Account				Cr
2017		Folio	€	2017		Folio		€
May 1	Balance	b/d	40	May 28	Cash	CB 64		38
				May 28	Discount	CB 64		2
			40					40

Trade Payables Ledger

Dr				U Singh Account				Cr
2017		Folio	€	2017		Folio		€
May 29	Bank	CB 64	57	May 1	Balance	b/d		60
May 29	Discount	CB 64	3					
			60					60

Dr				R Rossi Account				Cr
2017		Folio	€	2017		Folio		€
May 8	Bank	CB 64	95	May 1	Balance	b/d		100
May 8	Discount	CB 64	5					
			100					100

Dr				A Mendez Account				Cr
2017		Folio	€	2017		Folio		€
May 30	Bank	CB 64	429	May 1	Balance	b/d		440
May 30	Discount	CB 64	11					
			440					440

Nominal Ledger

Dr				Expenses Account				Cr
2017		Folio	€	2017		Folio		€
May 25	Cash	CB 64	92					

Nominal Ledger

Dr				Discounts Received Account				Cr
		Folio	€	2017		Folio		€
				May 31	Cash book	CB 64		19

Nominal Ledger

Dr				Discounts Allowed Account				Cr
2017		Folio	€			Folio		€
May 31	Cash book	CB 64	12					

▲ **Figure 5.18** Accounts book entries for worked example.

You can easily check whether the discounts have been entered correctly, as shown in **Figure 5.19**.

Discounts in Ledger Accounts	Debits		Credits	
		€		€
Discounts received	U Singh	3		
	R Rossi	5	Discounts received account	19
	A Mendez	11		
		19		
				€
Discounts allowed			B Schultz	3
	Discounts allowed account	12	N Ritter	7
			D Bernard	2
				12

▲ Figure 5.19 Checking discount entries.

You can see that the double entry has been carried out correctly since equal amounts, in total, have been entered on each side of the account.

5.10 BANK OVERDRAFTS AND THE CASH BOOK

Banks may offer overdraft facilities to businesses. An overdraft allows a business to pay more out of their bank account than the money available. In effect, a **bank overdraft** allows a business to borrow money on a temporary basis from the bank, as long as the bank has agreed to offer this facility. So far, the bank balances in the examples in this chapter have shown money in the bank, that is, debit balances brought down, an asset. When the account is overdrawn, the balance brought down becomes a credit balance, that is, a liability.

Look at the cash book in **Figure 5.18**. If the amount payable to A Mendez was €1429 instead of €429, the amount in the bank account, €1044, would be exceeded by the amount withdrawn. The cash book would appear as shown in **Figure 5.20**.

Dr					Cash Book						*Cr*
		Discount	Cash	Bank				Discount	Cash	Bank	
2017		€	€	€	2017			€	€	€	
May 1	Balances b/d		29	654	May 8	R Rossi		5		95	
May 2	B Schultz	3		117	May 11	Cash				100	
May 11	Bank		100		May 25	Expenses			92		
May 16	N Ritter	7		273	May 29	U Singh		3		57	
May 28	D Bernard	2	38		May 30	A Mendez		11		1429	
May 31	Balances c/d			637	May 31	Balances c/d			75		
		12	167	1,681				19	167	1681	
Jun 1	Balance b/d		75		Jun 1	Balance b/d				637	

▲ Figure 5.20 Entry of a bank overdraft in a cash book.

UNIT 2   5 BOOKS OF ORIGINAL ENTRY

On a statement of financial position, a bank overdraft is shown under the heading Current Liabilities.

WORKED EXAMPLE

A small company offering secretarial services to local businesses incurs the following items of expenditure during May 2017. First, these items must be entered in the petty cash book.

2017	
May 1	The petty cashier received a cash float of £200.00 from the cashier
May 2	Stationery £11.75 (see petty cash voucher no. 1)
May 4	Postage stamps, £22.00
May 6	Tea and coffee for office visitors, £8.00
May 9	Travel expenses, £16.00
May 10	Computer disks, £10.67
May 12	Postage on parcel, £3.60
May 15	Office cleaner, £25.00
May 22	Milk for office, £4.20
May 25	Received £6.00 from Luisa Moro, office manager, for personal postage*
May 27	Office cleaner, £25.00
May 27	Cleaning materials, £4.40
May 31	Travel expenses, £23.00
May 31	The cashier reimbursed the petty cashier with the amount spent during the month

For each of the above items, a petty cash voucher will be completed by the person who incurred the expenditure on behalf of the business. For illustration purposes, only one petty voucher is shown, in **Figure 5.21**.

Petty Cash Voucher

No. _1_
Date _2 May 2017_

Description	Amount	
	£	p
Stationery	11	75

Signature _Helena Kazim_
Authorised _Natasha Allen_

▲ Figure 5.21 A petty cash voucher.

5 BOOKS OF ORIGINAL ENTRY

All items of expenditure and receipts are entered in the petty cash book, as shown in **Figure 5.22**.

Receipts £ p	Date	Details	Voucher number	Total £ p	Postage £ p	Cleaning £ p	Travel expenses £ p	Stationery £ p	Other operating expenses £ p
	2017								
200.00	May 1	Cash	CB 19						
	May 2	Stationery	1	11.75				11.75	
	May 4	Postage stamps	2	22.00	22.00				
	May 6	Tea, coffee	3	8.00					8.00
	May 9	Travel expenses	4	16.00			16.00		
	May 10	Computer disks	5	10.67				10.67	
	May 12	Postage on parcel	6	3.60	3.60				
	May 15	Office cleaner	7	25.00		25.00			
	May 22	Milk	8	4.20					4.20
6.00	May 25	Luisa Moro postage	26						
	May 27	Office cleaner	9	25.00		25.00			
	May 27	Cleaning materials	10	4.40		4.40			
	May 31	Travel expenses	11	23.00			23.00		
				153.62	25.60	54.40	39.00	22.42	12.20
	May 31	Balance	c/d	52.38	GL 19	GL 29	GL 44	GL 56	GL 60
206.00				206.00					
52.38	June 1	Balance	b/d						
147.62	June 1	cash	CB 22						

Reimbursement equals the total amount spent in May 2017 (£153.62 − £6.00 receipt = £147.62 reimbursed)

Total amount spent in May 2017

▲ **Figure 5.22** Entries in a petty cash book.

ENTERING THE PETTY CASH BOOK

Look at **Figure 5.22**. On 1 May, the petty cashier receives £200.00 cash float from the senior cashier for the month.

The cashier enters this item on the credit side of the cash book. The money comes OUT of the bank. The debit entry is now shown on the 'Receipts' side of the petty cash book, as the money comes 'INTO' the petty cash. Note that the folio reference 'CB 19' (Cash Book page 19) is also entered to cross-reference the entry. Each petty cash voucher is entered in date order as follows:

- Enter the date.
- Enter the details of the payment.
- Give a number to the petty cash voucher. Enter the number on the voucher and in the 'voucher number' column.

- Enter the total expenditure incurred in the 'Total' column.
- Enter the expenditure in an appropriate expense column.
- Enter any money received from the sale of sundry items to a member of staff (such as Luisa Moro's personal postage) in the 'receipts' column. In this example the cost is £6.00. Also enter the date, details and receipt number in the appropriate columns.

The petty cashier will balance off the petty cash book at the end of the month as follows:

- Add up the 'Total' column.
- Add up each of the expense columns. The total of all the expense columns added together should equal the amount shown in the 'Total' column. In **Figure 5.22**, the total would be:

	£ p
Postage	25.60
Cleaning	54.40
Travel expenses	39.00
Stationery	22.42
Other operating expenses	12.20
Total	153.62

- Calculate the amount of money needed to restore the **imprest** to £200.00 for the beginning of the next period:

	£ p
Amount of float at beginning of May	200.00
Money received during month, Luisa Moro – postage	6.00
	206.00
Less Amount spent (see above)	153.62
Cash in hand at 31 May 2017	52.38
Amount of float	200.00
Less Cash in hand at 31 May 2017	52.38
Cash required to restore the imprest	157.62

- Enter the balance of cash in hand at 31 May 2017, £47.02, in the petty cash book. This shows as *Balance c/d*, £47.02 (see **Figure 5.22**).
- Add up the 'Receipts' and 'Total' columns. They should be equal to each other, that is, £206.00. These totals are shown on the same line and are both double underlined.
- Enter the *Balance b/d* on 1 June, £47.02, in the 'Receipts' column. Underneath that entry, enter the amount received from the cashier to restore the imprest, £152.98.

Now carry out the double entry for each of the expense columns:

- Debit the total of each expense column to the expense account in the nominal ledger.
- Enter the folio number of each nominal ledger account under each of the expense columns in the petty cash book. This enables cross-referencing and also means the double entry to the ledger account is complete.

> **SUBJECT VOCABULARY**
>
> **imprest** a sum of money given to someone in an organisation to make small payments

The double entry for all the items in **Figure 5.22** appear as shown in **Figure 5.23**.

Cash Book (Bank column only)

Dr				Cr
	2017		Folio	£
	May 1	Petty Cash	PCB 31	200.00
	June 1	Petty Cash	PCB 31	157.62

Nominal Ledger

Dr — Postages Account — Cr

2017		Folio	£	
May 31	Petty Cash	PCB 31	25.60	

Dr — Cleaning Account — Cr

2017		Folio	£	
May 31	Petty Cash	PCB 31	54.40	

Dr — Travel Expenses Account — Cr

2017		Folio	£	
May 31	Petty Cash	PCB 31	39.00	

Dr — Stationery Account — Cr

2017		Folio	£	
May 31	Petty Cash	PCB 31	22.42	

Dr — Other operating expenses Account — Cr

2017		Folio	£	
May 31	Petty Cash	PCB 31	12.20	

▲ **Figure 5.23** Accounting book entries for petty cash.

> **SUBJECT VOCABULARY**
>
> **other operating expenses** the indirect costs of a business, which are not directly involved in the production process. Examples are the cost of rent, advertising, stationary and bank charges

PAYING TRADE PAYABLES FROM PETTY CASH

Occasionally, a business will pay a creditor out of the petty cash. If this happens, the bookkeeper will enter the payment in the petty cash book, using a column headed 'Ledger accounts'. The bookkeeper will then post the item to the debit side of the creditor's account in the payables ledger. This type of transaction is very rare and only occurs when the item to be paid is small, or when a refund is made out of petty cash to a customer who may have overpaid their account.

5.11 THE JOURNAL

We know that transactions are first entered into a book of original entry. For example, we record all items involving receipts and payments in the cash book, while we enter purchase and revenue invoices in the respective day books. Occasionally, it is necessary to record a much less common transaction, such as writing off an irrecoverable debt. Another example of an unusual transaction is when a trade receivable is unable to pay an outstanding invoice and offers a non-current asset in full settlement of the debt. It is just as important to record these transactions as it is to record the purchase of goods for resale. These transactions are therefore recorded in another book of original entry – the journal.

The layout of the journal is shown in **Figure 5.24**.

The Journal

Date		Folio	Dr	Cr
	The name of the account to be debited			
	The name of the account to be credited			
	The narrative			

▲ Figure 5.24 The layout of the journal.

The journal is like a diary. Details of less common transactions are recorded here before they are posted to the ledger accounts. The following details are recorded for each transaction:

- the date
- the name of the accounts to be debited and credited and the amount
- a description and explanation of the transaction, known as the **narrative**
- a reference number for the source document as proof of the transaction.

TYPICAL USES OF THE JOURNAL

Some of the less common transactions that the journal may be used to record include:

- the purchase and sale of non-current assets on credit
- writing off irrecoverable debts
- other items: adjustments to any of the entries in the ledgers
- the correction of errors.

5.12 WRITING UP JOURNAL ENTRIES

Many students find it difficult to prepare journal entries, so let's look at some examples. These examples show:

1. the entries as they would appear in the double entry accounts
2. the journal entries for the transaction.

PURCHASE AND SALE OF NON-CURRENT ASSETS

Example 1: A business buys a drilling machine on credit from Toolmakers for Kenyan shilling 550,000 on 1 July 2017. This transaction involves the acquisition of a new drilling machine, which is an asset. But the business also incurs a liability because it has purchased the machine on credit from Toolmakers. The double entry for this transaction is a debit entry in the Machinery Account (since the business has acquired an asset) and a credit entry in the Toolmakers Account, which is a liability. This is shown in **Figure 5.25**.

Nominal Ledger

Dr			Machinery Account		(Folio NL 1) Cr
2017		Folio		Ks	
Jul 1	Toolmakers	PL 55		550 000	

Trade Payables Ledger

Dr		Toolmakers Account			(Folio PL 55) Cr
			2017	Folio	Ks
		Machinery	Jul 1	NL 1	550 000

▲ Figure 5.25 Double entry accounts for Example 1.

For the transaction above, the journal entry will appear as shown below. Remember, the journal is simply a kind of diary, not in account form but in ordinary written form. It says which account has to be debited and which account has to be credited, then gives a narrative that describes the nature of the transaction. For the transaction above, the journal entry will appear as shown in **Figure 5.26**.

The Journal					
Date	Details	Folio	Dr	Cr
2017			Ks	Ks
Jul 1	Machinery	NL 1	550 000	
	Toolmakers	PL 55		550 000
	Purchase of drilling machine on credit, purchase invoice no. 7/159			

▲ Figure 5.26 Journal entry for Example 1.

Example 2: Some office furniture that is no longer required is sold for £300 on credit to K De Silva on 2 July 2017. The double entry accounts and journal entries are shown in **Figure 5.27**.

Trade Receivables Ledger				
Dr		K De Silva Account		(Folio SL 79) Cr
2017		Folio	£	
Jul 2	Office furniture	GL 51	300	

Nominal Ledger				
Dr		Office Furniture Account		(Folio GL 51) Cr
		2017	Folio	£
		Jul 2	K De Silva	SL 79	300

The Journal				
Date	Details	Folio	Dr	Cr
2017			£	£
Jul 2	K De Silva	SL 79	300	
	Office furniture	GL 51		300
	Sale of some office furniture no longer required – see letter ref: CT 568			

▲ Figure 5.27 Double entry accounts and journal for Example 2.

WRITING OFF IRRECOVERABLE DEBTS

Example 3: A debt of HK$70 owed to a business by Y Li is written off as an irrecoverable debt on 31 August 2017. In this example, we need to cancel the amount owing by crediting Y Li's account. Since an irrecoverable debt is an expense, the irrecoverable debts account will need to be debited.

UNIT 2   5 BOOKS OF ORIGINAL ENTRY   57

> **DID YOU KNOW?**
> Luca Pacioli wrote *Summa de Arithmetica, Geometria, Proportioni et Proportionalita* in 1494. This book included a 27-page essay on bookkeeping, *Particularis de Computis et Scripturis* (Details of Calculation and Recording). This essay on the subjects of record keeping and **double entry accounting** became the reference text and teaching tool on those subjects for the next several hundred years.

The double entry accounts and journal entries are shown in **Figure 5.28**.

Nominal Ledger

Dr		Irrecoverable Debts Account		(Folio GL 16) Cr
2017		Folio	HK$	
Aug 31	Y Li	SL 99	70	

Trade Receivables Ledger

Dr		Y Li Account				(Folio SL 99) Cr
2017		Folio	HK$	2017	Folio	HK$
Aug 1	Balance	b/d	70	Aug 31	Irrecoverable debts GL 16	70

The Journal

Date	Details	Folio	Dr	Cr
2017			HK$	HK$
Aug 31	Irrecoverable debts	GL 16	70	
	Y Li	SL 99		70

▲ **Figure 5.28** Double entry accounts and journal for Example 3.

CORRECTION OF ERRORS

Most errors are discovered after a period of time has elapsed. Once identified, they need to be corrected properly via the journal. Do not cross out items, tear a page out of a ledger, or use correcting fluid. If these were allowed, there would be more risk of fraudulent transactions taking place.

Some errors do not affect the agreement of the trial balance. Other errors lead to the trial balance failing to balance.

END OF CHAPTER QUESTIONS

Choose the correct phrase to complete each sentence.

1. Purchase of _____ is recorded in the purchases journal.

   a. goods for cash
   b. goods for credit
   c. machinery for credit
   d. stationery for cash

2. We post the total of the discount recorded on the debit side of the cashbook in the _____ account.

   a. credit discount allowed
   b. credit discount received
   c. debit discount allowed
   d. debit discount received

3. Credit notes are recorded in the _____ .

   a. purchases journal
   b. purchases returns journal
   c. sales journal
   d. sales returns journal

4. Irrecoverable debts are written off in the _____ .

   a. cash book
   b. journal
   c. purchases book
   d. sales book

5 Entries in the purchases day book are made from _____.

    a credit notes   b delivery notes

    c invoices   d petty cash vouchers

6 Name the business document used to prepare the purchases day book.

7 Name the source document used to prepare the sales returns day book.

8 Name **one** use for the journal.

9 Which **two** accounts are prepared from entries in the purchases returns day book?

END OF CHAPTER CHECKLIST

- Ledger accounts must show the date, folio details, amount of the transaction and details of the opposite entry.
- All transactions must be entered in the books of original entry before posting to the ledgers.
- When goods or services are sold for cash, they do not need to be entered in the sales day book or trade receivables ledger.
- Credit control in a business is important in order to maintain a good cash position.

EXAM PRACTICE

A01 **A02** **A03**   Answer ALL questions in this section. Questions 1–5 must be answered with a cross in the appropriate box ⊠. If you change your mind about an answer, put a line through the box ⊠ and then mark your new answer with a cross ⊠.

1 A trader sells goods at a list price of Y6000 on credit. The trader offers his customers a trade discount of 10% and a cash discount of 5%. What amount will be recorded in the trader's sales journal?

☐ **A** Y5100
☐ **B** Y5130
☐ **C** Y5400
☐ **D** Y6000 **(1 mark)**

2 A sole trader withdraws cash from the business bank account for her personal use. How would this transaction be recorded in the ledger?

		Debit	Credit
☐	**A**	Bank	Cash
☐	**B**	Bank	Drawings
☐	**C**	Bank	Equity
☐	**D**	Drawings	Bank **(1 mark)**

3 Which of these accounts has a credit balance?

☐ **A** discount allowed
☐ **B** discount received
☐ **C** purchases
☐ **D** sales returns **(1 mark)**

4 In which books of original entry should an irrecoverable debt that has been written off be entered?

☐ **A** cash book
☐ **B** journal
☐ **C** purchases book
☐ **D** sales book **(1 mark)**

5 In which book do we record a credit note sent to a customer?

☐ **A** purchases returns day book
☐ **B** sales day book
☐ **C** sales returns day book
☐ **D** journal **(1 mark)**

6 Amir Kan commenced business on 1 July 2017. On that day he:

- purchased goods for resale, costing £5000 and fixtures and fittings for use in the business, costing £8000
- paid £3500 into a business bank account and kept £100 to pay for petty cash expenses
- received a £5000 loan from his brother, which he paid into the business bank account.

Show the opening journal entry to record these transactions. **(5 marks)**

(Total 10 marks)

6 LEDGER ACCOUNTING AND DOUBLE ENTRY BOOKKEEPING

▲ Ledger accounting is a slow and methodical task. Accuracy is very important.

HINT
For every debit entry, there must be a credit entry.

SKILLS CRITICAL THINKING

SUBJECT VOCABULARY
posting transferring balances from the accounts into the nominal ledger

LEARNING OBJECTIVES
- Explain the purpose of the:
  - nominal ledger
  - receivables ledger
  - payables ledger
- Record transactions in ledger accounts using the double entry principle

GETTING STARTED
The next stage in the accounting system is to allocate the information in the books of original entry to the ledgers. Be careful with the names of these accounts as they are not easy to learn. Make sure you allocate all the information to the correct ledger. Take your time so you do not make any errors in your figures. A mistake now will be carried through all the accounts.

ACTIVITY
Look at your source documents and entries from the previous chapter. See if you can decide which entries are good for the business and which ones are bad for the business.

6.1 THE LEDGERS

Ledger accounting is a slow and methodical task. Accuracy is very important. First, enter the details of the transaction that has been entered into the books of original entry. This information must be entered into the ledgers using the double entry system. This procedure is often referred to as **posting**. Revenue transactions are posted to the receivables ledger and purchase transactions are posted to the payables ledger. Other items are posted to the accounts in the general or nominal ledger. There is more information about the ledgers and other accounting books on page 37.

TYPES OF LEDGER
The different types of ledger used are as follows (their alternative names are shown in brackets).

TYPES OF LEDGER		
Trade receivables ledger (Receivables ledger)	**Trade payables ledger** (Payables ledger)	**Nominal ledger** (General ledger)
Shows records of customers' personal accounts.	Shows records of suppliers' personal accounts.	Contains the remaining double entry accounts, such as assets, equity, expenses and income.

PRIVATE LEDGER

Occasionally, a business may keep a private ledger in order to ensure the privacy of the proprietor(s) when recording transactions such as their equity, drawings accounts and other similar accounts.

6.2 INTRODUCTION AND HISTORY OF THE DOUBLE ENTRY SYSTEM OF ACCOUNTING

> **DID YOU KNOW?**
> The first book on double entry accounting was published by Luca Pacioli in 1494.

People have used various forms of record-keeping since early times to record such things as rents, taxes and fines due. There was, however, no formal or standard system of bookkeeping until the 15th century when Father Luca Pacioli invented the 'double entry system of accounting'. This was the beginning of the process of formalised bookkeeping and the start of accounting. Since that time, the principle of 'double entry' has developed into the worldwide system we see today.

Anyone in business today must keep accounting records that:

- record business transactions
- show how much the business owes and is owed at any time
- show how much cash the business has
- show whether or not the business is making a profit.

You will learn about the 'accounting equation' in Section 6.4. This equation states that the resources supplied by the owner of the business (i.e. the equity) always equal the resources owned by the business (i.e. the assets). In other words, each transaction affects two items: the equity and the assets. Double entry bookkeeping is based on the accounting equation because every transaction affects two sides of the account.

▲ Luca Pacioli.

6.3 THE DOUBLE ENTRY SYSTEM

The system of double entry bookkeeping is a method of recording transactions in the books of account for a business. As mentioned above, every transaction affects two items. The information for every item that is entered into the books of account is obtained from a source document – an invoice, credit note, cheque book stub, paying in book, etc.

Business transactions deal with money or money's worth and every transaction affects two things. For example, if a business buys stationery valued at Singapore dollars 40 and pays for it by cash, two things occur:

- the money in the business's cash account decreases by S$40
- the business acquires stationery to the value of S$40.

Similarly, if a business buys some equipment costing Emirati dirhams 2000 and pays for it by cheque, two things are affected:

- the money in the business's bank account decreases by AED2000
- the business acquires equipment to the value of AED2000.

Each transaction is entered into an **account** which shows the 'history' of the particular business item. The account is the place in the records where all the information referring to a particular item (for example, company cars in the motor vehicle account) is recorded. In manual records, each account is usually shown on a separate page. In a computerised system, each account is given a separate code number and the information is stored on the accounting package and back-up systems.

> **SUBJECT VOCABULARY**
> **account** a record showing money coming into and going out of a business, its profits, and its financial situation

THE ACCOUNTS FOR DOUBLE ENTRY

SUBJECT VOCABULARY

debit a record in financial accounts that shows money that has been spent or that is owed

credit an amount of money that is put into someone's bank account or added to another amount

Each account should be shown on a separate page. The double entry system divides each page into two halves. The left-hand side of each page is called the **debit** side. The right-hand side is called the **credit** side. The title of each account is written across the top of the account, as shown in **Figure 6.1**. Note that the word 'Debit' is often shown in a short form as *Dr*, while 'Credit' is often shown as *Cr*.

Dr			Title of account written here			Cr
Date	Details	£	Date	Details	£	

▲ **Figure 6.1** Setting up an account.

Left-hand side of the page. This is the 'debit' side.

Right-hand side of the page. This is the 'credit' side.

HINT

Use DEAD CLIC to show increases in:
- **D**ebit entry — **C**redit entry
- **E**xpenses — **L**iabilities
- **A**ssets — **I**ncome
- **D**rawings — **C**apital or equity

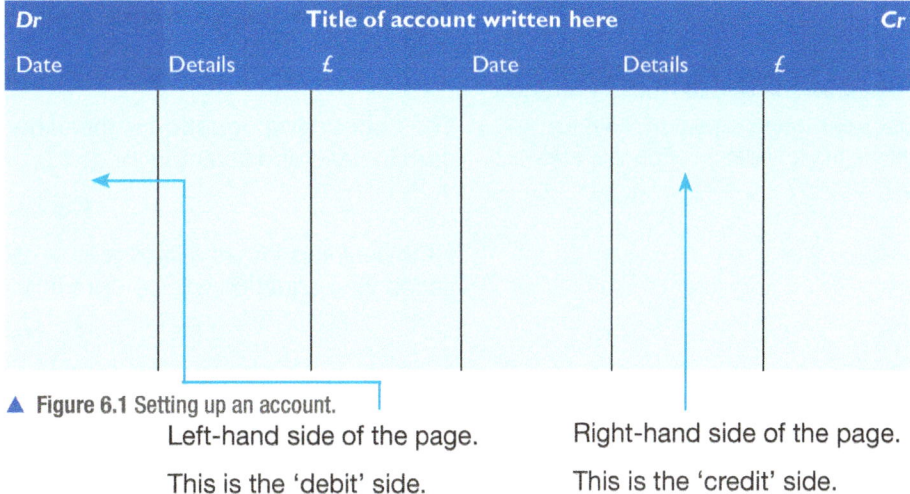

The words 'debit' and 'credit' do not mean the same in bookkeeping as in normal language. You may find it useful to think of IN when looking at the entry of a debit item, and to think of OUT when looking at the entry of a credit item (see pages 65–66).

6.4 RULES FOR DOUBLE ENTRY

Double entry is relatively easy to learn and understand if you follow these four rules:

1. Double entry means that every transaction affects two things. You should, therefore, enter every transaction twice: once on the Debit side and once on the Credit side. Later on in your studies, you may have to record a transaction in more than two accounts (for example, when an item is purchased and part of it is paid for in cash and part paid by cheque).

2. The order in which you enter items does not matter. You may find it easier to deal with any cash or bank transactions first, however, using the IN and OUT principle.

3. A **debit** entry is always an asset or an expense. A **credit** entry is a liability, capital or equity or income.

4. To increase or decrease assets, liabilities or capital or equity, the double entry rules are as shown in **Figure 6.2**.

ACCOUNTS	TO RECORD	ENTRY IN THE ACCOUNT
Assets	↑ an increase	Debit
	↓ a decrease	Credit
Liabilities	↑ an increase	Credit
	↓ a decrease	Debit
Equity	↑ an increase	Credit
	↓ a decrease	Debit

▲ **Figure 6.2** Double entry rules.

Look at the accounting equations below.

Capital (the owner's/owners' money) = Assets (cash in hand)

Capital = Assets

If the business then buys inventory of goods and pays for them by cash, the accounting equation will look like this:

Capital (the owner's/owners' money) = Assets (cash in hand less amount spent on the inventory) + inventory of goods

The accounting equation is the same except that we now have two assets: cash in hand and inventory of goods.

Capital = Assets

If the business incurs a liability (e.g. obtains a loan from the bank) the accounting equation will look like this:

Assets = Capital + Liabilities

An alternative way of using the accounting equation is:

Capital = Assets − Liabilities

In other words, the capital or equity always equals the assets less the liabilities. Using the example above, let us assume that the capital or equity is £10 000, which is deposited in the business's bank account. In addition, the business obtains a loan from the bank for £5000. The accounting equation is:

Capital = Assets − Liabilities = £10 000

Calculated as (Bank £10 000 + Loan £5000) − Bank Loan = £10 000

The double entry rules for assets, liabilities and equity are:

Equity account		Any asset account		Any liability account	
Decreases	Increases	Increases	Decreases	Decreases	Increases
−	+	+	−	−	+

SUBJECT VOCABULARY

the accounting equation the equation that is the foundation of double entry accounting

6.5 THE IN AND OUT APPROACH

If you are not sure which side of each account you should enter an item, you may find it helpful to think of the debit side being IN to the account, and the credit side being OUT of the account.

Two examples using this approach are shown below:

Example 1: Paid cash of £3000 to buy a second-hand van.

The double entry for this transaction is:

EFFECT	ACTION
Van comes IN.	A *debit* entry in the Van account.
Cash goes OUT.	A *credit* entry in the Cash account.

Example 2: Took £500 out of the business cash in hand and paid it into the business's bank account.

The double entry for this transaction is:

EFFECT	ACTION
Money comes IN to the bank.	A *debit* entry in the Bank account.
Cash goes OUT of the cash till.	A *credit* entry in the Cash account.

6.6 T ACCOUNTS

Business transactions are entered into accounts known as **T accounts**. These accounts are in the shape of a T as shown in **Figure 6.2**.

Account title here: the top stroke of the T

Debit side	Credit side

▲ Figure 6.2 The shape of a T account.

The line divides the two sides and is the downstroke of the T.

6.7 WORKED EXAMPLES: CASH TRANSACTIONS

This section examines double entry for cash transactions. In accounting terminology, the word 'cash' covers both items paid for or money received in cash, and also items paid for by cheque and cheques received. The transfer of money is also increasingly carried out electronically.

Example 3 shows a few entered transactions.

Example 3: The proprietor starts the business with €50 000 in cash on 1 January 2017.

EFFECT	ACTION
Increases the asset of cash.	Debit the cash account – cash goes IN.
Increases the equity.	Credit the equity account – cash comes OUT of the owner's money.

These transactions are entered as shown in **Figure 6.3**.

Dr		Cash Account			*Cr*
	IN			OUT	
2017			€		
Jan 1	Equity		50 000		

Dr		Equity Account			*Cr*
	IN			OUT	
			2017		€
			Jan 1	Cash	50 000

▲ Figure 6.3 Transactions for Example 3.

EXAM HINT
Always write the date in full, including the year. You could lose marks in the exam if you do not do this.

EXAM HINT
When completing double entry questions in the exam make sure the details (narratives) that you write are clear and relevant to that transaction.

The date of the transaction is entered on both accounts. A description is also included on each account so the transactions can be cross-referenced. The 'Cash Account' shows the entry 'Equity' while the 'Equity Account' shows the entry 'Cash'. The double entry rules have been met.

Some further examples are shown below.

Example 4: The business buys equipment for €4200 cash on 2 January 2017.

EFFECT	ACTION
Decreases the asset of cash.	Credit the cash account – cash goes OUT.
Increases the asset of equipment.	Debit the equipment account – equipment comes IN.

Dr	Cash Account		Cr
IN		OUT	
		2017	€
		Jan 2 Equipment	4200

Dr	Equipment Account		Cr
IN		OUT	
2017	€		
Jan 2 Cash	4200		

▲ Figure 6.4 Transactions for Example 4.

Example 5: The business buys goods for resale for €5000, paying by cash on 4 January 2017.

EFFECT	ACTION
Decreases the asset of cash.	Credit the cash account – cash goes OUT.
Increases the asset of purchases.	Debit the purchases account – purchases come IN.

Dr	Purchases Account		Cr
IN		OUT	
2017	€		
Jan 4 Cash	5000		

Dr	Cash Account		Cr
IN		OUT	€
		2017	
		Jan 4 Purchases	5000

▲ Figure 6.5 Transactions for Example 5.

Example 6: The business buys a motor van for €10 000, paying by cash on 5 January 2017.

EFFECT	ACTION
Decreases the asset of cash.	Credit the cash account – cash goes OUT.
Increases the asset of motor van.	Debit the motor van account – motor van comes IN.

> **NOTE**
> Goods bought for resale are recorded in a 'Purchases account' but are often referred to as 'inventory'.

Dr	Cash Account			Cr
	IN		OUT	
		2017		€
		Jan 5	Motor van	10 000

Dr	Motor Van Account			Cr
	IN		OUT	
2017		€		
Jan 5	Cash	10 000		

▲ **Figure 6.6** Transactions for Example 6.

Example 7: The business's transactions to date, shown in Examples 3–6, will be recorded as shown in **Figure 6.7**.

Dr	Cash Account			Cr
	IN		OUT	
2017		€	2017	€
Jan 1	Equity	50 000	Jan 2 Equipment	4200
			Jan 4 Purchases	5000
			Jan 5 Motor van	10 000

Dr	Equity Account			Cr
	IN		OUT	
		2017		€
		Jan 1	Cash	50 000

Dr	Equipment Account			Cr
	IN		OUT	
2017		€		
Jan 2	Cash	4200		

Dr	Purchases Account			Cr
	IN		OUT	
2017		€		
Jan 4	Cash	5000		

Dr	Motor Van Account			Cr
	IN		OUT	
2017		€		€
Jan 5	Cash	10 000		

▲ **Figure 6.7** Summary of transactions from Examples 3–6.

Example 8: This example introduces both cash and bank transactions. Remember that each item has to be entered twice:

- once on the debit side of the account
- once on the credit side of the account.

The order in which you enter the transactions does not matter, but it is often easier to deal with the monetary aspect of each transaction first:

1. Decide if the money is going IN or coming OUT and enter the item into the cash account or the bank account.
2. Enter the item into the other account, on the opposite side.

A business's transactions for July 2017 are shown below.

2017	
1 July	Started business with €20 000 cash.
1 July	Opened a bank account and deposited €19 000 of the cash into the account.
7 July	Paid rent for premises, €500 by cheque.
7 July	Bought goods for resale and paid €3000 by cheque.
12 July	Paid €2,000 by cheque for a second-hand van.
14 July	Sold some goods for cash, €600.
24 July	Bought fixtures and paid €800 by cheque.
28 July	Paid for motor expenses, €65 by cash.
30 July	Sold goods for €2000 and received a cheque which was paid into the bank.

The accounts for July are shown in **Figure 6.8**.

Dr		Cash Account			*Cr*
	IN			OUT	
2017		€	2017		€
July 1	Equity	20 000	July 1	Bank	19 000
July 14	Revenue	600	July 28	Motor expenses	65

Dr		Equity Account			*Cr*
	IN			OUT	
		€	2017		€
			July 1	Cash	20 000

Dr		Bank Account			*Cr*
	IN			OUT	
2017		€	2017		€
July 1	Cash	19 000	July 7	Rent	500
July 30	Revenue	2000	July 7	Purchases	3000
			July 12	Van	2000
			July 24	Fixtures	800

Dr		Rent Account			*Cr*
	IN			OUT	
2017		€			
July 7	Bank	500			

Dr		Purchases Account			*Cr*
	IN			OUT	
2017		€			€
July 7	Bank	3000			

Dr		Van Account			*Cr*
	IN			OUT	
2017		€			€
July 12	Bank	2000			

Dr		Revenue Account			*Cr*
	IN			OUT	
			2017		€
			July 14	Cash	600
			July 30	Bank	2000

Dr	Fixtures Account		Cr
	IN	OUT	
2017	€		€
July 24 Bank	800		

Dr	Motor Expenses Account		Cr
	IN	OUT	
2017	€		€
July 28 Cash	65		

▲ **Figure 6.8** Transactions for Example 8.

6.8 INTRODUCTION TO CREDIT TRANSACTIONS

Section 6.7 showed various double entry transactions involving items that had been bought and paid for by cash or cheque together with cash and cheques received. However, many businesses deal with items that are bought but paid for at a later date. These are known as 'credit transactions' and are in addition to cash and cheque transactions.

When an item is bought on credit, the customer obtains the goods without initially paying for them. The customer must then meet the supplier's 'terms and conditions' – usually, the customer will need to pay for the goods within 30 days. This credit facility helps the customer by providing short-term cash facilities, which improve the business's cash flow. A cash discount may be offered as an incentive to encourage the customer to pay within the 30 days. This means that the customer can deduct a small percentage (e.g. 2.5%) from their invoice if they pay promptly. Buying and selling on credit is widely used in most businesses today.

> **NOTE**
> Cash discounts are dealt with fully in Chapter 5.

When the customer receives goods 'on credit', they incur a liability: they owe the supplier for the cost of the goods supplied. At a later date, usually at the end of the month, the customer will pay the supplier for those goods.

The next section describes the double entry requirements for the purchase and sale of inventory.

6.9 PURCHASE OF INVENTORY ON CREDIT

Example 9: On 1 May 2017, J Hussein buys goods costing $2300 on credit from B White.

First, you must consider the effects of the transaction:

1 The asset of inventory is increased. An increase in an asset needs a debit entry in an account. This transaction involves the movement of 'purchases', so the account must be the purchases account.

2 There is an increase in a liability. This is a liability to B White's business because the goods supplied have not yet been paid for. An increase in a liability needs a credit entry, so a credit entry is made in B White's account.

As before, you can use the idea of the debit side being IN to the account and the credit side being OUT of the account. In this example, purchases have come IN, creating a debit in the Purchases account. The goods have come OUT of B White, so a credit is needed in the account of B White. This is shown in **Figure 6.9**.

J Hussein's Books

Dr	Purchases Account		Cr
IN		OUT	
2017	$		
May 1 B White	2300		

Dr	B White Account		Cr
IN		OUT	
		2017	$
		May 1 Purchases	2300

▲ **Figure 6.9** Transactions for Example 9: purchase of goods on credit.

On 30 May 2017, J Hussein pays B White a cheque for $2300 in full settlement of the goods supplied. The double entry to record the payment of the cheque to B White is shown in **Figure 6.10**.

- Credit the Bank account – the money goes 'OUT' of the bank.
- Debit B White's account – the money goes 'IN' to Whites's account.

Dr	Bank Account		Cr
IN		OUT	
		2017	$
		May 30 B White	2300

Dr	B White Account		Cr
'N		OUT	
2017	$	2017	$
May 30 Bank	2300	May 1 Purchases	2300

▲ **Figure 6.10** Transactions for Example 9: payment for goods bought on credit.

B White's account (above) shows the purchase of the goods on 1 May and the payment for those goods on 30 May. The account is now clear.

6.10 REVENUE OF INVENTORY ON CREDIT

Example 10: On 16 June 2017, Paine & Co sold goods on credit to M Chan for $1000. In this example:

1 An asset account is increased. This is the account showing that M Chan is a debtor, a person who owes money to Paine & Co for goods supplied. The increase in the asset of trade receivables requires a debit and the debtor is M Chan, so the account concerned is M Chan's account. (Goods have gone IN to M Chan – debit M Chan's account.)

2 The asset of inventory is decreased. For this, a credit entry to reduce an asset is needed. The movement of inventory is that of 'Revenue', so the account credited is the Revenue Account. (Revenue has gone OUT – credit the Revenue Account.)

This is shown in **Figure 6.11**.

Paine & Co's Books

Dr	M Chan Account			Cr
	IN		OUT	
2017		$		
June 16 Revenue		10 00		

Dr	Revenue Account			Cr
	IN		OUT	
			2017	$
			June 16 M Chan	1000

▲ Figure 6.11 Transactions for Example 10: sale of goods on credit.

On 12 July, M Chan sends Paine & Co a cheque for $1,000 in full settlement of the amount due. This is recorded in the books of Paine & Co shown in **Figure 6.12**.

- Debit the Bank account – the money goes IN to the Bank account.
- Credit M Chan's account – the money comes OUT of M Chan's account.

Dr	Bank Account			Cr
	IN		OUT	
2017		$		
July 12 M Chan		1000		

Dr	M Chan Account			Cr
	IN		OUT	
2017		$	2017	$
June 16 Revenue		1000	July 12 Bank	1000

▲ Figure 6.12 Transactions for Example 10: payment for goods sold on credit.

6.11 RETURNS

Purchases returns and revenue returns occur when goods that have been bought are returned to the supplier. This could be for various reasons, for example:

- the goods sent to the customer not to the correct specification
- the goods have been damaged in transit
- the goods are of poor quality.

The original purchase or sale will have been entered in the double entry system, so the return of the goods must also be entered.

Purchase returns represent goods that were purchased, and are then returned to the supplier for one of the reasons stated above. Example 11 considers a purchase return.

Example 11: On 14 April 2017, goods previously bought for £540 are returned by the business to I Glover. This is shown in **Figure 6.13**.

1 The liability of the business to I Glover is decreased by the value of the goods returned to him. The decrease in a liability needs a debit, this time in I Glover's Account. (The goods have gone IN to I Glover – debit the I Glover Account.)

2 The asset of inventory is decreased by the goods sent out. A credit representing a reduction in an asset is needed. The movement of inventory is that of 'Purchase Returns', so the entry will be a credit in the purchase returns account. (The returns have gone OUT – credit the Purchase Returns Account.)

Dr	I Glover Account			Cr
	IN		OUT	
2017		$		
April 14	Purchase returns	540		

Dr	Purchase Returns Account			Cr
	IN		OUT	
		2017		$
		April 14	I Glover	540

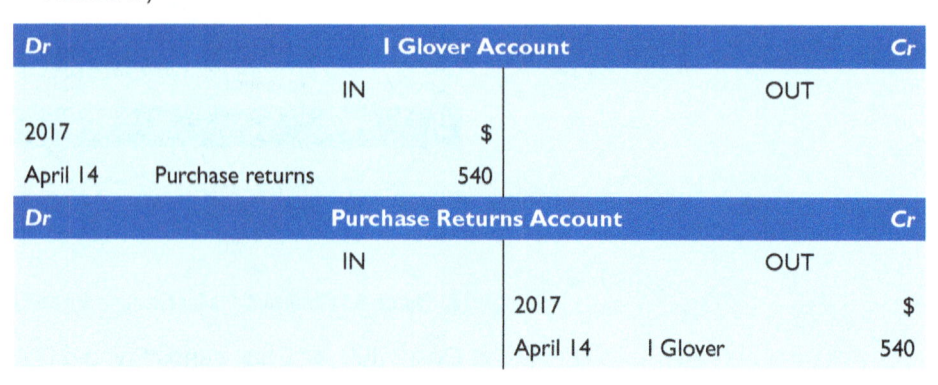

▲ Figure 6.13 Transactions for Example 11: a purchase return.

Revenue returns represent goods sold that are subsequently returned by a customer for one of the reasons stated above. Example 12 shows the double entry for revenue returns.

Example 12: On 19 March 2017, a business receives returned goods from Lucy Thang, which had previously been sold to her for £178. This is shown in **Figure 6.14**.

1 The asset of inventory is increased by the goods returned. A debit representing an increase of an asset is needed. This time the movement of inventory is that of 'Revenue Returns', so the entry required is a debit in the Revenue Returns Account. (The goods have come IN – debit the Revenue Returns Account.)

2 An asset is decreased. The debt of Lucy Thang to the business is reduced. A credit is required in Lucy Thang's account to record this. (The goods have come OUT of Lucy Thang's account – credit the Lucy Thang Account.)

Dr	Revenue Returns Account			Cr
	IN		OUT	
2017		£		
March 19	Lucy Thang	178		

Dr	Lucy Thang Account			Cr
	IN		OUT	
		2017		£
		March 19	Revenue returns	178

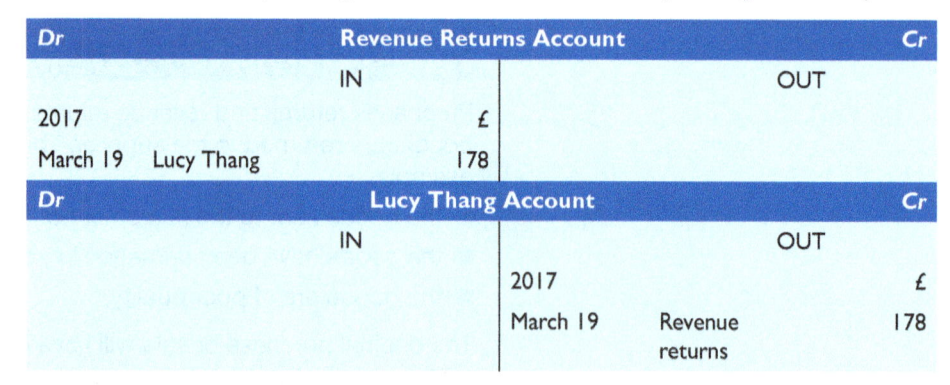

▲ Figure 6.14 Transactions for Example 12: a revenue return.

6.12 EXPENSES ON CREDIT

Businesses purchase and sell goods on credit. They may also incur business expenses and services that are initially provided to them on credit. The business agrees to pay at a later date.

Example 13: On 24 February 2017, a business asks Bangkos Garage to service the business's van. The business later receives an invoice for

$246, due for payment within 30 days. The initial double entry entries are as follows:

- Debit the Motor expenses account – services are received by the business; the benefit goes IN.
- Credit Bangkos Garage account – the business owes Bangkos Garage for the servicing of the van, so a liability has been incurred. A liability is always a credit entry.

Dr	Motor Expenses Account			Cr
	IN		OUT	
2017		$		
Feb 24	Bangkos Garage	246		

Dr	Bangkos Garage Account			Cr
	IN		OUT	
			2017	$
			Feb 24 Motor expenses	246

▲ Figure 6.15 Transactions for Example 13: expenses on credit.

On 20 March 2017, the business sends a cheque for $246 to Bangkos Garage in payment of the outstanding account. The double entry for the payment of the account is as follows:

- Credit the Bank account – the cheque is paid OUT of the bank account.
- Debit Bangkos Garage account – the cheque is paid to Bangkos Garage, so it goes IN to their account. The debt is now paid.

Dr	Bank Account			Cr
	IN		OUT	
			2017	$
			Mar 20 Bangkos Garage	246

Dr	Bangkos Garage Account			Cr
	IN		OUT	
2017		$	2017	$
March 20 Bank		246	Feb 24 Motor expenses	246

▲ Figure 6.16 Transactions for Example 13: settlement of expenses on credit.

6.13 WORKED EXAMPLE

A business's transactions for July 2017 are shown below.

2017	
July 1	Bought goods on credit, $1350 from Barsha & Co
July 5	Bought goods on credit, $3400 from Bhah & Sons
July 8	Bought stationery $83, for office use, on credit from PG Supplies
July 12	Sold goods on credit, $632 to Nayim
July 14	Returned goods to Barsha & Co, $190
July 16	Bought goods on credit, $2960 from Jogia
July 20	Van serviced by Nada Garage for $210 on credit
July 22	Sold goods for cash, $900
July 25	Nayim returned goods to us, $76
July 30	Paid PG Supplies $83 by cash

The double entry for these transactions is shown in **Figure 6.17**.

Dr		Purchases Account				Cr
2017		IN	$		OUT	
July 1	Barsha & Co		1350			
July 5	Bhah & Sons		3400			
July 16	Jogia		2960			

Dr		Barsha & Co Account				Cr
		IN			OUT	
2017			$	2017		$
July 14	Purchase Returns		190	July 1	Purchases	1350

Dr		Bhah & Sons Account				Cr
		IN			OUT	
				2017		$
				July 5	Purchases	3400

Dr		Stationery Account				Cr
		IN			OUT	
2017			$			
July 8	PG Supplies		83			

Dr		PG Supplies Account				Cr
		IN			OUT	
2017			$	2017		$
July 30	Cash		83	July 8	Stationery	83

Dr		Revenue Account				Cr
		IN			OUT	
				2017		$
				July 12	Nayim	632
				July 22	Cash	900

Dr		Nayim Account				Cr
		IN			OUT	
2017			$	2017		$
July 12	Revenue		632	July 25	Revenue Returns	76

Dr		Purchase Returns Account				Cr
		IN			OUT	
				2017		$
				July 14	Barsha & Co	190

Dr		Jogia Account				Cr
		IN			OUT	
				2017		$
				July 16	Purchases	2960

Dr		Motor Expenses Account				Cr
		IN			OUT	
2017			$			
July 20	Nada Garage		210			

Dr		Nada Garage Account				Cr
		IN			OUT	
				2017		$
				July 20	Motor Expenses	210

Dr		Cash Account			Cr
	IN			OUT	
2017		$	2017		$
July 22	Revenue	900	July 30	PG Supplies	83

Dr		Revenue Returns Account			Cr
	IN			OUT	
2017		$			
July 25	Nayim	76			

▲ **Figure 6.17** Transactions for worked example.

6.14 REVENUE AND PURCHASES

'Revenue' and 'purchases' have special meanings in accounting language:

- **Revenue** means the sale of those goods in which the business normally deals and that were bought with the main intention of resale. The description 'revenue' must never be given to the disposal of other items.

- **Purchases** means the purchase of those goods that the business buys with the main intention of selling. Sometimes the goods may be altered, added to or used in the manufacture of something else, but it is the element of resale that is important.

For example, a business that trades in computers will consider computers to be raw materials. If the business buys a motor van for use by the business, this cannot be called a purchase in accountancy terms because the van is not intended for resale.

6.15 COMPARISON OF CASH AND CREDIT TRANSACTIONS FOR PURCHASES AND REVENUE

You can now see the difference between the records for cash and credit transactions.

The complete set of entries for purchases, that are paid for immediately by cash, is as follows:

1 **debit the purchases account**
2 **credit the cash account.**

The complete set of entries for the purchase of goods on credit can be broken down into two stages: first, the purchase of the goods, and second, the payment for them. The entries for the first part are:

1 **debit the purchases account**
2 **credit the supplier's account.**

The entries for the second part are:

1 **debit the supplier's account**
2 **credit the cash account.**

With the cash purchase, there is no need to keep a copy of the supplier's account. This is because cash passes from buyer to supplier immediately, so there is no need to keep a record of indebtedness (money owing) to a supplier. In the credit purchase, the records should show to whom money is owed until payment is made. The table below shows a comparison of cash revenue and credit revenue:

CASH REVENUE	CREDIT REVENUE	
Complete entry: • debit cash account • credit revenue account	First part: Second part:	• debit customer's account • credit revenue account • debit cash account • credit customer's account

6.16 BALANCING THE ACCOUNTS

'Balancing off' accounts is a procedure carried out by most businesses on a monthly basis so they can keep a check on various accounting issues. These issues include:

- how much money they have in their cash account
- the balance in the bank account
- how much money they owe to other people (i.e. trade payables)
- how much money other people owe the business (i.e. trade receivables)
- the value of the business's assets
- the amount incurred on various expenses
- how much their inventory has cost (i.e. purchases)
- what the revenue figures are to date
- the equity invested in the business by the owner(s) and any drawings taken.

We use certain conventions to help us record accounts. Look at the account entries below before following example 14.

		Wages			
2017		€	2017		€
May 3	Cash	400	May 31	Balance c/d	1050
May 21	Bank	650			
		1050			1050
June 1	Balance b/d	1050			

		Wages			
2017		€	2017		€
June 1	Balance b/f	1050	June 30	Balance c/d	2200
June 8	Bank	800			
June 17	Cash	350			
		2200			2200
	Balance b/d	2200			

Example 14: In the example below, the bank account has been balanced off at the end of the period and the balance has been brought down to the next accounting period:

Dr		Bank Account			Cr
2017		$	2017		$
Oct 1	Equity	20 000	Oct 4	Purchases	2400
Oct 11	Revenue	550	Oct 7	Rent	500
			Oct 31	Balance c/d	17 650
		20 550			20 550
Nov 1	Balance b/d	17 650			

▲ Figure 6.18 Transactions for Example 14: Balancing off.

The procedure for 'balancing off' the bank account is as follows:

1. Add up both sides to find out their totals. Do not write anything permanent in the account at this stage. You could write the figures lightly in pencil or on a piece of paper. In the bank account (**Figure 6.18**), the debit side totals $20,550 while the credit side totals $2900.

KEY POINT

b/f = brought forward, the opening ledger balance for the period in question taken from the balance b/d from the previous period
c/d = carried down, the closing ledger balance for the period in question (this will be the balance b/d at the start of the next period).
b/d = brought down, the closing ledger balance that is used for the start of the next period

2 Deduct the smaller total from the larger total to find the balance. In **Figure 6.18**, this is $20 550 – $2900 = $17 650.

3 Now enter the balance on the side with the smallest total; in the example above, this is the credit side. Note that the date entered is usually the last day of the month – in our case, 31 October. Write 'Balance c/d', which stands for 'carried down', then enter the balance, $17 650.

4 Enter the totals on a level with each other. Note that totals in accounting are shown with a single line above them and a double line underneath.

5 Now enter the balance on the line below the totals. The balance below the totals should be on the opposite side to the balance shown above the totals. First enter the date, which is the first day of the next period – in the example above, 1 November. Then write 'Balance b/d', which stands for balance brought down. When you open a T account for the Bank Account for November you should start with 1 November, Balance b/f 17 650.

b/f stands for balance bought forward and means the amount that has been carried over or forward from the previous month or accounting period.

In **Figure 6.18**, there is a balance brought down of $17 650 on 1 November. This is a debit balance: $17 650 is the money available in the business's bank account. Remember, a debit balance is always an asset.

Example 15: Sometimes, the balances brought down are credit balances as shown in this example of K Grant, a creditor:

Dr			K Grant Account			Cr
2017		$	2017			$
Jan 30	Bank	120	Jan 1	Purchases		120
Jan 31	Balance c/d	1910	Jan 15	Purchases		610
			Jan 21	Purchases		1300
		2030				2030
			Feb 1	Balance b/d		1910

▲ Figure 6.19 A credit balance.

In K Grant's account, purchases in January totalled $2030 (120 + 610 + 1300 = 2030). Payment was made on 30 January of $120, leaving a balance outstanding of $1910 (2030 – 120 = 1910). This is shown as a **credit balance** brought down, showing that $1910 is owed to K Grant at the end of January. This is a liability and a liability is always a credit balance.

Example 16: In this example of D Araimi, a debtor, you will see that there is no balance outstanding at the end of the month.

Dr			D Araimi Account			Cr
2017		$	2017			$
May 1	Revenue	100	May 31	Bank		834
May 15	Revenue	734				
		834				834

▲ Figure 6.20 An account with no outstanding balance.

In this example, goods totalling $834 were sold to D Araimi during May. These were paid for in full on 31 May, so the account is clear.

EXAM HINT

When completing double entry questions in the exam, always remember to start with 'balance b/f' (if needed), 'balance c/d' and 'balance b/d'. Do not abbreviate 'Balance' to Bal or just write b/d or c/d.

SUBJECT VOCABULARY

credit balance a balance showing that more money has been received or is owed to a company than has been paid out or is owed by the company

SUBJECT VOCABULARY

debit balance a balance showing that more money has been paid out or is owed by a company than has been received or is owed to the company

Example 17: Sometimes. there is only one item in an account, as shown in the Machinery Account in **Figure 6.21**. In these circumstances it is not necessary to balance off the account since we can easily see that the amount shown – £6435 – represents the total machinery the business owns. Machinery is an asset, hence the **debit balance.**

Dr		Machinery Account		Cr
2017			£	
Sept 1	Bank		6435	

▲ Figure 6.21 An asset account containing only one item.

Example 18: The account in **Figure 6.22** shows that, for the month of March, £405 has been incurred in motor expenses. This is a **debit balance** which is always an asset or an expense. In this example it is an expense.

Dr		Motor Expenses Account				Cr
2017			£	2017		£
Mar 5	Cash		32	Mar 31	Balance c/d	405
Mar 16	Bank		301			
Mar 21	Bank		72			
			405			405
Apr 1	Balance b/d		405			

▲ Figure 6.22 An expense account with a debit balance.

EXAM HINT

Always check you have the correct date on your Balance b/d. It should always be the 1st of the next month.

6.17 THREE-COLUMN ACCOUNTS

Sometimes accounts are shown using three columns:
- a debit column
- a credit column
- a column showing the balance on the account.

This method of presenting accounts is used in computerised accounting packages. **Figures 6.23–6.26** show some three-column accounts.

T Baldwin Account					
		Debit	Credit	Balance (and whether debit or credit)	
2017		£	£	£	
May 1	Revenue	1200		1200	Dr
May 12	Revenue	411		1611	Dr
May 19	Bank		1,200	411	Dr
May 24	Revenue	260		671	Dr

▲ Figure 6.23 A debtor's account using a three-column account.

D Kemel Account					
		Debit	Credit	Balance (and whether debit or credit)	
2017		£	£	£	
May 7	Purchases		510	510	Cr
May 9	Purchases		82	592	Cr
May 26	Bank	510		82	Cr

▲ Figure 6.24 A creditor's account using a three-column account.

Equity Account		Debit	Credit	Balance (and whether debit or credit)
2017		£	£	£
May 1	Bank		30 000	30 000 Cr

▲ Figure 6.25 An equity account using a three-column account.

Stationery Account		Debit	Credit	Balance (and whether debit or credit)
2017		£	£	£
May 17	Cash	45		45 Dr
May 20	Bank	231		276 Dr
May 27	Cash	22		298 Dr

▲ Figure 6.26 An expense account using a three-column account.

6.18 WORKED EXAMPLE

The following accounts have been extracted from the books of John Roberts. Roberts runs a successful retail business. All the accounts have been balanced off by the bookkeeper and a trial balance has been prepared (see **Figures 6.27 and 6.28**), and note that details of trial balance will be covered in Chapter 8.

John Robert's books

Bank Account

Dr			£				Cr £
2017				2017			
June 1	Equity		20 000	June 3		Motor car	9000
June 30	A Cope		1,350	June 3		Rent	1500
				June 21		Computer	1650
				June 29		J Wang	2700
				June 30		G Moore	630
				June 30		Balance c/d	5870
			21 350				21 350
July 1	Balance b/d		5870				

Cash Account

Dr			£				Cr £
2017				2017			
June 5	Revenue		540	June 14		Stationery	55
June 12	Revenue		440	June 30		Balance c/d	925
			980				980
July 1	Balance b/d		925				

Revenue Account

Dr			£				Cr £
2017				2017			
June 30	Balance c/d		3350	June 5		Cash	540
				June 10		A Cope	1770
				June 12		Cash	440
				June 22		B Singh	600
			3350				3350
				July 1		Balance	3350

Revenue Returns Account

Dr			£				Cr £
2017				2017			
June 23	A Cope		420				

Dr		Purchases Account				Cr
2017			£	2017		£
June 3	J Wang		2700	June 30	Balance c/d	4800
June 4	G Moore		750			
June 18	G Moore		1350			
			4800			4800
July 1	Balance b/d		4800			

Dr		Purchase Returns Account				Cr
			£	2017		£
				June 6	G Moore	120

Dr		Computer Account				Cr
2017			£			£
June 21	Bank		1650			

Dr		Motor Car Account				Cr
2017			£			£
June 3	Bank		9000			

Dr		Rent Account				Cr
2017			£			£
June 3	Rent		1500			

Dr		Stationery Account				Cr
2017			£			£
June 14	Cash		55			

Dr		Equity Account				Cr
			£	2017		£
				June 1	Bank	20 000

Dr		B Singh Account				Cr
2017			£			£
June 22	Revenue		600			

Dr		A Cope Account				Cr
2017			£	2017		£
June 10	Revenue		1770	June 23	Revenue returns	420
				June 30	Bank	1350
			1770			1770

Dr		J Wang Account				Cr
2017			£	2017		£
June 29	Bank		2700	June 3	Raw materials/ordinary goods purchased	2700

Dr		G Moore Account				Cr
2017			£	2017		£
June 6	Purchase Returns		120	June 4	Purchases	750
June 30	Bank		630	June 18	Purchases	1350
June 30	Balance c/d		1350			
			2100			2100
				July 1	Balance b/d	1350

▲ **Figure 6.27** John Roberts' accounting books.

continued overleaf

John Roberts

Trial Balance as at 30 June 2017	Dr	Cr
	£	£
Bank	5870	
Cash	925	
Revenue		3350
Revenue returns	420	
Purchases	4800	
Purchase returns		120
Computer	1650	
Motor Car	9000	
Rent	1500	
Stationery	55	
Equity		20 000
B. Singh	600	
G. Moore		1350
	24 820	24 820

Figure 6.28 A trial balance for John Roberts.

6.19 ERRORS NOT REVEALED BY THE DOUBLE ENTRY SYSTEM

You should be aware that the trial balance will still appear to balance even if certain errors have occurred:

- **Error of transposition.** When the numbers are entered backwards in both accounts, e.g. £123 entered as £321.
- **Errors of original entry.** When an item is entered using an incorrect amount. For example, an invoice received showing goods purchased to the value of £260.00 is entered in both the purchases account and the supplier's account as £26.00.
- **Errors of principle.** When an item is entered in the wrong type of account. For example, a non-current asset is entered in an expense account.
- **Compensating errors.** When two errors of equal amounts, but on opposite sides of the accounts, cancel each other out.
- **Errors of omission.** When a transaction is completely omitted from the books. For example, when a cheque received is lost and therefore never entered in the books of account.
- **Errors of commission (wrong account).** When a correct amount is entered, but in the wrong person's account. For example, when a sale of goods to J Roberts is entered, in error, in J Robertson's account.
- **Complete reversal of entries.** When the correct amounts are entered in the correct accounts but the item is shown on the wrong side of each account.

HINT
Use the acronym **TOPCOCC** to remember your errors: Transposition, Original Entry, Principle, Compensating, Omission, Commission and Complete Reversal.

SKILLS REASONING, ARGUMENTATION

▲ Indian Railways has issues with its assets.

CASE STUDY: ADOPTION OF DOUBLE ENTRY ACCOUNTING IN INDIA

The Institute of Chartered Accountants of India (ICAI) have asked the Indian Railways to introduce a double entry accounting system from 2017. It is hoped that using a double entry accounting system will allow Indian Railways to improve their financial recording and help them manage their accounts more effectively.

END OF CHAPTER QUESTIONS

1 Yuri keeps a full set of accounting records. Name the ledger in which each of the following accounts is found.
   a insurance
   b sales
   c purchases
   d Lottie, a credit supplier
   e Matthew, a credit customer
   f equity

2 Lynch bought goods worth $100, on credit, but he recorded this as $1000. Name the type of error he has made.

3 Ruth provides the following information.
   Ruth took goods costing $60 for her own use. An invoice was received from PJ Motors for $15 600. This included $600 for repairs to a motor vehicle and $15 000 for the purchase of an additional motor vehicle. It was discovered that the purchase of stationery, $20, had been debited to the purchases account. This error should now be corrected.
   a Prepare the necessary journal entries to record this information. Narratives are required.
   b In connection with journal entries, explain what is meant by the term 'narrative'.
   c Explain why a narrative should be shown as part of a journal entry.

4 Put the following entries into T accounts.

1 Sep	Started a business with £2000 in a bank account.
3 Sep	Bought goods £200 paying by cheque.
5 Sep	Bought goods £150 on credit from D Smith.
6 Sep	Sold goods £95, a cheque being received.
7 Sep	Some of the goods (value £50) bought from D Smith are found to be faulty, and are returned.
10 Sep	Sold goods £105 on credit to I Wain.
12 Sep	Bought a machine for use in the business £500 on credit from Rowcester Machinery Co.
14 Sep	Paid D Smith the amount owing by cheque.
17 Sep	I Wain returns goods to the value of £25.
20 Sep	Sold goods £55, a cheque being received.
22 Sep	I Wain pays the amount owing to us by cheque.
24 Sep	The purchaser of the goods on 20 Sep returns them – a refund is made by cheque.
27 Sep	Paid Rowcester Machinery Co by cheque.

END OF CHAPTER CHECKLIST

- The purchase and sale revenue of goods on credit is recorded using the double entry system of bookkeeping.
- Transactions involving expenses and services that are supplied on credit are recorded using the double entry system.
- Various accounts are used to record the movement of inventory because inventory is normally sold at a higher price than its cost.
- The accounts used to record the movement of inventory are:
  - the purchases account – purchases of inventory are recorded as debit entries in this account since the goods come IN to the business
  - the sales revenue account – sales of goods are recorded as credit entries in this account because the goods go OUT of the business
  - the revenue returns account – goods that a customer returns to the business are recorded as debit entries since the goods are returned IN to the business
  - the purchase returns account – goods that the business returns to its suppliers are recorded as credit entries as the goods go OUT of the business.
- Remember the special meaning in accounting terms of 'purchases' and 'revenue'. 'Purchases' are goods bought for resale. Purchases of assets, such as a motor van to be used in the business, are recorded separately in the asset account, motor van. 'Sales' are goods sold in the normal course of business. The disposal of an asset such as equipment should never be recorded in the sales account; instead, it should be recorded separately in a disposal account. This will be discussed later.
- Purchases for cash are **never** entered in the supplier's account while purchases on credit are **always** entered in the supplier's (trade payables) account.

EXAM PRACTICE

A01 A02 A03 Answer ALL questions in this section. Questions 1–14 must be answered with a cross in the box ☒. If you change your mind about an answer, put a line through the box ☒ and then mark your new answer with a cross ☒.

1 Where are the accounts of credit customers found?
- A purchases journal
- B payables ledger
- C sales journal
- D trade receivables ledger (1 mark)

2 The purchase of a new computer has been posted to the repairs account in error.
What type of error is this?
- A commission
- B complete reversal of entries
- C original entry
- D principle (1 mark)

3 Which of the following is an error of omission?
- A No entry has been made for the purchase of stationery by cheque.
- B Purchase of stationery has been entered only in the cash book.
- C Purchase of stationery has been entered only in the stationery account.
- D The stationery account has been missed out of the trial balance. (1 mark)

4 The totals of a trial balance agreed. It was later found goods sold on credit for $230 had been correctly entered on the trade receivables account, but incorrectly entered on the sales account as $320.
Which type of error is this?
- A compensating
- B complete reversal
- C original entry
- D principle (1 mark)

5 Maresh Samdi sells motor vehicles at his garage in Mumbai. Maresh sold a car to J.Hussein on credit. How will this be shown in the books of Maresh?

	Debit	Credit
A	motor vehicles	J Hussein
B	J Hussein	sales
C	sales	J Hussein
D	J Hussein	motor vehicles

(1 mark)

6 Which account is contained in the receivables ledger?
- A customer's account
- B sales account
- C sales returns account
- D supplier's account (1 mark)

7 What is the correct treatment of a sale on credit?

	Nominal ledger	Trade receivables ledger
A	debit cash	credit sales
B	credit sales	debit cash
C	credit sales	debit customer
D	debit customer	credit sales

(1 mark)

8 A business keeps a three-column cash book.
Where is the total of the discount column on the debit side posted?
- A to the credit side of the discounts allowed account
- B to the credit side of the discounts received account
- C to the debit side of the discounts allowed account
- D to the debit side of the discounts received account (1 mark)

9 How should the purchase of a machine for your business, paid for by cheque, be recorded in the double entry accounts?

	Debit	Credit
☐ A	Cash Account	Machinery Account
☐ B	Machinery Account	Cash Account
☐ C	Bank Account	Machinery Account
☐ D	Machinery Account	Bank Account

(1 mark)

10 The bank account in a firm's double entry system appears as:

Bank					
1 May	Equity	£2000	10 May	Purchases	£250
20 May	Sales	£200	12 May	Typewriter	£125
			25 May	Purchases	£125

What is the balance on this account?

☐ A A debit balance of £1700

☐ B A credit balance of £1700

☐ C A debit balance of £2200

☐ D A credit balance of £500

(1 mark)

11 What is the meaning of a debit balance of £425 on P Ross's account in the books of B Harris?

☐ A P Ross owes B Harris £425

☐ B B Harris owes P Ross £425

☐ C P Ross has paid B Harris £425

☐ B Harris has paid P Ross £425

(1 mark)

12 What is the meaning of a debit balance of £1000 on the Machinery Account in the books of Smith?

☐ A Smith owes £1000 for machinery purchased

☐ B Smith has sold machinery for £1000

☐ C Smith owns machinery which cost £1000

☐ D Smith's Equity Account has a credit balance of £1000

(1 mark)

13 Which one of the following accounts normally has a debit balance?

☐ A Cash Account

☐ B Returns Outwards Account

☐ C Sales Account

☐ D Purchases Account

(1 mark)

UNIT 2   **6 LEDGER ACCOUNTING AND DOUBLE ENTRY BOOKKEEPING**

14 Which one of the following accounts normally has a credit balance?

- [ ] A Returns Inwards Account
- [ ] B Sales Account
- [ ] C Machinery Account
- [ ] D Cash Account

(1 mark)

15 Complete the double entry transaction for Kai Loo.

Date	Transactions	Gain	Loss
01-Apr	Started business with £2000 in cash	Cash	Equity
02-Apr	Paid £1750 cash into the bank	Bank	Cash
04-Apr	Bought a second-hand van for £1000, paying by cheque	Van	Bank
06-Apr	Bought a typewriter for £250 on credit from Business Equipment	Typewriter	Business Equipment
11-Apr	Bought a photocopier for £350 on credit from Johnson Brothers	Photocopier	Johnson Brother
12-Apr	Paid the amount owing to Business Equipment by cheque	Business Equipment	Bank
17-Apr	Paid the amount owing to Johnson Brothers by cheque	Johnson Brothers	Bank

(14 marks)

16 S.A. Nary is just starting business as a fishmonger. Put the following transactions into the double entry system for S.A. Nary.

July 1st	Opened a business bank account and paid in £6000.
July 1st	Paid rent for month of £100 by cheque.
July 1st	Purchased fittings for £1200 by cheque.
July 1st	Paid for refrigerators £700 by cheque.
July 2nd	Purchased motor van £2000 paid by cheque.
July 2nd	Paid for motor insurance £55 by cheque.
July 2nd	Paid for licence for van £40 by cheque.
July 3rd	Obtained £800 of fish and canned goods from J Eulie on credit of seven days.
July 4th	Cash sales £643.
July 5th	Paid for cleaning £3 cash.
July 6th	Banked £600

(20 marks)

(Total 48 marks)

7 DEPRECIATION

LEARNING OBJECTIVES

- Explain the causes of depreciation
- Distinguish between straight line and reducing balance methods of depreciation
- Calculate and record depreciation in the books of account
- Calculate and record profit or loss of non-current assets

GETTING STARTED

Depreciation is a very important part of accounting. There are two methods of depreciation: straight line and reducing balance. Depreciation is linked closely to the accounting concept of consistency and accruals.

ACTIVITY

Look at your list of non-current assets and order them according to which will depreciate or lose their value more quickly. Why do you think non-current assets will have different valuations for depreciation? Will some of the non-current assets increase in value in the future?

7.1 CAUSES OF DEPRECIATION

Non-current assets such as machinery, motor vehicles, plant and equipment tend to fall in value (depreciate) for various reasons. These reasons are described more fully below.

PHYSICAL DEPRECIATION

1 **Wear and tear.** Non-current assets as described above eventually wear out. Some last many years, while others wear out more quickly.

2 **Erosion, rust, rot and decay.** Equipment may be eroded or wasted away by the action of wind, rain, sun or the other elements of nature. The metals in motor vehicles or machinery will rust away. Wood will rot eventually. Decay is a process caused by the elements of nature and a lack of proper attention.

ECONOMIC FACTORS

Economic factors are the reasons for an asset being put out of use even though it is in good physical condition. The two main economic factors are obsolescence and inadequacy.

DID YOU KNOW?

Certain former top executives of Waste Management Inc., an American environmental services company, were sued in 2002 by U.S. Securities and Exchange Commission for mixing up its capital and revenue expenditure and inflating its profits by a reported $1.7 billion.

1 **Obsolescence.** This occurs when an asset becomes out of date due to advanced technology or a change in processes. For example, in the car industry much of the assembly work is now done by robots. Computer hardware and software tend to go out-of-date very quickly and need updating and replacing regularly.

2 **Inadequacy.** This arises when an asset is no longer used because of the growth and change in the size of the business due to new regulations. The transport industry is now able to use much larger vehicles than before, resulting in many businesses selling off their smaller vehicles.

Both obsolescence and inadequacy do not necessarily mean that an asset is destroyed. It is merely put out of use by the business. Another business will often buy it.

THE TIME FACTOR

Some assets have a legal life fixed in terms of years, for example, a lease. A business may decide to rent a property for ten years, so it takes out a lease. A legal agreement is drawn up between the parties. Each year, a proportion of the cost of the lease is depreciated until the lease expires and the value is nil. In such cases, the term **amortisation** may be used instead of the term depreciation.

DEPLETION

Some assets are of a 'wasting nature' such as the extraction of raw materials from mines or quarries, or oil from oil wells. Such natural resources are often sold in their raw state to other businesses for processing. Providing for the consumption of an asset of a wasting character is known as provision for depletion.

> **SUBJECT VOCABULARY**
>
> **depletion** when a quantity of something is greatly reduced or nearly all used up

7.2 METHODS OF CALCULATING DEPRECIATION CHARGES

The two main methods used for calculating depreciation charges are the **straight line method** and the **reducing balance**. Most accountants think that the straight line method is usually most suitable, although other methods are needed in certain cases.

STRAIGHT LINE METHOD

This method involves the cost price of an asset, the estimated years of its use and the expected disposal value. The depreciation charge each year can be calculated as:

$$\text{depreciation charge per year} = \frac{\text{cost price} - \text{disposal value}}{\text{number of years of use}}$$

For example, a business purchases a car for £22 000. It decides to keep it for four years and then sell it for £2000. The depreciation to be charged is:

$$\frac{\text{cost price} - \text{disposal value}}{\text{number of years of use}} = \frac{£22\,000 - £2000}{4} = £5000 \text{ depreciation per year}$$

The depreciation charge of £5,000 will be charged for four years.

If, after four years, the car had no disposal value, the charge for depreciation would be:

$$\frac{\text{cost price}}{\text{number of years of use}} = \frac{£22\,000}{4} = £5500 \text{ depreciation each year for 4 years}$$

CASE STUDY: STRAIGHT LINE METHOD

Demi owns a factory in Macau producing cash registers. She recently purchased a new machine for MOP22 000. She expects it to last for 10 years. After this it will be scrapped. It is estimated to have a scrap value of MOP500.

Calculate the annual depreciation charge for Demi using the straight line method.

FIXED INSTALMENT METHOD

In the exam, you may be asked to calculate straight line depreciation using a percentage. The percentage is derived from the number of years of use, and the scrap value is taken into consideration, but it is just given as a percentage.

Example 1: A question may say:

Mic purchased a motor vehicle at a cost of $25 000. He wants to use the straight line method at 20%.

You would therefore work out 20% of $25 000, which is $5000.

REDUCING BALANCE METHOD

Calculating the amount of depreciation to be charged involves deciding on a percentage amount to be used each year. This percentage is deducted from the cost price in the first year and deducted from the new (reduced) balance in subsequent years. This is illustrated in Example 2.

Example 2: A machine is bought for £10 000 and depreciation is to be charged at 20%. The calculations for the first three years are:

	£
Cost	10 000
First year: depreciation (20% of £10 000)	2000
	8000
Second year: depreciation (20% of £8000)	1600
	6400
Third year: depreciation (20% of £6400)	1280
Carrying value at the end of the third year	5120

> **HINT**
>
> carrying value = cost price – depreciation to date

SKILLS PROBLEM SOLVING

CASE STUDY: REDUCING BALANCE METHOD

John owns a motor vehicle repair company in Bangkok. He recently purchased a new van to help with the running of his business. The van was purchased on 1 January 2016 at a cost of $20 000. John wants to calculate the depreciation using the reducing balance method. He has provided the rate of 40%.

Calculate the annual charge for depreciation for 2016, 2017 and 2018.

The reducing balance method means that much larger amounts are charged in the earlier years of use, compared with the later years of use. It is often said that repairs and upkeep in the early years will cost less than when the asset becomes old. This means that:

In the early years
a higher charge for depreciation
+
a lower charge for repairs and upkeep

is usually approximately equal to

In the later years
a lower charge for depreciation
+
a higher charge for repairs and upkeep

A comparison of the two methods is shown in the worked example.

> **WORKED EXAMPLE**
>
> A joinery manufacturer has bought a machine for £16 000. It has an expected life of four years and a disposal value of £1000. The owner asks for a comparison of the depreciation to be charged using both methods. A percentage of 50% is to be used for the reducing balance method.
>
> The depreciation for the straight line method is calculated as follows:
>
> $$\text{depreciation per year} = \frac{\text{cost price} - \text{disposal value}}{\text{number of years of use}}$$
>
> $$= \frac{£16\,000 - £1000}{4} = \frac{15\,000}{4}$$
>
> $$= £3750$$
>
> A percentage figure of 50% is used for the reducing balance method:
>
> | | Method 1 Straight line | | Method 2 Reducing balance |
> |---|---|---|---|
> | | £ | | £ |
> | Cost | 16 000 | | 16 000 |
> | Depreciation: year 1 | 3750 | (50% of £16,000) | 8000 |
> | | 12 250 | | 8000 |
> | Depreciation: year 2 | 3750 | (50% of £8000) | 4000 |
> | | 8500 | | 4000 |
> | Depreciation: year 3 | 3750 | (50% of £4000) | 2000 |
> | | 4750 | | 2000 |
> | Depreciation: year 4 | 3750 | (50% of £2000) | 1000 |
> | Disposal value | 1000 | | 1000 |

Using the straight line method, the depreciation charge remains the same each year. Using the reducing balance method, the depreciation charges are much higher in the early years than in the later years.

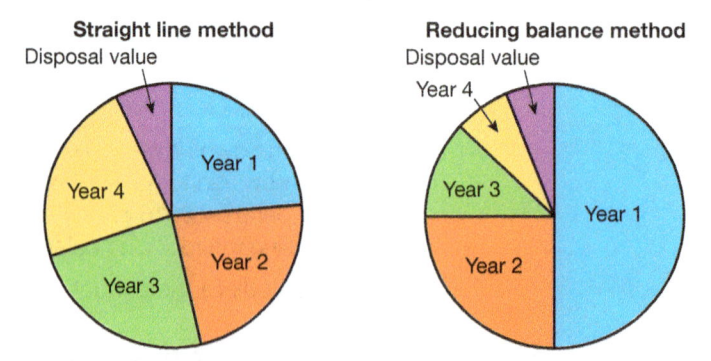

▲ **Figure 7.1** Comparing depreciation charges for the above worked example.

7.3 RECORDING DEPRECIATION

When a business purchases non-current assets, the cost price is recorded in the respective non-current asset account. Any depreciation subsequently charged on that asset is recorded separately in a **provision for depreciation account.** The depreciation charge accumulates each year. Example 4 illustrates the purchase of machinery and the depreciation charge. The transaction is recorded using double entry principles.

Example 3: A business purchases machinery for use in its workshop for €2,000 on 1 January 2014. The company uses the reducing balance method of depreciation and a rate of 20% per annum. Their year end is 31 December. The accounting records for the first three years are shown below:

> Recording purchase of a non-current asset:
> 1 Debit – Asset account
> 2 Credit – Bank account (if paid)

1 The machinery is purchased on 1 January 2014 and paid for by cheque:
debit the machinery account €2000
credit the bank account €2000 (not shown in our example).

2 At the end of the year, the asset is depreciated at 20% per annum using the reducing balance method. First of all, the amount of depreciation to be charged each year needs to be calculated:

	€
Cost of machinery	2000
First year: depreciation (20% of €2000)	400
Reduced balance year 1	1600
Second year: depreciation (20% of €1600)	320
Reduced balance year 2	1280
Third year: depreciation (20% of €1280)	256
Carrying Value at end of third year	1024

Note: Carrying Value = cost price – depreciation = 2,000 – 976 = €1024

> Recording depreciation charges:
> 1 Debit – Income statement
> 2 Credit – Provision for depreciation account

3 To record the depreciation:
- **debit** the income statement with the amount of depreciation each year.
- **credit** the provision for depreciation – machinery account with the amount of the depreciation charged each year.

> Statement of financial position entries:
> 1 Asset is always shown at cost price
> 2 Total depreciation to date is shown as a deduction from the cost price to arrive at the carrying value

4 In the statement of financial position, the asset and total depreciation are shown under the non-current asset section as follows:
- The asset, i.e. machinery, is always shown at **cost price**, i.e. €2000.
- The total depreciation to date, i.e. €400 + €320 + €256 = €976, is shown as a deduction from the cost price of the machinery. This gives **carrying value**, €2000 – €976 = €1024.

Dr			Machinery Account			Cr
2014		€	2014			€
Jan 1	Cash	2000	Dec 31	Balance c/d		2000
2015			2015			
Jan 1	Balance b/d	2000	Dec 31	Balance c/d		2000
2016			2016 2003			
Jan 1	Balance b/d	2000	Dec 31	Balance c/d		2000
2017						
Jan 1	Balance b/d	2000				

Dr			Provision for Depreciation – Machinery Account			Cr
2014		€	2014			€
Dec 31	Balance c/d	400	Dec 31	Income statement		400
2015			2015			
Dec 31	Balance c/d	720	Jan 1	Balance b/d		400
			Dec 31	Income statement		320
		720				720
2016			2016			
Dec 31	Balance c/d	976	Jan 1	Balance b/d		720
			Dec 31	Income statement		256
		976				976
			2017			
			Jan 1	Balance b/d		976

▲ **Figure 7.2** Recording depreciation using double entry principles.

Income Statement (extracts) for the year ended 31 December		
		€
2014	Depreciation	400
2015	Depreciation	320
2016	Depreciation	256

The balance on the machinery account is shown on the statement of financial position at the end of each year (**Figure 7.3**). The figure is less the balance on the provision for depreciation – Machinery Account.

Statement of financial position (extracts) as at 31 December			
	Cost	Total depreciation	Carrying Value
2014	€	€	€
Machinery	2000	400	1600
2015			
Machinery	2000	720	1280
2016			
Machinery	2000	976	1,24

▲ **Figure 7.3** Statement of financial position.

Example 4: This example is for a business with a year end of 30 June. The business buys a motor car on 1 July 2016 for £8000. They buy another car on 1 July 2017 for £11 000. They expect each car to be in use for five years. They expect the disposal value of the first car to be £500, and the second car to be £1000. They use the straight line method of depreciation.

First, we need to calculate the depreciation charge, as follows:

Depreciation per year – straight line method:

Motor Car No. 1: Bought on 1 July 2015 at a cost price of £8000

$$\text{depreciation charge per year} = \frac{\text{cost price} - \text{disposal value}}{\text{number of years of use}}$$

$$= \frac{8000 - 500}{5}$$

$$= £1500 \text{ depreciation charge per year}$$

Motor Car No. 2: Bought on 1 July 2016 at a cost price of £11 000

$$\text{depreciation charge per year} = \frac{\text{cost price} - \text{disposal value}}{\text{number of years of use}}$$

$$= \frac{11\,000 - 1000}{5}$$

$$= £2000 \text{ depreciation charge per year}$$

The bookkeeping entries for the first two years are shown in **Figure 7.4**.

> **NOTE**
> The entries in the cash book have not been shown in this example.

Dr		Motor Cars Account			Cr
2015		£	2016		£
Jul 1	Bank	8000	Jun 30	Balance c/d	8000
2016			2017		
Jul 1	Balance b/d	8000	Jun 30	Balance c/d	19 000
Jul 1	Bank	11 000			
		19 000			19 000
2017					
Jul 1	Balance b/d	19 000			

Dr		Provision for Depreciation – Motor Cars Account			Cr
2016		£	2016		£
Jun 30	Balance c/d	1500	Jun 30	Income Statement	1500
			Jul 1	Balance b/d	1500
2017			2017		
Jun 30	Balance c/d	5000	Jun 30	Income Statement	3500
		5000			5000
			Jul 1	Balance b/d	5000

Income Statement (extracts) for the year ended 30 June		
		£
2016	Depreciation	1500
2017	Depreciation	3500

Statement of financial position (extract) as at 30 June 2016			
	Cost	Total depreciation	Carrying Value
	£	£	£
Motor cars	8000	1500	6500

Statement of financial position (extract) as at 30 June 2017			
	Cost	Total depreciation	Carrying Value
	£	£	£
Motor cars	19 000	5000	14 000

▲ **Figure 7.4** Recording depreciation.

7.4 THE DISPOSAL OF A NON-CURRENT ASSET

REASON FOR ACCOUNTING ENTRIES

When an asset is sold, it must be deleted from the accounts. This means that the cost of the asset is taken out of the asset account. In addition, the depreciation of the asset that has been sold from the depreciation provision needs to be removed. Finally, the profit or loss on the sale must be calculated.

Depreciation charges can only be estimated. When a business purchases an asset, they do not know exactly when they will dispose of the asset or how much they will be able to sell the asset for, if anything. When they do eventually dispose of the asset, the amount they receive for it is usually different from the original estimate.

ACCOUNTING ENTRIES NEEDED

On the sale of a non-current asset, e.g. machinery, the following entries are needed:

A Transfer the cost price of the asset sold to an assets disposal account (in this case, a machinery disposals account):
- **debit** the machinery disposals account
- **credit** the machinery account.

B Transfer the depreciation already charged to the assets disposal account:
- **debit** the provision for depreciation – machinery account
- **credit** the machinery disposals account.

C Record the amount received on disposal:
- **debit** cash book
- **credit** machinery disposals account.

D Transfer the difference (i.e. the amount to balance the machinery disposals account) to the income statement.

  a If the machinery disposals account shows a difference on the debit side of the account, there is a profit on the sale:
  - **debit** the machinery disposals account
  - **credit** the income statement.

  b If the machinery disposals account shows a difference on the credit side of the account, there is a loss on the sale:
  - **debit** the income statement
  - **credit** the machinery disposals account.

These entries can be illustrated using figures from **Figure 7.2**. **Presume** that the machinery shown is sold. The records to 31 December 2016 show that the cost of the machine was €2000. A total of €976 has been written off as depreciation,

> **KEY POINT**
> Learn the entries for disposal of an asset shown here.

> **GENERAL VOCABULARY**
> **presume** accept something as true and base something else on it

leaving a carrying value of (€2000 − €976) = €1024. If the machine is sold on 2 January 2017 for more than €1024, a profit on sale will be made. If the machine is sold for less than €1024, then a loss on disposal will be incurred.

Figure 7.5 shows the entries needed if the machine is sold for €1070 and a small profit is made on sale. **Figure 7.6** shows the entries if the machine is sold for €950, incurring a loss on the sale. In both cases the sale is on 2 January 2017 and no depreciation is charged for the two days' ownership in 2017. The letters (A) to (D) in **Figures 7.5** and **7.6** refer to the sequence of instructions shown above.

> **NOTE**
> Cash book entries are not shown.

Dr				Machinery Account				Cr
2014			€	2017				€
Jan 1	Cash		2000	Jan 2	Machinery disposals	(A)		2000

Dr				Provision for Depreciation: Machinery Account				Cr
2017			€	2017				€
Jan 2	Machinery disposals	(B)	976	Jan 1	Balance b/d			976

Dr				Machinery Disposals Account				Cr
2017			€	2017				€
Jan 2	Machinery	(A)	2000	Jan 2	Cash	(C)		1070
Dec 31	Income Statement	(D)	46	2	Provision for depreciation	(B)		976
			2046					2046

Income Statement for the year ended 31 December 2017

	€
Gross Profit	xxx
Add Profit on sale of machinery (D)	46

▲ Figure 7.5 Machinery sold for a profit.

> **SUBJECT VOCABULARY**
> **gross profit** the difference between revenue and costs of sales. It is the profit figure before operating expenses have been deducted

Dr				Machinery Account				Cr
2016			€	2017				€
Jan 1	Cash		2000	Jan 2	Machinery disposals	(A)		2000

Dr				Provision for Depreciation: Machinery Account				Cr
2017			€	2017				€
Jan 2	Machinery disposals	(B)	976	Jan 1	Balance b/d			976

Dr				Machinery Disposals Account				Cr
2017			€	2017				€
Jan 2	Machinery	(A)	2000	Jan 2	Cash	(C)		950
				Jan 2	Provision for depreciation	(B)		976
				Jan 2	Income Statement	(D)		74
			2000					2000

> **DID YOU KNOW?**
> Tangible (physical) non-current assets are depreciated, whereas intangible non-current assets are **amortised**.

Income Statement for the year ended 31 December 2017

	€
Gross Profit	xxx
Less Loss on sale of machinery (D)	74

▲ Figure 7.6 Machinery sold for a loss.

> **SUBJECT VOCABULARY**
> **amortise** gradually write off the initial cost of an intangible non-current asset over a period of time

END OF CHAPTER QUESTIONS

1. Define the term depreciation.
2. Explain the main differences between straight line and reducing balance depreciation.
3. What two concepts are applied when calculating depreciation?
4. What is meant by the term 'carrying value'?
5. Which account is debited and which account is credited with the annual charge for depreciation?

END OF CHAPTER CHECKLIST

- Depreciation is provided on all non-current assets except land.
- The method of depreciation should not be changed each year.
- Depreciation measures the use of the non-current asset over a specific time period. The time period is normally a year.

EXAM PRACTICE

A01 **A02** **A03** Answer ALL questions in this section. Questions 1–9 must be answered with a cross in the box ☒. If you change your mind about an answer, put a line through the box ☒ and then mark your new answer with a cross ☒.

1 A sole trader depreciates his motor vehicles at 25% per annum on a reducing balance basis.

The vehicles cost £16 000 on 1 January Year 1.

What is the depreciation for year 2?

☐ A £3000
☐ B £4000
☐ C £7000
☐ D £8000 **(1 mark)**

2 An office machine cost S$8500 and is estimated to have a useful life of four years. Its scrap value at the end of this time is estimated at S$1000.

What is the annual charge for depreciation using the straight line method?

☐ A S$1000
☐ B S$1875
☐ C S$2125
☐ D S$2375 **(1 mark)**

3 Why does a business depreciate a non-current asset?

☐ A to know the profit or loss on disposal
☐ B to know the value at the end of its useful life
☐ C to provide cash for its replacement
☐ D to spread the cost over its expected useful life **(1 mark)**

4 Yin bought a machine for HK$6000 and depreciated it at the rate of 20% each year, using the reducing balance method.

What is the total depreciation for years 1 and 2?

☐ A HK$1200
☐ B HK$1440
☐ C HK$2160
☐ D HK$2400 **(1 mark)**

5 Paul purchased a motor vehicle for $15 000. He estimated that it would be used for five years and then be sold for $2000. Paul decided to spread the depreciation of the motor vehicle equally over its working life at a rate of 20% per annum.

What is the accumulated depreciation at the end of year 2?

☐ A $4680
☐ B $5200
☐ C $5400
☐ D $6000 **(1 mark)**

6 An office machine cost MOP8500 and is estimated to have a useful life of four years. Its scrap value at the end of this time is estimated at MOP1000.

What is the annual charge for depreciation using the straight line method?

☐ A MOP1000
☐ B MOP1875
☐ C MOP2125
☐ D MOP2375 **(1 mark)**

7 A sole trader has omitted depreciation from his financial statements.

What are the effects on the Statement of Financial Position?

	Non-current assets	Profit for the year
☐ A	overstated	overstated
☐ B	overstated	understated
☐ C	understated	overstated
☐ D	understated	understated

(1 mark)

8 Paul Williams improves the layout of his shop by spending £12 000 on new Fixtures and Fittings on 1 April 2015. He decides to depreciate using the reducing balance method at 20% per annum. Depreciation of £2400 is included in the income statement for the year ended 31 March 2016.

Which amount will be included for depreciation of motor vehicles in the income statement for the year ended 31 March 2017?

- [ ] **A** $1920
- [ ] **B** $2000
- [ ] **C** $2400
- [ ] **D** $960 **(1 mark)**

9 A vehicle was purchased for $20 000 in January 2015. Two years later, the vehicle has a carrying value of $10 000. Depreciation was calculated using the straight line method. What annual depreciation rate has been used?

- [ ] **A** 16%
- [ ] **B** 25%
- [ ] **C** 50%
- [ ] **D** 33.3% **(1 mark)**

10 Anwar Healie produces his accounts to 31 March each year. He bought a motor vehicle on 1 April 2014 for $22 000. Depreciation is to be charged at 15% each year using the straight line method.

a Calculate the depreciation charge in his accounts for the years ended 31 March 2015, 31 March 2016 and 31 March 2017.

b Calculate the carrying value for the Motor Vehicle at 31 March 2017.

c Show the journal entries for the depreciation charged over the three-year period.

(8 marks)

11 Equipment was bought for $76 000. It has an estimated useful life of five years, after which their scrap value is expected to be £16 000. Use the straight line method and show your workings to calculate:

a the annual amount of depreciation to be charged

b the annual percentage rate of depreciation to be charged. **(8 marks)**

12 Jason owns a hairdresser's salon and he bought a new set of chairs on 1 April 2016 for £1000. He calculates depreciation using the reducing balance method at 20%. On 1 April 2017 he bought a new air conditioner for £8000. He calculates depreciation for the delivery van at 20% using the straight line method.

a Calculate the entries in the income statement for the year ending 31 March 2018.

b Complete the non-current assets section for Jason's Statement of Financial position at 31 March 2018. **(10 marks)**

(Total 35 marks)

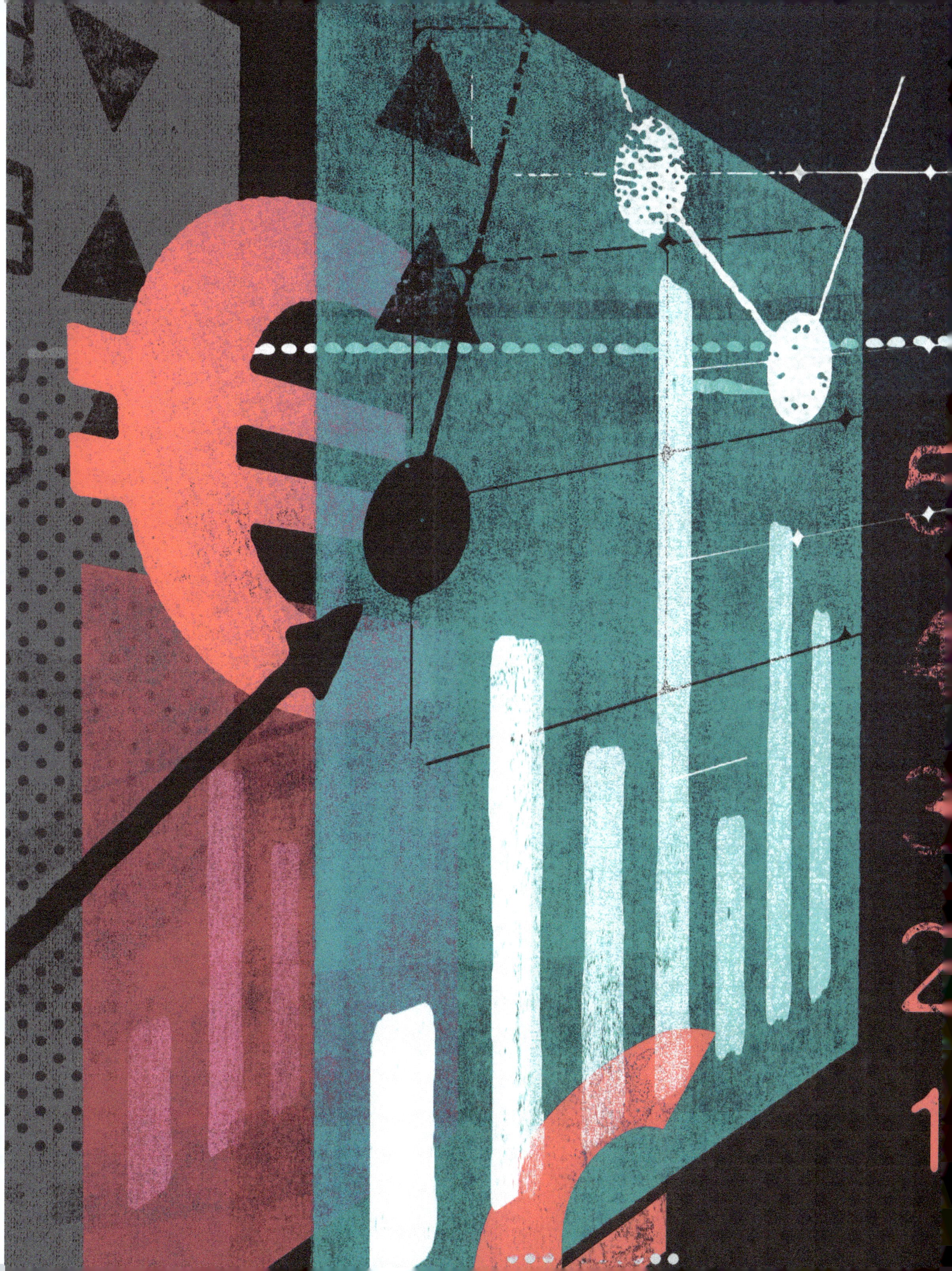

8 TRIAL BALANCE | 100   9 CORRECTION OF ERRORS | 108   10 CONTROL ACCOUNTS | 121
11 BANK RECONCILIATION STATEMENTS | 132

UNIT 3
INTRODUCTION TO CONTROL PROCESSES

Assessment Objective AO1
Demonstrate a knowledge and understanding of accounting terminology, principles, procedures and techniques

Assessment Objective AO2
Select and apply their knowledge and understanding of accounting procedures to a variety of accounting problems

Assessment Objective AO3
Analyse, evaluate and present information in appropriate accounting formats and communicate reasoned explanations

All businesses need to check that their accounts are accurate. Mistakes and errors can often occur when we use double entry bookkeeping. We may record the figures incorrectly or enter the wrong name for a customer or supplier. We also need to check that cash has not been taken out of the business incorrectly.

Unit 3 explains the three main ways of checking your accounts are accurate – the trial balance, control accounts and the bank reconciliation statement – and shows you how to correct any errors that have been discovered. The content covered in this unit will be tested in Paper 1, but will also help you with your understanding of questions in Paper 2.

8 TRIAL BALANCE

LEARNING OBJECTIVES

- Explain the purpose of a trial balance
- Prepare a trial balance
- Understand the limitations of a trial balance

▲ 'Balancing off' reveals some but not all accounting errors.

GETTING STARTED

The focus of this chapter is on 'balancing off' accounts. This procedure is usually carried out at the end of each month, before the preparation of the trial balance. The trial balance will reveal some errors, but not all of them. It provides an arithmetical check on the accuracy of the ledgers and makes the preparation of the financial statements easier.

SKILLS ANALYSIS

ACTIVITY

Look at Chapter 6 and go through your notes on double entry bookkeeping. Note that some entries are always on the same side. For example, sales revenue is always a credit from the business's point of view and purchases are always a debit entry. Which other accounts only have entries on the debit or credit side?

8.1 BALANCING OFF

HINT

Assets, Expenses and Drawings will normally have a debit balance. Income, Liabilities and Capital will always have a credit balance.

SUBJECT VOCABULARY

balancing off finding the difference between the two sides of an account

Balancing off simply means finding the difference between the two sides of an account (i.e. the difference between the total debit entries and the total credit entries in the account). The 'difference' between the two sides is known as the 'balance'. This figure is inserted on the side of the account that shows the least amount of money. If both sides of the account are then totalled up, they should agree, because the balance has been inserted. If they do not agree, there is an error and you must check the calculation again. Sometimes an account simply requires closing off. This is when the debit and credit sides total up to exactly the same amount so there is no balance.

8.2 THE TRIAL BALANCE

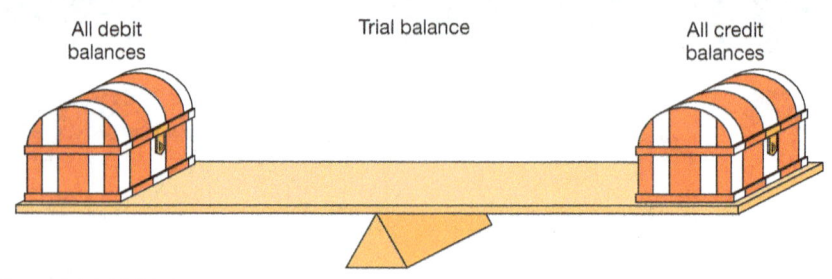

▲ Figure 8.1 A trial balance.

A trial balance is essential to ensure the accuracy of the bookkeeping entries before preparing the financial statements. It is a list of account titles and their balances in the ledger on a specific date. The trial balance gives the name of each account together with the balance shown in the debit or credit columns. Since every entry in double entry bookkeeping should have a corresponding credit entry, the two columns should agree when they are totalled. If they do not, an error has occurred.

8.3 WORKED EXAMPLE

The following accounts are extracted from the books of James Lau. James runs a successful retail business. You will see that the bookkeeper has balanced off all the accounts and prepared a trial balance.

James Lau's books

Dr			Bank Account			Cr
2017			£	2017		£
June 1	Equity		20 000	June 3	Motor car	9000
June 30	A Cope		1350	June 3	Rent	1500
				June 21	Computer	1650
				June 29	J Wang	2700
				June 30	G Moore	630
				June 30	Balance c/d	5870
			21 350			21 350
July 1	Balance b/d		5870			

Dr		Cash Account			Cr
2017		£	2017		£
June 5	Revenue	540	June 14	Stationery	55
June 12	Revenue	440	June 30	Balance c/d	925
		980			980
July 1	Balance b/d	925			

Dr		Revenue Account			Cr
2017		£	2017		£
June 30	Balance c/d	3350	June 5	Cash	540
			June 10	A Cope	1770
			June 12	Cash	440
			June 22	B Singh	600
		3350			3350
			July 1	Balance b/d	3350

Dr			Revenue Returns Account			Cr
2017			£	2017		£
June 23	A Cope		420	June 30	Balance c/d	420
July 1	Balance b/d		420			

Dr			Purchases Account			Cr
2017			£	2017		£
June 3	J Wang		2700	June 30	Balance c/d	4800
June 4	G Moore		750			
June 18	G Moore		1350			
			4800			4800
July 1	Balance b/d		4800			

Dr			Purchase Returns Account			Cr
			£	2017		£
June 30	Balance c/d		120	June 6	G Moore	120
				July 1	Balance b/d	120

Dr			Computer Account			Cr
2017			£			£
June 21	Bank		1650	June 30	Balance c/d	1650

Dr			Motor Car Account			Cr
2017			£			£
June 3	Bank		9000	June 30	Balance c/d	9000
July 1	Balance b/d					

Dr			Rent Account			Cr
2017			£			£
June 3	Rent		1500	June 30	Balance c/d	1500
July 1	Balance b/d		1500			

Dr			Stationery Account			Cr
2017			£			£
June 14	Cash		55	June 30	Balance c/d	55
July 1	Balance b/d		55			

Dr			Equity Account			Cr
			£	2017		£
June 30	Balance c/d		20 000	June 1	Bank	20 000
				July 1	Balance b/d	20 000

Dr			B Singh Account			Cr
2017			£			£
June 22	Revenue		600	June 30	Balance c/d	600

Dr			A Cope Account			Cr
2017			£	2017		£
June 10	Revenue		1770	June 23	Revenue returns	420
				June 30	Bank	1350
			1770			1770

Dr			J Wang Account			Cr
2017			£	2017		£
June 29	Bank		2700	June 3	Purchases	2700

UNIT 3   8 TRIAL BALANCE

Dr			G Moore Account			Cr
2017		£	2017			£
June 6	Purchase Returns	120	June 4	Purchases		750
June 30	Bank	630	June 18	Purchases		1350
June 30	Balance c/d	1350				
		2100				2100
			July 1	Balance b/d		1350

▲ Figure 8.2 James Lau's accounting books.

James Lau

Trial Balance as at 30 June 2017	Dr	Cr
	£	£
Bank	5870	
Cash	925	
Revenue		3350
Revenue returns	420	
Purchases	4800	
Purchase returns		120
Computer	1650	
Motor Car	9000	
Rent	1500	
Stationery	55	
Equity		20000
B. Singh	600	
G. Moore		1350
	24820	24820

▲ Figure 8.3 A trial balance for James Lau.

EXAM HINT

In the exam you may just be given a list of balances and asked to calculate a trial balance. Always use the acronym **DEAD CLIC** to help you. Debit entries will always be Expenses, Assets or Drawings (DEAD) while Credit entries will always be Liabilities, Income or Capital (CLIC).

CASE STUDY: TRIAL BALANCE

Stuart is a motorcycle mechanic in Marcheto. He has prepared the following balances from his ledgers but he needs help putting them into a trial balance. Complete the trial balance for Stuart using the balances given below.

	$
Revenue	52000
Rent	4000
Wages	12000
Electricity	5000
Discount received	5200
Discount allowed	2300
Trade Payables	7200
Trade Receivables	8500
Purchases	35200
	131400

It is often assumed that if the trial balance 'balances', the entries in the accounts must be correct. However, this may not be true.

Certain types of error will not be revealed by a trial balance: look at Chapter 9, pages 108–120 for more information about these types of error.

8.4 STEPS TO TAKE IF THE TRIAL BALANCE DOES NOT BALANCE

If the trial balance does not balance (i.e. the two totals are different) this shows that one or more errors have been made in the double entry bookkeeping or in the preparation of the trial balance itself. Take the following steps to locate the error(s).

1. If the trial balance is badly written and contains many alterations, rewrite it.
2. Add each side of the trial balance again. If you added the numbers 'upwards' the first time, then start at the top and work 'downwards' the second time, or vice versa.
3. Find the amount of the discrepancy and check the accounts for a transaction of this amount. If you find a transaction for this amount, ensure the double entry has been carried out correctly.
4. Halve the amount of the discrepancy and look in the accounts for a transaction for this amount. If you find one, ensure the double entry has been carried out correctly. This type of error may occur if an item is entered on the wrong side of the trial balance.
5. If the amount of the discrepancy is divisible by nine, the digits may have been transposed when the figure was originally entered. For example, £63 may have been entered as £36, or £27 entered as £72.
6. Check that the balance on each account has been calculated correctly and entered into the trial balance in the right column using the correct amount.
7. Make sure every outstanding balance (from all the ledgers and the cash book) has been included in the trial balance and ensure each balance has been entered correctly.
8. If you have not identified the error after steps 1–7, you must re-check the accounts themselves. You may need to check all entries from the date of the last trial balance.

If the trial balance does not balance, you will have to open a suspense account. A suspense account is a T account that is used to locate errors in the books of prime entry and the double entry bookkeeping process, and is shown in **Figure 8.4**.

Suspense Account

Trial balance difference	800	Rent error	400
Sales revenue error	300	Wages error	700
	1100		1100

▲ Figure 8.4 A suspense account.

Notice that the account does not have any balances b/d or c/d. This is because it is only temporary. An example has been given on the next page.

SUBJECT VOCABULARY

overcast when the amount recorded in the accounts is more than the original amount. For example, rent that should be recorded as £200, but is recorded as £250, has been overcast by £50
undercast when the amount recorded in the accounts is lower than the original amount. For example, if electricity should be recorded as $500, but is recorded as $400, it has been undercast by $100

WORKED EXAMPLE

Daniel Marris has drawn up a suspense account at 31 July 2016 following the discovery of errors.

From the following list of errors, make the necessary entries in the suspense account and calculate the trial balance difference.
1. The sales day book has been **overcast** by £2000.
2. The returns inward has been entered as a credit of £3000. It actually totalled £2000.
3. A discount received of £800 was entered in the cash book but omitted from the general ledger.
4. A cheque for £1200 paid to G Mitchell was entered in the account of B Mitchell in error.

Answer
1. Debit: Sales: £2000 and Credit: Suspense Account £2000.
2. Debit: Returns Inwards: £3000 and Credit: Suspense Account £3000. Then Debit: Returns Inwards: £2000 and Credit: Suspense Account £2000.
3. Debit: Suspense Account £800 and Credit: Discount Received: £800.
4. Debit: G Mitchell £1200 and Credit: B Mitchell £1200. No suspense account entry is needed.

The Suspense Account is shown in **Figure 8.5** and the trial balance difference can now be calculated.

		Suspense Account				
31-Jul	Trial balance difference	6200	31-Jul	Sales overcast	2000
31-Jul	Discount Rec	800	31-Jul	Returns in	3000
			31-Jul	Returns in	2000
		7000			7000

▲ **Figure 8.5** Suspense account worked example.

END OF CHAPTER QUESTIONS

1. Which side of the trial balance usually has more entries?
2. What is the major weakness of preparing a trial balance?
3. What is an advantage of preparing a trial balance?
4. What dos b/d and c/d mean when balancing off?
5. Which account should you open if the trial balance doesn't balance?

END OF CHAPTER CHECKLIST

- A trial balance is extracted from the three ledgers.
- The debit column lists Expenses, Assets and Drawings.
- The credit column lists Liabilities, Income and Capital.
- The trial balance is an arithmetical check on the accuracy of the ledgers.
- Not all errors are revealed by the trial balance – remember TOPCOCC.

EXAM PRACTICE

A01 A02 A03 Answer ALL questions in this section. Questions 1–8 must be answered with a cross in the box ☒. If you change your mind about an answer, put a line through the box ☒ and then mark your new answer with a cross ☒.

1 Which of the following is not a purpose of preparing a trial balance?
- A to aid the preparation of financial statements
- B to check the arithmetical accuracy of the double entry bookkeeping
- C to help locate arithmetical errors
- D to prove that the double entry has been carried out without errors **(1 mark)**

2 Which error will affect the balancing of a trial balance?
- A a purchase invoice, KES20 000, completely omitted from the books
- B a sale on credit, KES5000, entered in the sales journal as KES550
- C purchase of a machine, KES50 000, entered in the purchases account
- D the purchases journal undercast by KES10 000 **(1 mark)**

3 Why is a trial balance prepared?
- A to calculate profit for the year
- B to check the amount of the owner's equity
- C to check the arithmetical accuracy of the double entry
- D to find out how much is owed to a trade payable **(1 mark)**

4 A cheque for LKS9600 to Mahesh Perera was entered into his account as LKS6900. When the trial balance was prepared, the difference was entered into a suspense account.

Which entries are required to correct this error?

	account to be debited	account to be credited
A	Mahesh Perera 2700	suspense 2700
B	Mahesh Perera 5400	suspense 5400
C	Mahesh Perera 6900	suspense 6900
D	Mahesh Perera 9600	suspense 9600

(1 mark)

5 Which error will affect the balancing of the trial balance?
- A A cheque from Sam is debited in the bank account but not entered in Sam's account.
- B A cheque paid to Smith is debited in Smythe's account.
- C An invoice from a supplier has been lost and not recorded.
- D A payment of rent was debited to the bank account and credited to the rent account. **(1 mark)**

6 Which will appear on the credit side of a trial balance?
- A loan interest received
- B motor vehicles at cost
- C rent paid
- D electricity **(1 mark)**

7 Wai-Yee receives payment from a trade payable. She debits the trade payable's account and credits the bank account.

Which type of error is this?
- A compensating
- B complete reversal
- C original entry
- D principle **(1 mark)**

8 The totals of a trial balance agreed. It was later found that goods sold on credit for HK$230 had been entered on the correct side of both the trade receivables account and the revenue account as HK$320.

Which type of error is this?
- A compensating
- B complete reversal
- C original entry
- D principle **(1 mark)**

9

Colin Tate has a business providing spare parts for washing machines. His financial year ends on March 2017.

At 31 March 2017, his accounts showed the following balances:

Non-current assets at cost	$24 200
Provision for depreciation	$7400
Inventory (at 1 April 2016)	$4500
Balance at bank	$(Dr) 1250
Revenue	$72 340
Revenue returns	$800
Purchases	$38 150
Carriage outwards	$200
Salaries	$5000
Marketing	$7200
Heating and Lighting	$8940
Equity	$9650
Drawings	$2000

Prepare Colin's trial balance at 31 March 2017.
(6 marks)

10

The following list of balances was taken from the books of Rafa, a sole trader, on 30 April 2017.

	£
Bank (overdraft)	4350
Capital	16 650
Drawings	9000
Expenses	42 500
Inventories	16 500
Machinery	12 000
Purchases	84 000
Sales revenue	135 000
Trade payables	1700
Trade receivables	700

a Prepare Rafa's trial balance at 30 April 2017. Include a suspense account to show any difference.

After the trial balance was prepared, the following **three** errors were found:

1) Cash sales of £9000 had been paid into the bank but had not been posted to the sales account.

2) Drawings of £1100 had been correctly entered in the cash book but posted to the drawings account as £600.

3) The cash account of £1500 had been omitted from the list of balances.

b Complete a suspense account to correct the errors.

c Prepare a correct trial balance for Rafa.
(15 marks)

11

The following trial balance was prepared by Imisi. It contains several mistakes.

Trial Balance – 31 January 2017

	$	$
Equity	10 500	
Cash in hand	1320	
Discount received	96	
Drawings	3600	
Fixtures and fittings		2050
General expenses	1050	
Inventory 1 February 2016		2567
Purchases	4720	
Revenue returns		92
Sales revenue		8430
Trade payables		3455
Trade receivables		3203
	21 286	19 797

In addition to the mistakes in the trial balance, the following errors were also discovered:

1) A purchase of fittings for $120 had been included in the purchases account.

2) A payment of $75 made to a trade payable had not been posted from the cash book into the payables ledger.

3) A cheque of $56 received from a customer had been correctly entered into the cash book but posted to the customer's account as $50.

4) A page of the sales day book was correctly totalled as $564 but carried forward as $456.

Prepare the trial balance for Imisi after all the errors have been corrected. Please show all your workings.
(11 marks)

(Total 40 marks)

9 CORRECTION OF ERRORS

▲ A methodical approach to finding and correcting errors is very important.

LEARNING OBJECTIVES

- Identify and explain errors that do, and do not, affect the balancing of the trial balance
- Prepare journal entries to correct errors
- Prepare a suspense account

GETTING STARTED

In this chapter, we will learn about the mistakes that can be made when preparing accounts using double entry. This can be a particularly challenging topic for students as some errors are not revealed by the preparation of the trial balance. This can be confusing, as the trial balance is supposed to balance. Remember that this is the weakness of the trial balance: just because it balances does not mean it is correct.

ACTIVITY

Look back at the previous chapters on double entry and the trial balance. Here, the acronyms DEAD vs CLIC were used. What do they mean?

9.1 ERRORS NOT REVEALED BY A TRIAL BALANCE

As you have learned, the trial balance will appear to balance even if certain errors have occurred. Remember the acronym **TOPCOCC** to remind you of the different types of error, described below.

- **(T) Error of transposition.** When a number is recorded incorrectly on both sides. For example, instead of writing $123, you write £321 on both sides of the entry.
- **(O) Error of original entry.** When an item is entered using an incorrect amount. For example, an invoice received, showing goods purchased to the value of $260.00, is entered in both the purchases account and the supplier's account as $26.00.
- **(P) Errors of principle.** When an item is entered in the wrong class of account. For example, a non-current asset is entered in an expense account.
- **(C) Complete reversal of entries.** When the correct amounts are entered in the correct accounts, but each item is shown on the wrong side of the account.

EXAM HINT
Examiners like to ask questions about how the correction of errors will affect the profit for the year.

EXAM HINT
If a transaction has no effect on the financial statements, tell the examiner.

EXAM HINT
Use the acronym **TOPCOCC** in the exam. Write it down as soon as the exam starts.

- **(O) Error of omission.** When a transaction is completely omitted from the books. For example, a cheque received is lost and therefore never entered in the books of account.
- **(C) Errors of commission (wrong account).** When a correct amount is entered, but in the wrong person's account or wrong account. For example, a sale of goods to J Roberts is entered in J Robertson's account.
- **(C) Compensating errors.** Where two or more errors are cancelled off by two other errors. These can be on the same side or on opposite sides.

9.2 ERRORS NOT AFFECTING TRIAL BALANCE AGREEMENT

Examples of each type of error are shown below.

Example 1: Errors of commission

A Chang paid us £50 by cheque on 18 May 2017. The transaction was entered correctly in the cash book, but it was entered by mistake in the account for A Chung. The trial balance will still balance because there is a debit of £50 and a credit of £50. This transaction appears in the personal account as:

Dr	A Chung Account		Cr
2017			£
May 18		Bank	50

The error was found on 31 May 2017. We now have to correct it. This requires two entries:

▼ ACCOUNTING ENTRIES	▼ EXPLANATION
Debit A Chung account	To cancel out the error on the credit side of that account
Credit A Chang account	To enter the amount in the correct account

The accounts and journal entry are shown in **Figure 9.1**.

Dr		A Chung Account				Cr
2017			£	2017		£
May 31	A Chang: Error corrected		50	May 18	Bank	50

Dr		A Chang Account				Cr
2017			£	2017		£
May 1	Balance b/d		50	May 31	Cash entered in error A Chung's account	50

The Journal				
			Dr	Cr
2017			£	£
May 31	A Chung		50	
	A Chang			50
	Cheque received. Entered in wrong personal account, now corrected.			

▲ **Figure 9.1** Accounts and journal entry for Example 1.

Example 2: Errors of principle

A motor car is purchased for AED35 500 by cheque on 14 May 2017. It is debited in error to a motor expenses account. In the cash book, it is shown correctly. The trial balance will still balance because there is a debit of AED35 500 and a credit of AED35 500.

This transaction appears in the expense account as:

Dr	Motor Expenses Account		Cr
2017		AED	
May 14	Bank	AED35 500	

A bookkeeper detects the error on 31 May 2017 and corrects it. She adds two entries.

▼ ACCOUNTING ENTRY	▼ EXPLANATION
Debit Motor Car account	To put the amount in the correct account
Credit Motor Expenses account	To cancel the error previously made in the Motor Expenses account

The corrected accounts and journal entry are shown in **Figure 9.2**.

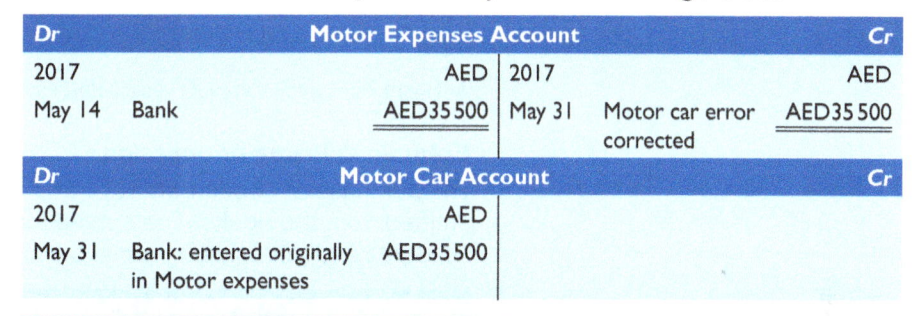

Dr	Motor Expenses Account					Cr
2017			AED	2017		AED
May 14	Bank		AED35 500	May 31	Motor car error corrected	AED35 500

Dr	Motor Car Account			Cr
2017			AED	
May 31	Bank: entered originally in Motor expenses		AED35 500	

The Journal			
		Dr	Cr
2017		AED	AED
May 31	Motor car	35 500	
	Motor expenses		35 500
	Correction of error – purchase of motor car was debited to motor expenses account.		

▲ **Figure 9.2** Corrected accounts and journal entry for Example 2.

Example 3: Errors of original entry

Revenue of £150 to C Higgins on 13 May 2017 is entered as both a debit and a credit of £130. This transaction appears in the accounts as:

Dr	C Higgins Account		Cr
2017		£	
May 13	Revenue	130	

Dr	Revenue Account		Cr
		2017	£
		May 13 Sales day book (part of total)	130

The error is found on 31 May 2017. The corrected accounts and journal entry are shown in **Figure 9.3**.

Dr			C Higgins Account		Cr
2017		£			
May 13	Revenue	130			
May 31	Revenue: error	20			

Dr			Revenue Account		Cr
			2017		£
			May 13	Sales day book	130
			May 31	C Higgins: error corrected	20

The Journal				
			Dr	Cr
2017			£	£
May 31	C Higgins		20	
	Revenue			20
	Correction of error. Revenue of £150 had been incorrectly entered as £130.			

▲ **Figure 9.3** Corrected accounts and journal entry for Example 3.

Example 4: Errors of omission

The purchase of goods from K Oke for $250 on 13 May 2017 is completely omitted from the books. The error is found on 31 May 17. The corrected accounts and journal entry are shown in **Figure 9.4**.

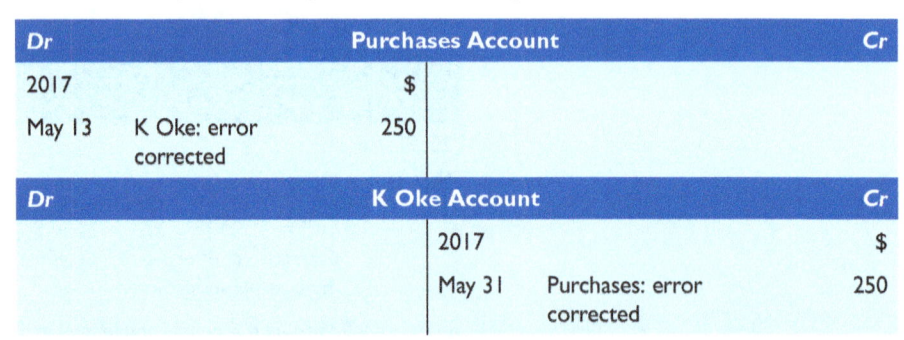

Dr			Purchases Account		Cr
2017		$			
May 13	K Oke: error corrected	250			

Dr			K Oke Account		Cr
			2017		$
			May 31	Purchases: error corrected	250

The Journal				
			Dr	Cr
2017			$	$
May 31	Purchases		250	
	K Oke			250
	Correction of error. Purchase omitted			

▲ **Figure 9.4** Corrected accounts and journal entry for Example 4.

Example 5: Compensating errors

A business's books contain two incorrect totals: purchases (MOP7900) and revenue (MOP9900). The purchases day book adds up to MOP100 too much. In the same period, the sales day book also adds up to MOP100 too much.

If these are the only errors in the books, the trial balance totals will equal each other. Both totals are wrong, as they are both MOP100 too high – but they will be equal. The accounts will look like this:

Dr		Purchases Account			Cr
2017		MOP			
May 31	Purchases	7900			

Dr		Revenue Account			Cr
			2017		MOP
			May 31	Revenue	9900

The corrected accounts and journal entry are show in **Figure 9.5**.

Dr		Purchases Account			Cr
2017		MOP	2017		MOP
May 31	Purchases	7900	May 31	The Journal: error corrected	100

Dr		Revenue Account			Cr
2017		MOP	2017		MOP
May 31	The Journal: error corrected	100	May 31	Revenue	9900

The Journal			
		Dr	Cr
2017		MOP	MOP
May 31	Revenue	100	
	Purchases		100
Correction of compensating errors.			
Totals of both purchases and sales day book added up to MOP100 too much.			

▲ Figure 9.5 Corrected accounts and journal entry for Example 5.

Example 6: Complete reversal of entries

On 28 May 2017, a cheque for £200 is paid to A Lowe. This is entered in the accounts as shown below. The trial balance will balance because there has been a debit of £200 and a credit of £200.

Dr		Cash Book (A)				Cr
		Cash	Bank		Cash	Bank
2017		£	£		£	£
May 28	A Lowe		200			

Dr		A Lowe (A)			Cr
			2017		£
			May 28	Bank	200

This is incorrect. The transaction should have been entered as a debit in A Lowe's account and as a credit in the Bank account. Both items have been entered in the correct accounts, but each item is on the wrong side of its account.

This type of error is more difficult to correct than the other errors as we need to enter the figures twice. The figure below shows how the accounts would have looked if the transaction had been entered correctly in the first place.

Dr			Cash Book (B)				Cr
		Cash	Bank			Cash	Bank
		£	£	2017		£	£
				May 28	A Lowe		200

Dr		A Lowe (B)			Cr
2017		£			
May 28	Bank	200			

The error was discovered on May 31 and corrected as follows:

1 First we have to cancel the error. We enter these amounts:

Dr	A Lowe	£200	
Cr	Bank		£200

2 Then we have to enter up the transaction:

Dr	A Lowe	£200	
Cr	Bank		£200

The entries to correct the error are twice the amounts first entered.

The corrected accounts, labelled (C), are shown in **Figure 9.6**.

You can see that the accounts labelled (C) give the same final answer as the accounts labelled (B).

Dr			Cash Book (C)				Cr
		Cash	Bank			Cash	Bank
2017		£	£	2017		£	£
May 28	A Lowe		200	May 31	A Lowe: error corrected		400

Dr		A Lowe Account (C)				Cr
2017		£	2017			£
May 31	Bank: error corrected	400	May 28	Bank		200

				£	£
(B)	Dr	A Lowe		200	
	Cr	Bank			200
(C)	Dr	A Lowe (£400 – £200)		200	
	Cr	Bank (£400 – £200)			200

▲ Figure 9.6 Corrected accounts for Example 6.

The journal entries to correct this error are shown in **Figure 9.7**.

The Journal			
		Dr	Cr
2017		£	£
May 31	A Lowe	400	
	Bank		400
	Payment of £200 on 28 May 2017 to A Lowe incorrectly credited to his account, and debited to bank. Error now corrected.		

▲ Figure 9.7 Journal entry for Example 6.

> **HINT**
> If the error is caused by complete reversal of entries, the amount will always be doubled in both accounts during correction.

9.3 ERRORS AFFECTING TRIAL BALANCE AGREEMENT

There are various types of error that will affect the balancing of the trial balance:
- incorrect additions in any account
- making an entry on only one side of the accounts, for example, a debit but no credit, or a credit but no debit
- entering a different amount on the debit side from the amount on the credit side
- errors in writing up the trial balance
- account balances not picked up to the trial balance.

EXAM HINT

If the transaction has no effect on the trial balance it is important to tell the examiner this. Otherwise, the examiner will assume you haven't answered the question.

SUSPENSE ACCOUNTS AND ERRORS

SUBJECT VOCABULARY

suspense account an account in the general ledger in which amounts are temporarily recorded

If a trial balance does not balance, it is important to locate and correct the errors as soon as possible. If the errors cannot be found, the trial balance totals need to be made to agree with each other by inserting the amount of the difference between the two sides in a **suspense account**.

In the **Figure 9.8** there is a difference of £40.

To make the two totals the same, a figure of £40 has been added to the credit side of the trial balance. Then a suspense account needs to be opened. The £40 difference is also shown on the credit side.

Trial Balance as at 31 December 2017

	Dr	Cr
	£	£
Totals after all the accounts have been listed	100 000	99 960
Suspense account		40
	100 000	100 000

Dr	Suspense Account	Cr
		£
	Dec 31 Difference per trial balance/ balance b/d	40

▲ Figure 9.8 Trial balance and suspense account.

SUSPENSE ACCOUNT AND THE STATEMENT OF FINANCIAL POSITION

If the errors cannot be found before the financial statements are prepared, the suspense account balance will be included in the statement of financial position. If the balance is a credit balance, it should be included under current liabilities on the statement of financial position. If the balance is a debit balance, it should be shown under current assets on the statement of financial position. Wherever possible, however, errors should be found before the financial statements are drawn up.

CORRECTION OF ERRORS: ONE ERROR ONLY

SUBJECT VOCABULARY

undercast undervalue

When errors are found, they must be corrected using double entry. Each correction must be described by an entry in the journal. Here are two examples to consider:

Example 7: Assume that the error of £40 shown in the example above is found in the following year on 31 March 2017. The error is that the revenue account was **undercast** (see sections 8.4 and 9.5) by £40. The action taken to correct this is:
- debit the suspense account to close it: £40
- credit the revenue account to show where the item should have been: £40.

The double entry accounts and journal entry are shown in **Figure 9.9**.

Dr	Suspense Account				Cr
2017		£	2016		£
Mar 31	Revenue	40	Dec 31	Difference per trial balance	40

Dr	Revenue Account				Cr
			2017		£
			Mar 31	Suspense	40

The Journal			
		Dr	Cr
2017		£	£
Mar 31	Suspense	40	
	Revenue		40
	Correction of undercasting of revenue by £40 in last year's accounts.		

▲ **Figure 9.9** Double entry accounts and journal entry for Example 7.

Example 8: The trial balance on 31 December 2016 shows a difference of £168, caused by a **shortage** on the debit side. A suspense account is opened and the difference of £168 is entered on the debit side.

On 31 May 2017 the error is found. A payment of £168 had been made to D Miguel to close his account. It was correctly entered in the cash book, but it was not entered in D Miguel's account.

To correct the error, the account of D Miguel is debited with £168, as it should have been in 2016. The suspense account is credited with £168 so that the account can be closed. The double entry accounts and journal entry are shown in **Figure 9.10**.

Dr	D Miguel Account				Cr
2017		£	2017		£
May 31	Bank	168	Jan 1	Balance b/d	168

Dr	Suspense Account				Cr
2016		£	2017		£
Dec 31	Difference per trial balance	168	May 31	D Miguel	168

The Journal			
		Dr	Cr
2017		£	£
Mar 31	D Miguel	168	
	Suspense		168
	Correction of non-entry of payment last year in D Miguel's account.		

▲ **Figure 9.10** Double entry accounts and journal entry for Example 8.

> **GENERAL VOCABULARY**
>
> **shortage** a situation in which there is not enough of something

CORRECTION OF ERRORS: MORE THAN ONE ERROR

Look at example 9, where the suspense account difference has been caused by more than one error.

Example 9: A business's trial balance at 31 December 2016 shows a difference of £77. The shortage is on the debit side. The bookkeeper opens a suspense account, and enters the difference of £77 on the debit side of the account. The bookkeeper finds all the errors from the previous year on 28 February 2017:

a A cheque of £150 paid to L Park was correctly entered in the cash book, but was not entered in Park's account.

b The purchases account was undercast by £20.

c A cheque of £93 received from K Garcia was correctly entered in the cash book but was not entered in Garcia's account.

These three errors have resulted in a net error of £77. The error is seen in the debit of £77 on the debit side of the suspense account. The three errors are corrected by:

- making correcting entries in the accounts for (a), (b) and (c)
- recording the double entry for these items in the suspense account.

The double entry accounts and journal entry are shown in **Figure 9.11**.

Dr		L Park Account			Cr
2017		£			
Jan 28	Suspense (a)	150			

Dr		Purchases Account			Cr
2017		£			
Jan 28	Suspense (b)	20			

Dr		K Garcia Account			Cr
			2017		£
			Jan 28	Suspense (c)	93

Dr		Suspense Account			Cr
2017		£	2017		£
Jan 1	Balance b/d	77	Jan 28	L Park (a)	150
Jan 28	K Garcia (c)	93	Jan 28	Purchases (b)	20
		170			170

The Journal				
			Dr	Cr
2017			£	£
Jan 28	L Park		150	
	Suspense			150
	Cheque paid omitted from Kent's account			
Jan 28	Purchases		20	
	Suspense			20
	Undercasting of purchases by £20 in last year's accounts			
Jan 28	Suspense		93	
	K Garcia			93
	Cheque received omitted from Garcia's account			

▲ **Figure 9.11** Double entry accounts and journal entry for Example 9.

UNIT 3 9 CORRECTION OF ERRORS 117

It is only necessary to correct those errors that make the trial balance totals different from each other. This is done via the suspense account.

CASE STUDY: TESCO LOSES £2 BILLION IN VALUE

SKILLS REASONING, DECISION MAKING

In 2014, Tesco shares lost over £2 billion in value due to the misallocation of some expenses. The error was discovered after a **whistleblower** had raised an alert to highlight the errors. The correction of the errors meant that Tesco's profit had been overstated by £250 million.

What should Tesco have done when they discovered the error?

How can Tesco stop this happening in the future?

SUBJECT VOCABULARY

whistleblower a person who exposes any kind of information or activity that is deemed illegal, dishonest, or not correct within an organisation that is either private or public

END OF CHAPTER QUESTIONS

1 What is the purpose of the journal?

2 What is the purpose of a suspense account?

3 What is an error of commission?

4 What does the term overcast mean?

5 What would be the impact of an expense credited in the journal? Would it increase or decrease profit?

6 What side are liabilities on in the trial balance?

7 A business has a suspense account. The amount in the suspense account is in respect of a cash sale to Tahir, which was omitted from the sales account. Which entries will correct the error?

	account debited	account credited
a	sales	suspense
b	suspense	sales
c	suspense	Tahir
d	Tahir	suspense

8 Which error requires a correcting entry in a suspense account?

   a cash paid to Gideon debited to Gibson's account

   b motor vehicles account omitted from the trial balance

   c purchase of fixtures for cash debited to the purchases account

   d no entry made for cash paid for stationery

9 Which is an error of omission?

   a No entry is made for the purchase of stationery by cheque.

   b Purchase of stationery is entered only in the cash book.

   c Purchase of stationery is entered only in the stationery account.

   d The stationery account is missed out of the trial balance.

10 When is a suspense account opened?

   a when a Statement of Financial Position fails to balance

   b when a trial balance fails to balance

   c when an error of omission is corrected

   d when a cash book fails to balance

11 The purchase of a new computer has been posted to the repairs account in error.

   What type of error is this?

   a commission

   b complete reversal of entries

   c original entry

   d principle

12 Rent received of $100 has been debited to the rent paid account and credited to the cash account.

   What is the journal entry to correct this?

	account debited $	account credited $
a	cash 100	rent received 100
b	cash 200	rent paid 100 rent received 100
c	rent received 100 rent paid 100	cash 200
d	rent paid 100	rent received 100

13 The total of the discounts received account, $400, is entered on the wrong side of a trial balance.

   Which suspense account entry will balance the trial balance?

   a $400 credit   b $800 credit

   c $400 debit   d $800 debit

14 Saddique's trial balance failed to balance. The debit column totalled $12 250 and the credit column totalled $12 200.

The following errors were discovered and corrected.
- No entry had been made for cash sales, $150.
- The total of the discount received account, $50, had been omitted from the trial balance.

What will be the totals of the amended trial balance?

a $12 250   b $12 300
c $12 350   d $12 400

15 The difference on a trial balance was entered in a suspense account. It was found later that a payment of $1600 for rent had been entered correctly in the cash book but credited in the rent account.

Which entry corrects this error?

	account to be debited $	account to be credited $
a	rent 1600	suspense 1600
b	rent 3200	suspense 3200
c	suspense 1600	rent 1600
d	suspense 3200	rent 3200

16 Mohammed deals in office equipment. A desk intended for use by the business was recorded as the purchase of goods for resale.

Which entry corrects this error?

	account to be debited	account to be credited
a	purchases	office equipment
b	office equipment	purchases
c	sales	office equipment
d	office equipment	sales

17 A purchase of equipment is debited to the equipment repairs account in error.

What is the effect of this error on the business's financial statements?

	profit for the year	non-current assets
a	too high	too high
b	too high	too low
c	too low	too high
d	too low	too low

END OF CHAPTER CHECKLIST

- The trial balance can be incorrect even if it balances.
- A suspense account is used if the debit and credit columns of the trial balance do not balance.
- When you have corrected the errors, the suspense account should not exist anymore.
- Do not balance off the suspense account.
- A narrative is a brief explanation of what you are doing.

EXAM PRACTICE

A01 **A02** **A03** Answer ALL questions in this section.

1 Bill Williams prepares his draft financial statements for the year ended 30 April 2017. Hugh discovers that he has recorded a cash sales transaction for £200 as debit sales £200 and credit cash £200.

   a Name this type of error.

   b State the effects of this error on Bill's financial statements. **(3 marks)**

2 A cheque received from Susan Zafar is correctly entered in the cash book but is debited to Susan Zafar's account. Only **one** of the above errors will require a correcting entry in the suspense account. Explain why you will not need to open a suspense account. **(3 marks)**

3 Kamilla's financial year ends on 31 January 2018. Her trial balance did not balance. Kamilla entered the difference between the totals in the trial balance into a suspense account.

   a Explain why it is necessary to open a suspense account when the trial balance fails to balance.

   The following errors were later discovered:

   1. Rent paid, $387, was entered in the cash book but not in the rent account.
   2. $863 paid to K Long, a supplier, was credited to the account of L Kong, another supplier.
   3. The purchase of fixtures and fittings at, $7500, was credited to the cash book and debited to the purchases account.
   4. No entry was made for payment of $400 by Tamara, a trade receivable.
   5. The total of the sales returns journal, $680, was credited to the purchases return journal as $850.

   b Prepare the entries for Kamilla's journal to correct these errors.

   c Before the errors were discovered Kamilla calculated that she had made a profit of the year for $22 500. Calculate Kamilla's adjusted profit for the year after these errors have been corrected. **(10 marks)**

4 Laxmi owns a shop in Mumbai. She writes up the books of account herself but is not an experienced bookkeeper. Her financial year ends on 28 March. The trial balance she prepared on 30 March 2017 showed a debit shortage of $720. Laxmi entered this in a suspense account and then prepared a draft income statement which showed a profit for the year of $5200.

The following errors were later discovered:

1. A cheque payment of $520 to repay a loan from Jan was correctly entered in the cash book, but $750 was debited from the loan account.
2. Cash sales of $1200 were not included in the books.
3. A cheque payment for $800 for goods has was entered in the cash book but no other entry was made.
4. The purchase of new carpeting for $1400 was debited from the repairs account.

   a Show the journal entries required to correct the above errors. The date and narrative are not required.

   b Prepare the suspense account for Laxmi's ledger from the above journal entries.
   (12 marks)

   (Total 28 marks)

10 CONTROL ACCOUNTS

▲ Control accounts save time when checking accounting records.

LEARNING OBJECTIVES

- Explain the purpose of control accounts
- Prepare a trade receivables ledger control account and a trade payables ledger control account

GETTING STARTED

In this chapter, we will learn how businesses keep a check on their credit customers (receivables) and credit suppliers (payables). These two groups are very important to a business. If customers do not pay, the business will lose money. If the business does not pay its suppliers, it will not have any inventory to sell. Remember that control accounts do not look at cash sales or cash purchases.

ACTIVITY

Can you name the three ledgers? Most of a business's entries should appear in the receivables ledger and the payables ledger. Why do you think we need to 'control' these ledgers?

10.1 THE PRINCIPLE OF CONTROL ACCOUNTS

Chapter 5 introduced the books of account, including books of original entry and ledgers. At the end of an accounting period, the accounts are balanced off and a trial balance is prepared to check the accuracy of the bookkeeping entries. If the trial balance fails to balance, this usually indicates that an error or errors have been made. The error(s) needs to be identified. As a business expands, its accounting requirements will increase. This may lead to more errors occurring, which are very difficult to find.

To make it easier to identify errors, a type of mini trial balance for the revenue and payables ledgers is drawn up. This is recorded in a **control account**. The two main control accounts are:

- **trade receivables ledger control account.** An account that summarises the customer accounts (trade receivables) in the receivables ledger. It only includes sales that are on credit.
- **trade payables ledger control account.** An account that summarises all the credit supplier accounts (trade payables) in the payables ledger.

Control accounts are often referred to as 'total accounts'. This is because they contain the 'totals' of the various transactions that have taken place during the period. If the total of the opening balances for each individual ledger account is known, and the total additions and total deductions made into these accounts during a period are also known, the total amount outstanding at the end of that period can be calculated.

The total amount outstanding in the control account can then be checked against a list of the individual balances of the ledger accounts. If no errors have occurred, the two total figures should agree. If an error has occurred in the ledger, it can be identified more easily if control accounts are maintained: if a control account fails to balance, you know the error lies within that particular ledger.

> **HINT**
>
> A trade receivables control account compares all the totals taken from the books of prime entry with the totals in the trade receivables ledger accounts to check that they balance.

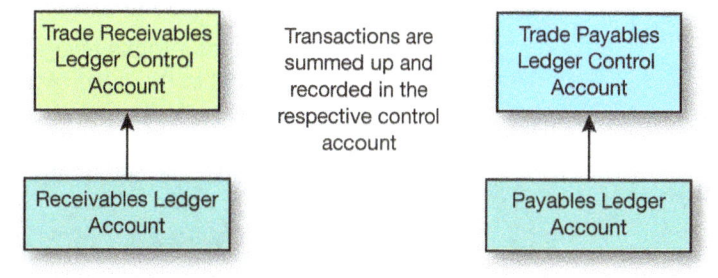

▲ Figure 10.1 Control accounts.

10.2 EXAMPLE: A TRADE RECEIVABLES LEDGER CONTROL ACCOUNT

Look at the trade receivables ledger in **Figure 10.2**. There were only four accounts in the trade receivables ledger for the month of May 2017.

Trade receivables Ledger

Dr		T Allen Account				Cr
2017			£	2017		£
May 1	Balance b/d		850	May 7	Bank	820
May 4	Credit sales		900	May 7	Discounts allowed	30
May 30	Credit sales		350	May 31	Balance c/d	1250
			2100			2100
Jun 1	Balance b/d		1250			

Dr		P May Account				Cr
2017			£	2017		£
May 1	Balance b/d		1500	May 9	Sales returns	200
May 28	Credit sales		400	May 14	Bank	900
				May 14	Discounts allowed	20
				May 31	Balance c/d	780
			1900			1900
Jun 1	Balance b/d		780			

Dr		K White Account				Cr
2017			£	2017		£
May 1	Balance b/d		750	May 20	Sales returns	110
May 15	Credit sales		600	May 31	Balance c/d	1240
			1350			1350
Jun 1	Balance b/d		1240			

Dr		C Young Account				Cr
2017			£	2017		£
May 1	Balance b/d		450	May 28	Irrecoverable debts	450

▲ Figure 10.2 Trade receivables ledger for May 2017.

UNIT 3　10 CONTROL ACCOUNTS

A control account, in this case a trade receivables ledger control account, would consist only of the totals of the items in the trade receivables ledger. Start by listing the totals for each type of item.

May 1 Balances b/d:	£850 + £1500 + £750 + £450 = £3550
Credit sales in May:	£900 + £350 + £400 + £600 = £2250
Cheques received in May:	£820 + £900 = £1720
Discounts allowed in May:	£30 + £20 = £50
Sales returns in May:	£200 + £110 = £310
Irrecoverable debts written off in May:	£450

> **HINT**
>
> Entries in the control accounts go on the same side as in the personal accounts, i.e. trade receivables or trade payables.

Then use these totals to draw up a trade receivables ledger control account. Transactions in the control account should be entered on the same side as they would be in the personal accounts:

Dr		Trade receivables ledger control account				Cr
2017			£	2017		£
May 1	Balance b/d		3550	May 31	Bank	1720
May 31	Credit sales for the month		2250	May 31	Discounts allowed	50
				May 31	Sales returns	310
				May 31	Irrecoverable debts	450
				May 31	Balance c/d (A)	?
			5800			5800
Jun 1	Balance b/d (B)		?			

▲ Figure 10.3 Trade receivables ledger control account for May 2017.

From your studies of double entry accounting you can see that the Balance c/d (A) is the figure needed to balance the account. This figure is the difference between the two sides, which is £5800 – £2530 = £3270.

Now look at the trade receivables ledger (**Figure 10.2**) to see if this is correct. The balances are £1250 + £780 + £1240 = £3270. This is correct, so the figure of £3270 can be recorded in the trade receivables ledger control account (**Figure 10.3**) as the balance carried down (A) and the balance brought down (B).

Remember that the main purpose of a control account is to act as a check on the accuracy of the entries in the ledgers. The total of a list of all the balances extracted from the ledger should equal the balance on the control account. If it does not, a mistake (or mistakes) has been made; this will have to be found.

> **EXAM HINT**
>
> Do not forget to bring balances down – if you fail to do so, you may lose easy marks. In this example, there were only four ledger accounts. For big businesses, however, there could be 400 – or 4000 or 40 000 – ledger accounts. In these cases, it is more difficult for us to obtain the information concerning the totals of each type of item.

> **EXAM HINT**
>
> The most common error that students make on control accounts is reversing all the entries.

> **EXAM HINT**
>
> Cash sales do not go in the trade receivables account.

CASE STUDY: TRADE RECEIVABLES ACCOUNT

Tamara is new to bookkeeping and is not quite sure about control accounts. She is able to balance off her accounts in the trade receivables ledger and has included them below.

	£
Sales Returns	840
Credit Sales	8678
Money paid by receivables	5762
Discounts allowed	342
Cash Sales Revenue	4500
Irrecoverable debts	45

Complete the trade receivables ledger control account for Tamara.

10.3 INFORMATION FOR CONTROL ACCOUNTS

The following tables show where you can find the information you need to draw up control accounts.

	TRADE RECEIVABLES LEDGER CONTROL ACCOUNT	SOURCE
A	Opening trade receivables	List of trade receivables' balances drawn up at the end of the previous period.
B	Credit trade receivables	Total from sales day book.
C	Sales returns	Total from sales returns day book.
D	Cheques received	Cash book: Bank column on debit (received) side. List extracted or total of a special column for cheques that have been included in the cash book.
E	Cash received	Cash book: Cash column on debit (received) side. List extracted or total of a special column that has been included in the cash book.
F	Discounts allowed	Total of discounts allowed column in the cash book.
G	Closing trade receivables*	List of trade receivables' balances drawn up at the end of the period.
H	Total figure	Total of entries for that period. The totals should be the same.

NOTE

The final total of outstanding trade receivables at the end of the period is shown on the Statement of Financial Position under the heading Current Assets. This is covered in Chapter 14.

	PAYABLES LEDGER CONTROL ACCOUNT	SOURCE
A	Opening trade payables	List of trade payables' balances drawn up at the end of the previous period.
B	Credit trade payables	Total from purchases day book.
C	Purchase returns	Total from purchase returns day book.
D	Cheques paid	Cash book: Bank column on credit (payments) side. List extracted or total of a special column that has been included in the cash book.
E	Cash paid	Cash book: Cash column on credit (payments) side. List extracted or total of a special column that has been included in the cash book.
F	Discounts received	Total of discounts received column in the cash book.
G	Closing trade payables*	List of trade payables' balances drawn up at the end of the period.
H	Total figure	Total of entries for that period. The totals should be the same.

Control accounts are normally prepared in the same way as any other account. The totals of the debit entries in the ledger are recorded on the left-hand side of the control account. The totals of the various credit entries in the ledger are recorded on the right-hand side.

Figure 10.4 shows how information is used to construct a trade receivables ledger control account for the month of May 2017. The letters A, B, C, etc. in the diagram relate to the items in the tables above.

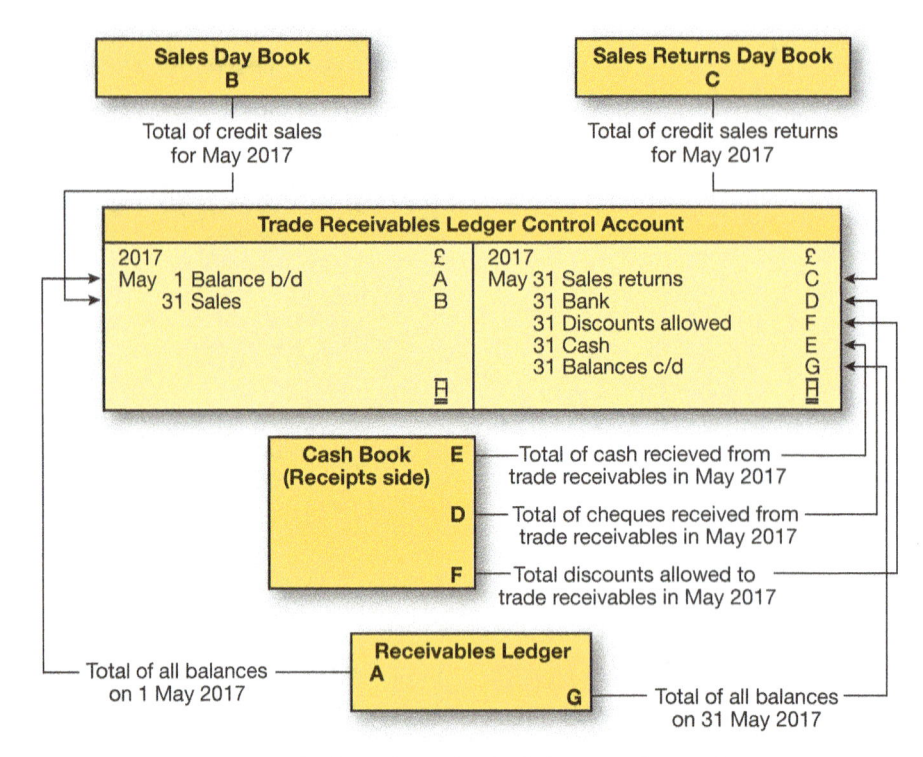

Sales Day Book
B

Total of credit sales for May 2017

Sales Returns Day Book
C

Total of credit sales returns for May 2017

Trade Receivables Ledger Control Account

2017		£	2017		£
May 1	Balance b/d	A	May 31	Sales returns	C
31	Sales	B	31	Bank	D
			31	Discounts allowed	F
			31	Cash	E
			31	Balances c/d	G
		H			H

Cash Book (Receipts side)
- **E** — Total of cash received from trade receivables in May 2017
- **D** — Total of cheques received from trade receivables in May 2017
- **F** — Total discounts allowed to trade receivables in May 2017

Receivables Ledger
- **A** — Total of all balances on 1 May 2017
- **G** — Total of all balances on 31 May 2017

▲ **Figure 10.4** Sources of data for the trade receivables ledger control account.

Figure 10.5 shows how information is used to construct a trade payables control account for May 2017.

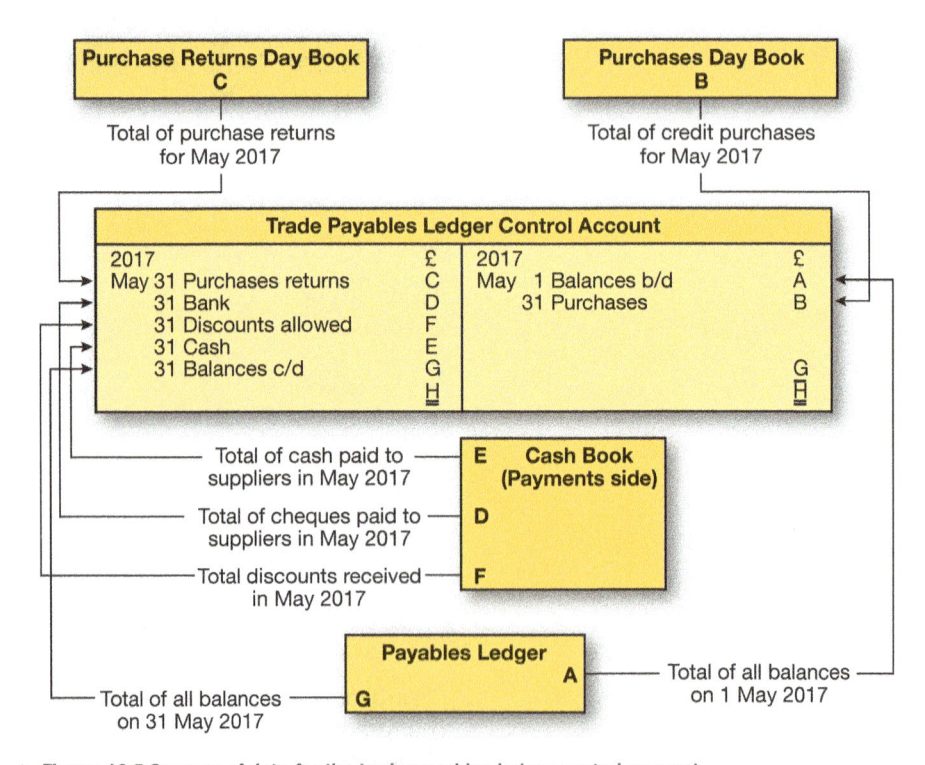

Purchase Returns Day Book
C

Total of purchase returns for May 2017

Purchases Day Book
B

Total of credit purchases for May 2017

Trade Payables Ledger Control Account

2017		£	2017		£
May 31	Purchases returns	C	May 1	Balances b/d	A
31	Bank	D	31	Purchases	B
31	Discounts allowed	F			
31	Cash	E			
31	Balances c/d	G			G
		H			H

Cash Book (Payments side)
- **E** — Total of cash paid to suppliers in May 2017
- **D** — Total of cheques paid to suppliers in May 2017
- **F** — Total discounts received in May 2017

Payables Ledger
- **G** — Total of all balances on 31 May 2017
- **A** — Total of all balances on 1 May 2017

▲ **Figure 10.5** Sources of data for the trade payables ledger control account.

10.4 FURTHER EXAMPLES

Figure 10.6 shows an example of a trade receivables ledger control account for a trade receivables ledger in which all the entries are arithmetically correct.

Trade receivables ledger	HK$
Debit balances on 1 July 2017	11 364
Total credit trade receivables for the month	61 740
Cheques received from customers in the month	43 704
Cash received from customers in the month	7 416
Trade receivables returns from customers during the month	1 776
Debit balances on 31 July as extracted from the trade receivables ledger	20 208

Dr			Trade receivables ledger control account			Cr
2017			HK$	2017		HK$
July 1	Balance b/d		11 364	July 31	Bank	43 704
31	Credit sales		61 740	31	Cash	7 416
				31	Sales returns	1 776
				31	Balances c/d	20 208
			73 104			73 104

▲ **Figure 10.6** A trade receivables ledger control account.

The ledger has proved to be arithmetically correct because the totals of the control account equal each other. If they were not equal, this would show that an error had occurred.

Figure 10.7 shows an example in which an error has been made in a payables ledger. The ledger will have to be checked in detail so the error can be found and the control account corrected.

Trade payables ledger	S$
Credit balances on 1 July 2017	11 670
Cheques paid to suppliers during the month	10 860
Purchase returns to suppliers in the month	285
Bought from suppliers in the month	14 808
Credit balances on 31 July as extracted from the payables ledger	15 453

Dr		Trade Payables Ledger Control Account			Cr
2017		S$	2017		S$
July 31	Bank	10 860	July 1	Balances b/d	11 670
31	Purchase returns	285	31	Credit purchases	14 808
31	Balance c/d	15 453			
		26 598*			26 478*

*The totals at the bottom of the control do not agree: there is a S$120 (S$26 598 − S$26 478) error in the payables ledger. The ledger will need to be checked in detail to find the error.

▲ **Figure 10.7** A trade payables ledger control account containing an error.

Notice that there is no double line under the totals in **Figure 10.7**. The account cannot be finalised and ruled off until the error has been traced and corrected.

10.5 OTHER TRANSFERS

Irrecoverable debts. This phrase describes a customer (trade receivable) who has bought goods on credit but is unable to pay this debt. The debt will be transferred to an irrecoverable debt account. This will have to be recorded in the trade receivables ledger control account because it involves entries in the trade receivables ledgers.

Contra account. In a contra account, the same business is both a supplier and a customer, so inter-indebtedness is 'set off'. These transactions are also entered in the control accounts.

Example 1:

i   A business has sold A Oduya KES60 000 goods on 1 May.
ii A Oduya has supplied the business with KES88 000 goods on 12 May.
iii The KES60 000 that Oduya owes is set off against the KES88 000 owing to him on 30 May.
iv This leaves KES28 000 owing to Oduya on 31 May.

Trade receivables Ledger

Dr		A Oduya Account		Cr
				KES
May 1	Trade receivables	(i)		60 000

Trade payables Ledger

Dr		A Oduya Account		Cr
				KES
May 12	Trade payables	(ii)		88 000

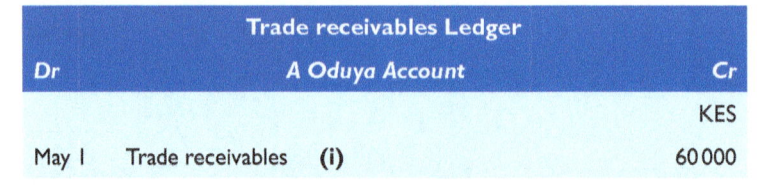

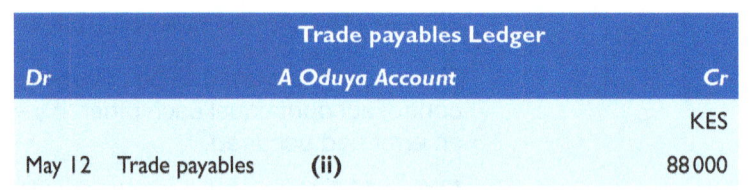

▲ Figure 10.8 A Oduya is both a supplier and a customer.

The transactions can be set off as shown in **Figure 10.9**.

Trade receivables Ledger

Dr		A Oduya Account					Cr
				KES			KES
May 1	Trade receivables	(i)		60 000	May 30	Set-off: Trade payables ledger (iii)	60 000

Trade payables Ledger

Dr		A Oduya Account					Cr
				KES			KES
May 30	Set-off: Trade receivables ledger	(iii)	60 000	May 12	Trade payables (ii)	88 000
May 31	Balance c/d	(iv)	28 000			
			88 000			88 000
				Jun 1	Balance b/d (iv)	28 000

▲ Figure 10.9 Transactions are set off.

> **HINT**
> When dealing with contra items (i.e. set-offs) think of the set-off as cash received or paid; the entries go on the same side of the control accounts as these items.

The transfer of the KES60 000 appears on the **credit side** of the trade receivables ledger control account. It also appears on the **debit side** of the trade payables ledger control account.

Students often find it difficult to work out where to put contra items (set-offs) – i.e. on which side of each control account they should be shown. Think of the 'set-off' as cash received or cash paid. The entries go on the same sides of the control accounts as these items. A contra item will appear on the credit side of the trade receivables ledger control account (the same side as cash received from trade receivables). It will appear on the debit side of the trade payables ledger control account (the same side as cash paid to trade payables would appear). Remember this and you will not get it wrong.

10.6 CONTROL ACCOUNTS AND COMPUTERISED ACCOUNTING SYSTEMS

Many businesses use control accounts, especially businesses that use manual accounting systems. In computerised accounting systems, the control accounts are an integral part of the accounting package and are prepared automatically. Computerised systems ensure that all double entry transactions are completed upon entry. This ensures that the ledgers balance. However, even businesses with computerised accounting packages often prepare their own manual control accounts to ensure the ledgers balance and to detect any errors.

10.7 ADVANTAGES OF CONTROL ACCOUNTS

There are several advantages to using control accounts:

- **Location of error.** Preparation of control accounts will reveal any arithmetical errors that may have occurred. It will also show if a clerk has mistakenly omitted to enter an invoice or payment in the personal accounts. This is because the control account acts as a mini trial balance. However, there are some errors that will not be revealed by control accounts. These include mispostings or compensating errors.
- **Prevention of fraud.** Control accounts are usually under the supervision of a senior member of the accounting team or the accounts manager. This makes fraud more difficult since any transaction entered into a ledger account must also be included in the control account. If different members of staff are responsible for maintaining the ledgers and the control accounts, it will be more difficult to carry out fraudulent transactions: the supervisor or manager provides an internal check on the procedures.
- **Information for management.** The balances on the control accounts can be assumed to equal trade receivables and trade payables; if the control accounts are up to date, it is not necessary to extract these balances from the ledgers. This helps management control because information can be obtained quickly. Speed is one of the prerequisites of efficient control.

10.8 DISADVANTAGES OF CONTROL ACCOUNTS

Not all errors are revealed by control accounts. Control accounts only check the arithmetical accuracy of the ledger. Some errors will not be revealed by the control accounts. For example:

- compensating errors and errors of original entry in the business documents will be carried through
- errors of omission will not be revealed
- errors of commission will not be revealed.

> **HINT**
>
> When it comes to errors **not** revealed in the control accounts, remember the acronym COCO:
> - **C**ompensating error
> - **O**mission
> - **C**ommission
> - **O**riginal entry

END OF CHAPTER QUESTIONS

1 Why does a business keep control accounts?

2 What is 'contra'?

3 How often does a business prepare control accounts?

4 In which control account would you find irrecoverable debts?

5 Name the three ledgers.

6 Explain how a trade receivables ledger control account should be used to verify the balances in the receivables ledger.

7 Explain two ways in which the trade payables ledger control account can act as an aid to managing the business.

END OF CHAPTER CHECKLIST

- Receivables control accounts are used to deal with any sales revenue from credit customers.
- Payables control accounts are used to deal with purchases from credit suppliers.
- Irrecoverable debts are recorded in the receivables control account; the allowance for irrecoverable debts will not appear because it is an estimate and does not relate to actual trade receivables.
- Contra (set-offs) are credited to the receivables control account and debited to the payables control account.
- Control accounts help to reveal errors in the two personal ledgers.
- A control account will be prepared every month.

EXAM PRACTICE

A01 **A02** **A03** Answer ALL questions in this section. Questions 1–5 must be answered with a cross in the box ☒. If you change your mind about an answer, put a line through the box ☒ and then mark your new answer with a cross ☒.

1 How can trade payables be calculated?

☐ **A** closing trade payables + payments to trade payables − opening trade payables

☐ **B** closing trade payables + payments to trade payables + opening trade payables

☐ **C** closing trade payables − payments to trade payables − opening trade payables

☐ **D** closing trade payables − payments to trade payables + opening trade payables

(1 mark)

2 Look at the account below and answer the question that follows.

Dr			K Jagath Account			Cr
2017		LKR	2017			LKR
May 1	Balance b/d	450 000	May 9	Sales returns		?
May 28	Credit sales	1 040 000	May 14	Bank		890 000
			May 14	Discounts allowed		102 000
			May 31	Balance c/d		78 000

Calculate the missing figure for sales returns.

☐ **A** LKR420 000

☐ **B** LKR520 000

☐ **C** LKR320 000

☐ **D** LKR498 000

(1 mark)

3 On what side(s) will a contra (set-off) appear in the two control accounts?

	Trade receivables	**Trade payables**
☐ **A**	debit	debit
☐ **B**	debit	credit
☐ **C**	credit	debit
☐ **D**	credit	credit

(1 mark)

4 Which of the following does not appear in the trade payables ledger control account?

☐ **A** discount received

☐ **B** returns outward

☐ **C** cash paid

☐ **D** irrecoverable debt

(1 mark)

UNIT 3 — 10 CONTROL ACCOUNTS

5 Which of the following does not appear on the credit side of the trade receivables ledger control account?

☐ **A** credit sales revenue
☐ **B** discount allowed
☐ **C** cheque from trade receivables
☐ **D** contra   (1 mark)

6 Jan Tharshini sells electrical goods. All sales and purchases are on credit. The following information has been extracted from the books of account.

	£
Trade payables at 1 April 2017	85 301
Trade receivables at 1 April 2017	1 028 944

Cashbook
30 April
Received from customers: Discount £724
                           Cheque £54 754

30 April
Paid to suppliers   Discount £1276
                           Cheque £35 234

Purchases Day Book
30 April
                           Total   £34 123

Sales Day Book
30 April
                           Total   £43 123

Returns Inwards Day Book
30 April
                           Total   £2345

Returns Outwards Day Book
30 April
                           Total   £1234

Journal   Dr   Cr
                           £   £
Irrecoverable debts written off 182
L Pilar   182

Additional information

1 Kali Ltd is both a customer and a supplier. A contra entry should be made to clear the balance owing to Kali Ltd of £899.

2 A cheque for £1362 received from Dario Fang, a credit customer, was returned unpaid by Dario Fang's bank. The cheque was in full settlement of an invoice for £1262.

3 Discount allowed of £71 was not entered in the cash book.

Prepare a trade receivables ledger control account at 30 April 2017 for Jan Thashini.

(12 marks)

(Total 17 marks)

11 BANK RECONCILIATION STATEMENTS

LEARNING OBJECTIVES

- Explain the purpose of bank reconciliation statements
- Understand the process of bank reconciliation
- Prepare a bank reconciliation statement

▲ Cash books should be checked against bank statements at least once a month.

GETTING STARTED

In this chapter, we will learn how to check a cash book against the bank statement issued by the bank. This is usually carried out each month. If the cash book and bank statement do not correspond, a Bank Reconciliation Statement should be used.

SKILLS ANALYSIS

ACTIVITY

Try to find a bank statement and some receipts from that account. Look carefully at the details on the statement. Match the receipts with the figures on the bank statement. Check the dates to see how long some payments take to **clear**.

SUBJECT VOCABULARY

clear a cheque or payment clears when the money is sent from one bank to another

11.1 INTRODUCTION TO RECORDING TRANSACTIONS

In Chapter 5, you learned how businesses record monies coming into and out of the business in their cash book. The business's bookkeeper enters cash items in the cash columns. He enters cheques and other bank items in the bank columns.

The bank also records the business's bank transactions. If all the items the bookkeeper enters in the cash book are the same as the items the bank enters in the business's account at the bank, the bank balance in the business's books will be equal to the bank balance in the bank's books. However, this is not usually the case.

DID YOU KNOW?

Most countries have their own bank transfer system.
In Sri Lanka, it is called SLIPS – Sri Lanka Interbank Payment System.

A bookkeeper may not record every item that is paid into or out of the business bank account in the cash book. The bookkeeper may also enter items in the cash book that the bank has not yet entered in the bank's records of the business's account. The bookkeeper needs to compare his own records with the bank's to see if there are any differences between the two balances and check whether any errors have been made. He will need to obtain a bank statement from the bank. Banks usually issue bank statements to their customers on a regular basis, but a customer can request a bank statement at any time.

HINT

Tick items that are the same in the cash book and on the bank statement, before preparing a bank reconciliation statement.

Figure 11.1 is an example of a cash book and a bank statement. The items that are the same in both sets of records have been ticked off.

11 BANK RECONCILIATION STATEMENTS

Dr	Cash Book (bank columns only)						Cr
2017			£	2017			£
June 1	Balance b/f	✓	80	June 27	I Gordon	✓	35
June 28	D Jones	✓	100	June 29	B Tyrell		40
				June 30	Balance c/d		105
			180				180
July 1	Balance b/d		105				

Bank Statement		Dr	Cr	Balance
2017			£	£
June 26	Balance b/f	✓		80 Cr
June 28	Banking	✓	100	180 Cr
June 30	I Gordon	✓	35	145 Cr

▲ **Figure 11.1** A cash book and bank statement for the same period.

A bank statement is the record of the transactions made by an account holder over a period of time, usually a month. A bank statement will show any cheques paid or received, any cash withdrawals from the business, direct debits, standing order, bank transfers as well as any interest paid or received. Bank statements reflect the position of the bank, therefore debit entries in the business records will appear as credit entries in the bank statement and vice versa. A business should regularly check or reconcile the bank statement against its own records. This will help identify any mistakes or discrepancies by yourself or the bank.

Compare the cash book and the **bank statement** in **Figure 11.1**. The only item that is not in both of them is the cheque payment to B Tyrell for £40 in the cash book. This is simply an issue of timing. The cheque was posted to B Tyrell on 29 June. There has been no time for it to be banked by Tyrell and passed through the banking system. Such a cheque is called an **unpresented cheque** because it has not yet been presented at the drawer's bank.

A bookkeeper must prove that the difference in the balance is not due to error, so he draws up a **bank reconciliation statement**. This statement compares the cash book balance with the bank statement balance, as shown in **Figure 11.2**.

Bank Reconciliation Statement as at 30 June 2017	
	£
Balance in hand as per cash book	105
Add unpresented cheque: Tyrell	40
Balance in hand as per bank statement	145

▲ **Figure 11.2** A bank reconciliation statement starting with the cash book balance.

Alternatively, you may begin the bank reconciliation statement with the bank statement balance, as shown in **Figure 11.3**.

Bank Reconciliation Statement as at 30 June 2017	
	£
Balance in hand as per bank statement	145
Less unpresented cheque: Tyrell	40
Balance in hand as per cash book	105

▲ **Figure 11.3** A bank reconciliation statement starting with the bank statement balance.

SUBJECT VOCABULARY

bank statement a statement issued by the bank to show the balance in a bank account and the amounts that have been paid into it and withdrawn from it

bank reconciliation statement a statement comparing the cash book balance with the bank statement balance

unpresented cheque a cheque that has not yet cleared through the banking system

EXAM HINT

Don't only check the dates and names in the cash book and bank statement. Always check the amounts as well, since errors can be made here and the examiner may be testing you on this.

NOTE

In the business's cash book, the bank account shows a debit balance brought down because, to the business, the balance is an asset. This is because it is money in the bank. In the bank's book, however, the account shows a credit balance because it is a liability. It is money owed by the bank to the business.

11.2 REASONS FOR DIFFERENT BALANCES

A more complicated example is shown in **Figure 11.4**. Similar items in both the cash book and bank statement have been ticked.

Dr	Cash Book					Cr
2016		AED	2016			AED
Dec 27	Total b/f	2000	Dec 27	Total b/f		1600
Dec 29	J Kattan ✓	60	Dec 28	J Cham	✓	105
Dec 31	M Qureshi (B)	220	Dec 30	M Haddad (A)		15
			Dec 31	Balance c/d		560
		2280				2280
2017						
Jan 1	Balance b/d	560				

> **HINT**
> Remember that the debit column in the cash book is the credit column in the bank statement and vice versa.

	Bank Statement			
		Dr	Cr	Balance
2016		AED	AED	AED
Dec 27	Balance b/f			400 Cr
Dec 29	Cheque ✓		60	460 Cr
Dec 30	J Cham ✓	105		355 Cr
Dec 30	Bank transfer L Seif (C)		70	425 Cr
Dec 30	Bank charges (D)	20		405 Cr

▲ **Figure 11.4** A cash book and bank statement for December 2016.

The balance brought forward in the bank statement, AED400, is the same figure as in the cash book: it totals b/f AED2000 – AED1600 = AED400. However, items (A) and (B) are in the cash book only, while items (C) and (D) are on the bank statement only. Let's consider these items in detail:

A This is a cheque that we recently sent to Mr Haddad. It has not yet passed through the banking system. It has not been presented to our bank. It is therefore an unpresented cheque.

B This is a cheque that we banked on our visit to the bank when we collected the copy of our bank statement. It would not appear on the statement.

C A customer, L Seif, paid his account by instructing his bank to pay us directly through the banking system, instead of paying by cheque. This type of transaction is usually called a bank transfer.

D The bank has charged us AED20 for operating our account.

Now that the above differences have been taken into account, we can prepare the bank reconciliation statement. As mentioned earlier, there are two ways in which this can be done. We can start with the balance as shown in the cash book (see **Figure 11.5**) or, alternatively, we can start with the balance as shown on the bank statement (see **Figure 11.6**). Examining bodies may ask for either method of presentation, so make sure you know exactly which method is required before attempting the question.

11 BANK RECONCILIATION STATEMENTS

Bank Reconciliation Statement as at 31 December 2016

	AED	AED
Balance in hand as per cash book		560
Add Unpresented cheque – M Haddad	15	
Bank transfer	70	
		85
		645
Less Bank charges	20	
Bank lodgement not yet entered on bank statement	220	
		240
Balance in hand as per bank statement		405

▲ **Figure 11.5** A bank reconciliation statement starting with the cash book balance.

SUBJECT VOCABULARY

lodgement a receipt that has been entered in the cash book but has not yet appeared on the bank statement

Bank Reconciliation Statement as at 31 December 2016

	AED	AED
Balance in hand as per bank statement		405
Add Bank charges	20	
Bank lodgement not yet entered on bank statement	220	
		240
		645
Less Unpresented cheque – M Haddad	15	
Bank transfers	70	
		85
Balance in hand as per cash book		560

▲ **Figure 11.6** A bank reconciliation statement starting with the bank statement balance.

HINT

It is usually easier to update the cash book before preparing the bank reconciliation statement.

11.3 UPDATING THE CASH BOOK BEFORE ATTEMPTING A RECONCILIATION

The easiest way to prepare a reconciliation statement is to complete any outstanding entries in the cash book first. Next, enter all items on the bank statement into the cash book. After this, the only differences will be items in the cash book. There will be no differences on the bank statement. At the same time, any errors found in the cash book during this check can be corrected.

This is the normal way to proceed before drawing up a bank reconciliation statement. However, it is possible that an examiner will ask you to do it differently. Look again at the example in **Figure 11.4**. If we had written up the cash book before drawing up the bank reconciliation statement, the cash book and the reconciliation statement would appear as shown in **Figures 11.7** and **11.8**.

Dr		Cash Book				*Cr*
2016			AED	2016		AED
Dec 27	Total b/fwd		2000	Dec 27	Total b/fwd	1600
Dec 29	J Kattan		60	Dec 28	J Cham	105
Dec 31	M Qureshi		220	Dec 30	M Haddad	15
Dec 31	BGC: L Seif*		70	Dec 31	Bank charges*	20
			2350	Dec 31	Balance c/d	610
						2350
2017						
Jan 1	Balance b/d		610			

*Add items that appear in the bank statement but not in the cash book.

▲ **Figure 11.7** The amended cash book.

Bank Reconciliation Statement as on 31 December 2016	
	AED
Balance in hand as per cash book	610
Add Unpresented cheque – M Haddad	15
	625
Less Bank lodgement not yet entered on bank statement	220
Balance in hand as per bank statement	405

▲ Figure 11.8 A bank reconciliation statement drawn up after the cash book has been amended.

SKILLS CRITICAL THINKING

CASE STUDY: BANK RECONCILIATION STATEMENT

Marcus owns a home improvement business in Colombo. He prepares his cash book for January 2017. He then receives his bank statement. His cash book and bank statement are shown below.

Dr			Cash book			Ch No	
Jan 02	Balance b/d	451	Jan 03	T Gramson	114		91
Jan 10	N Jennings	860	Jan 12	D Cowling	115		384
Jan 27	J Sahif	168	Jan 14	K Patak	116		22
			Jan 23	C Evans	117		164
			Jan 29	V Masig	118		123
			Jan 31	Balance c/d			695
		1479					1479
Feb 01	Balance b/d	695					

Bank Statement

Transaction		Dr	Cr	Balance
Date	Details			
Jan 01	Balance b/d			451
Jan 08	Cheque 114	291		160
Jan 19	N Jennings		860	1020
Jan 26	Cheque 117	164		856
Jan 26	Cheque 116	22		834
Jan 27	J Sahif		186	1020

Prepare a bank reconciliation statement for 31 January 2017.

EXAM HINT

Always tick your entries off as you go through the cash book and bank statement. Check the opening balances of the cash book and bank statement before ticking, as an outstanding item could be from the previous month.

11.4 BANK OVERDRAFTS

When there is a bank overdraft (shown by a credit balance in the cash book), the adjustments needed for reconciliation work are opposite to those needed for a debit balance.

Figure 11.9 shows a cash book and a bank statement showing an overdraft. Only the cheque for G Canton (A) £106 and the cheque paid to J Kelly (B) £63 need to be adjusted.

Dr			Cash Book (bank columns only)			Cr
2016			£	2016		£
Dec 5	I Howe		308	Dec 1	Balance b/f	709
Dec 24	L Mason		120	Dec 9	P Davies	140
Dec 29	K King		124	Dec 27	J Kelly (B)	63
Dec 31	G Canton (A)		106	Dec 29	United Trust	77
Dec 31	Balance c/f		380	Dec 31	Bank charges	49
			1038			1038
				2017		
				Jan 1	Balance b/f	380

Bank Statement

		Dr	Cr	Balance
2016		£	£	£
Dec 1	Balance b/f			709 O/D
Dec 5	Cheque		308	401 O/D
Dec 14	P Davies	140		541 O/D
Dec 24	Cheque		120	421 O/D
Dec 29	K King: BGC		124	297 O/D
Dec 29	United Trust: Standing order	77		374 O/D
Dec 31	Bank charges	49		423 O/D

▲ Figure 11.9 A cash book and bank statement showing an overdraft.

NOTE
On a bank statement, an overdraft is often shown with the letters O/D following the amount. It may also be shown as a debit balance, indicated by the letters DR after the amount.

The bank reconciliation statement for the accounts in **Figure 11.9** is shown in **Figure 11.10**.

Bank Reconciliation Statement as on 31 December 2016	
	£
Overdraft as per cash book	(380)
Add Unpresented cheque	63
	317
Less Bank lodgements not on bank statement	106
Overdraft per bank statement	(423)

▲ Figure 11.10 A bank reconciliation statement involving a bank overdraft.

11.5 DISHONOURED CHEQUES

SUBJECT VOCABULARY

dishonoured cheque a cheque that the bank will not pay because there is not enough money in the account to pay it

When a bank receives a cheque from a customer, the bank records the cheque on the debit side of the cash book. The cheque also appears on the customer's bank statement as a deposit to the bank. At a later date, the customer may find that the bank will not pay them the amount due on the cheque. It is known as a **dishonoured cheque**.

A cheque may be dishonoured for several reasons. For example, K Aguta gives us a cheque for KES300 000 on 20 May 2017. We bank it. On 25 May 2017 our bank returns the cheque to us. This may be because:

- Aguta wrote KES300 000 in figures on the cheque, but wrote two hundred thousand Kenyan shillings in words. We will have to give the cheque back to Aguta for amendment or reissue.

- Aguta wrote the year 2016 on the cheque, instead of 2017. Normally, cheques are considered 'stale' six months after the date on the cheque. In other words, banks will not pay cheques that are more than six months old.

- Aguta did not have sufficient funds in his bank account and his bank will not allow him to have an overdraft. In such a case, the cheque will be dishonoured. The bank will write on the cheque 'refer to drawer'. We will have to contact Aguta about settling his account.

In all of these cases, the bank will show the original banking as being cancelled, i.e. they will show the cheque paid out of our bank account. The bank will notify us as soon as this happens. We will then amend our accounts to show the cheque being cancelled by a credit in the cash book. We will then debit that amount to Aguta's account.

When Aguta originally paid his account, our records were as shown in **Figure 11.11**.

Dr			K Aguta Account			Cr
2017			KES	2017		KES
May 1	Balance b/d		300 000	May 20	Bank	300 000

Dr			Bank Account			Cr
2017			KES			
May 20	K Aguta		300 000			

▲ **Figure 11.11** Statement of Aguta's account.

Once we have recorded the dishonoured cheque, the records will appear as shown in **Figure 11.12**.

Dr	K Aguta Account				Cr
2017		KES	2017		KES
May 1	Balance b/d		May 20		300 000
May 25	Bank: cheque dishonoured	300 000			

Dr	Bank Account				Cr
2017		KES			KES
May 20	K Aguta	300 000	May 25	K Aguta: cheque dishonoured	300 000

▲ Figure 11.12 Amendment of accounts to show dishonoured cheque.

In other words, Aguta is once again shown as owing us KES300 000.

11.6 OTHER REASONS FOR DIFFERENCES IN THE BALANCES

A difference between the balance in the business's cash book and the balance on the bank statement may also be caused by:

- **direct debits.** A direct debit is when a business gives permission for an organisation to collect amounts owing directly from its bank account. This method is often used to pay mortgages, insurance premiums, etc.
- **standing orders.** A standing order is when a business instructs a bank to pay a specified amount on a given date.
- **bank charges.** Costs charged by the bank. These costs could include overdraft fees or costs to maintain the account.
- **interest.** This could be interest received on a credit balance or interest paid on a debit balance.

All four of these payments are made by the bank on behalf of the business. Entries in the cash book cannot be made until the business receives the bank statement.

In the UK, a more recent method of making payments is by **Bankers' Automated Clearing Service** (**BACS**). This is a computerised payment transfer system used to pay trade payables, wages and salaries. Details of these payments will appear on the bank statement and will need to be entered into the business's cash book.

FINAL CHECKLIST FOR PREPARING A BANK RECONCILIATION STATEMENT

- Balance the cash book.
- Compare the bank columns of the cash book with the bank statement. Tick off the entries that are the same.
- Update the cash book with any items not ticked on the bank statement. For example, standing orders, direct debits, bank charges, interest and dishonoured cheques.
- If there are any errors on the bank statement, ask the bank to correct them.
- Prepare the bank reconciliation statement.

HINT

Always check that the opening balances in the cash book and the bank statement are the same.

END OF CHAPTER QUESTIONS

1 Zafira's cash book shows a balance in the bank column of $620 Dr on 30 April 2015.

She compares her cash book with the bank statement at 30 April. She finds the following items were included on the bank statement but are not yet in the cash book.

Bank charges	$15
Direct debit paid for insurance	$40
Bank interest received	$ 20
Bank (credit) transfer from customer, Aisha	$130
Dishonoured cheque, Yanni	$ 65

a Write up the cash book at 30 April 2015 and bring down the updated balance.

At 30 April 2015, Zafira discovers the following:
- She has recorded a receipt in her cash book of $310 but has not yet deposited the money at the bank.
- She has written a cheque for $250 and entered it in the cash book but it has not yet been paid by the bank.

b Prepare the bank reconciliation statement at 30 April 2015.

c Zafira's bank statement shows a balance that is different from the bank reconciliation statement. Suggest **two possible errors** that may have caused this difference.

2 On 31 January 2017, Chelsey, a trader, obtained a statement from her bank and compared it with the bank account in her cash book.

The bank balance shown in the cash book was an overdraft of $1780. This differed from the balance shown on the bank statement because:
- a cheque for $270 payable to Katy had not yet been presented for payment
- cash paid into the bank amounting to $800 had not yet been credited to Chelsey's account.

Prepare a bank reconciliation statement to show the balance that appeared on the bank statement on 31 January 2017.

3 Ky Lo is a trader. Her financial year ends on 30 April.

The bank columns of her cash book for the month of April 2017 were as follows:

Cash Book (bank columns only)					
2017		$	2017		$
Apr-01	Balance b/d	2210	Apr-09	Aston Stores	436
12	Kobiashi Traders	314	16	General expenses	125
30	Cash	500	26	Ganges & Co	390
			30	Balance c/d	2073
		3024			3024
01-May	Balance b/d	2073			

Bank Statement 30 April 2017				
Date	Details	Debit $	Credit $	Balance $
Apr-01	Balance			2120 Cr
10	JC Insurance	360		1760
11	Credit Transfer		62	1822
17	Aston Stores	436		1386
18	Kobiashi Traders		314	1700
21	General Expenses	125		1575
29	Kobiashi Traders (dishonoured)	314		1261
30	Bank charges	11		1250

The following errors were discovered:
- The cash book balance brought forward on 1 April should have been $2120.
- The bank had credited a dividend of $62 to Ky Lo's business account instead of her personal account.

Update the cash book and prepare a bank reconciliation statement for Ky Lo.

END OF CHAPTER CHECKLIST

- We use bank reconciliation statements to check the accuracy of transactions recorded in the cash book.
- You need to update the cash book first and then prepare a bank reconciliation statement.

EXAM PRACTICE

A01 A02 A03 Answer ALL questions in this section. Questions 1–8 must be answered with a cross in the box ☒. If you change your mind about an answer, put a line through the box ☒ and then mark your new answer with a cross ☒.

1 What is a bank reconciliation statement?
- A A statement presented by a business to the bank listing cheques to be credited by the bank.
- B A statement sent by a business to a customer who has purchased goods on credit.
- C A statement sent to a customer each month by the bank.
- D A statement showing the differences between a business's cash book balance and the bank statement balance.

(1 mark)

2 A bank statement showed a balance of $1650 credit. Dishonoured cheques, $310, and standing orders, $55, paid by the bank, have not been entered in the cash book.

What was the debit balance on the cash book before it was updated?
- A $1285
- B $1395
- C $1905
- D $2015

(1 mark)

3 A business prepares a bank reconciliation statement and starts with the balance as per the bank statement.

What is deducted from this balance in the bank reconciliation statement?
- A amounts not yet credited by the bank
- B bank charges not recorded in the cash book
- C standing orders paid by the bank but not entered in the cash book
- D unpresented cheques

(1 mark)

4 A business receives a bank statement and updates its cash book.

Which item will increase the bank balance in the cash book?
- A bank charges
- B credit transfers received
- C interest charges
- D standing orders paid

(1 mark)

5 The following information is available at the end of the month.
- bank statement balance   €4000 credit
- cash book balance   €5000 debit
- unpresented cheques   €800

What is the value of receipts in the cash book that have not yet appeared on the bank statement?
- A €200
- B €1200
- C €1800
- D €800

(1 mark)

6 What is the purpose of preparing a bank reconciliation statement?
- A to check that all expenses have been paid
- B to check on the amount owed by trade receivables
- C to explain the difference between the bank statement balance and cash book balance
- D to see by how much the bank balance has increased during the accounting period

(1 mark)

7 Which of the following would appear on a bank statement?

☐ **A** cheques issued but not yet presented
☐ **B** cheques paid but not yet credited
☐ **C** dishonoured cheques
☐ **D** lost cheques   **(1 mark)**

8 Xinyi started a business on 1 January.

On 31 January her cash book showed that she had S$2100 in the bank.

On that date cheques not yet presented for payment totalled S$600 and a deposit of S$900 had not been credited by the bank.

What was the balance shown on Xinyi's bank statement on 31 January?

☐ **A** S$1500 credit
☐ **B** S$1800 credit
☐ **C** S$2400 credit
☐ **D** S$2700 credit   **(1 mark)**

9 Why would you prepare a bank reconciliation statement?   **(2 marks)**

10 How often is a bank reconciliation statement prepared?   **(2 marks)**

11 Explain the term 'payee'.   **(2 marks)**

12 What is the difference between a standing order and a direct debit?   **(2 marks)**

13 What is meant by 'OD' on a bank statement?   **(2 marks)**

14 What is a lodgement?   **(2 marks)**

(Total 20 marks)

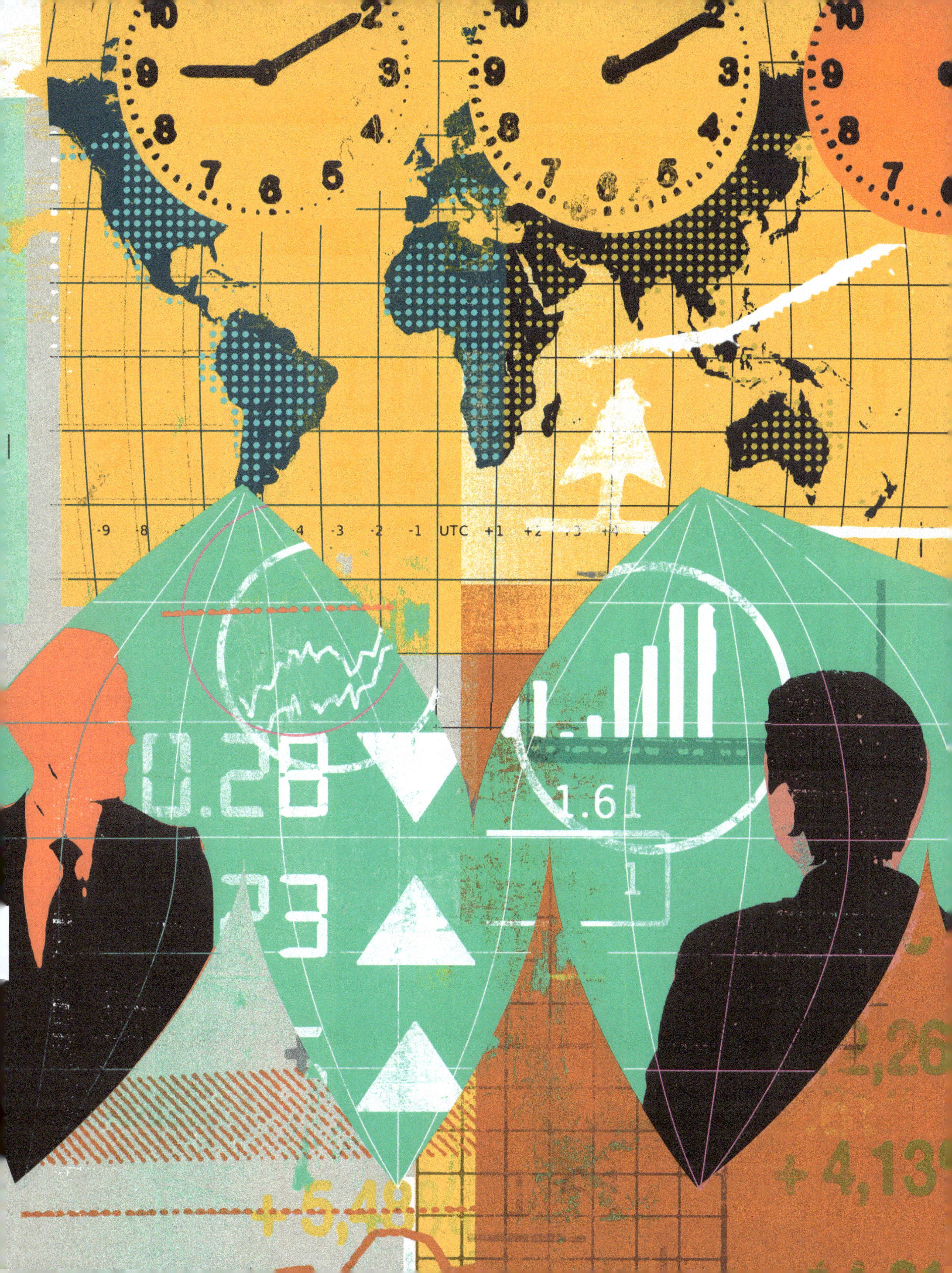

UTC
1.61

12 CAPITAL AND REVENUE EXPENDITURE	146	13 ACCOUNTING CONCEPTS	152
14 FINANCIAL STATEMENTS OF A SOLE TRADER	158	15 OTHER RECEIVABLES AND PAYABLES	169
16 IRRECOVERABLE DEBTS	183	17 INCOMPLETE RECORDS	190
18 THE CALCULATION AND INTERPRETATION OF ACCOUNTING RATIOS	206
19 FINANCIAL STATEMENTS OF A PARTNERSHIP	217	20 FINANCIAL STATEMENTS OF A MANUFACTURER	228

UNIT 4
THE PREPARATION OF FINANCIAL STATEMENTS AND END OF PERIOD ADJUSTMENTS

Assessment Objective AO1
Demonstrate a knowledge and understanding of accounting terminology, principles, procedures and techniques

Assessment Objective AO2
Select and apply their knowledge and understanding of accounting procedures to a variety of accounting problems

Assessment Objective AO3
Analyse, evaluate and present information in appropriate accounting formats and communicate reasoned explanations

In this unit, we will focus on the financial statements for a sole trader, partnership and a manufacturing business. We will also look at evaluating the financial statements of a business by introducing ratio analysis. We will look at the differences between capital and revenue expenditure as well as making adjustments to the financial statements using depreciation, other receivables and payables and irrecoverable debts.

The content covered in this unit will be tested in Paper 2 but will also help you to clarify your understanding of the topics in Paper 1.

12 CAPITAL AND REVENUE EXPENDITURE

▲ Capital expenditure includes building or renovation work.

SKILLS ADAPTIVE LEARNING

LEARNING OBJECTIVES

- Explain the terms:
  - capital expenditure
  - revenue expenditure
- Explain the importance of the correct procedure for capital expenditure and revenue expenditure

GETTING STARTED

In this chapter, we will examine the difference between capital and revenue expenditure. Capital expenditure is linked to the statement of financial position and revenue expenditure is linked to the income statement.

ACTIVITY

Go into a local supermarket or shopping centre. Look around and write a list of 10 items you would class as assets (things the business owns, not for resale) and 10 items you would class as expenses (costs involved in the day-to-day running of the business). Compare your list with your friends' to see if you have the same responses. Check with a teacher if you need more guidance.

12.1 CAPITAL EXPENDITURE

SUBJECT VOCABULARY

capital expenditure appears on the statement of financial position. Capital expenditure tends to last longer than a year and usually involves non-current assets

Capital expenditure occurs when a business spends money to:
- buy non-current assets
- add to the value of an existing non-current asset.

This expenditure includes:
- the costs of acquiring non-current assets
- the costs of bringing non-current assets into the business
- the legal costs of buying premises
- the carriage inwards (cost of transport) on machinery/equipment purchased
- any other cost involved in preparing the non-current asset for use, e.g. installation costs
- upgrades to existing assets.

Example 1: Mike buys a new van for $15 000 for his fish delivery business. He fits the van out with a refrigerator unit costing $1000. He puts his logo on the side of the van, which costs $250. Therefore, the total capital expenditure for his van is $16 250.

UNIT 4   12 CAPITAL AND REVENUE EXPENDITURE   147

SUBJECT VOCABULARY

capital receipts the sale of non-current assets

Capital receipts are the sale of non-current assets. They should not be included in the business's revenue as they are not the normal day-to-day sales of the business. These transactions should be recorded as cash or bank. Only the profit or loss made on the sale of non-current assets should be included in the income statement.

12.2 REVENUE EXPENDITURE

SUBJECT VOCABULARY

revenue expenditure expenditure that does not increase the value of non-current assets but is incurred in the day-to-day running expenses of the business

Revenue expenditure is expenditure that does not increase the value of non-current assets but is incurred in the day-to-day running expenses of the business. It can include inventories, purchases of inventory, wages, heating and lighting. Expenditure impacts on profit.

The difference between capital and revenue expenditure can be explained when considering the cost of purchasing and running a motor vehicle. The expenditure we incur in acquiring the motor vehicle is classed as capital expenditure. The cost of the petrol we use to run the vehicle, and any maintenance costs, are revenue expenditure. The revenue expenditure is used up in a few days and does not add to the value of the non-current asset.

HINT

Revenue expenditures are recorded in the Income Statement. They are normal, everyday running expenses.

▲ Buying a van is capital expenditure.

▲ Repairs to a van are revenue expenditure.

▼ The cost of the petrol used to run a vehicle is revenue expenditure.

SUBJECT VOCABULARY

revenue receipts receipts from the normal trading activities of the business

Revenue receipts are receipts from the normal trading activities of the business. They include selling inventory to customers. They are included in revenue on the income statement.

12.3 DIFFERENCE BETWEEN EQUITY AND REVENUE EXPENDITURE

Revenue expenditure is the day-to-day running expenses of the business. As such, it is chargeable to the income statement. Equity expenditure, in contrast, results in an increase in the non-current assets shown in the statement of financial position. The difference between equity and revenue expenditure is explained more generally in **Figure 12.1**.

▼ Capital expenditure	▼ Revenue expenditure
Premises purchased	Rent of premises
Legal charges for conveyancing	Legal charges for debt collection
New machinery	Maintenance of assets
Installation of machinery	Repairs to van
Additions to assets	Carriage on purchases and revenue
Motor van	Redecorating existing offices
Delivery charges on new assets	Interest on loan to purchase air-conditioning
Extension costs of new offices	
Cost of adding air-conditioning to offices	

▲ Figure 12.1 The difference between capital expenditure and revenue expenditure.

GENERAL VOCABULARY

conveyancing work done, usually by a lawyer, to change the possession of property from one person to another

▲ Tamara has different types of expenditure after setting up her newsagent's business.

CASE STUDY: CAPITAL EXPENDITURE AND REVENUE EXPENDITURE

Tamara has recently opened a newsagent in Mumbai. She sells books and magazines as well as some stationery. She also sells food and drink. Can you categorise the following purchases for her as capital or revenue expenditure?

- Purchase of magazines and books   Revenue / Capital
- Purchase of shop fittings   Revenue / Capital
- Purchase of a cash register   Revenue / Capital
- Purchase of stationery   Revenue / Capital
- Purchase of a refrigerator   Revenue / Capital

12.4 INCORRECT TREATMENT OF EXPENDITURE

If capital expenditure is incorrectly treated as revenue expenditure, or vice-versa, the figures on both the statement of financial position and the income statement will be incorrect. This means that the figure showing the profit for the year will also be incorrect.

UNIT 4   12 CAPITAL AND REVENUE EXPENDITURE   149

> **EXAM HINT**
>
> The exam often includes multiple-choice questions about capital expenditure and revenue expenditure. Make sure you understand the difference otherwise you will lose marks.

Example 2: A bookkeeper posts the purchase of a photocopier to the stationery account. The purchase of the photocopier should have been posted to the office equipment account.

In this example, capital expenditure has been incorrectly posted to revenue expenditure, so:

- profit for the year will be understated
- the statement of financial position values will not include the value of the asset.

Example 3: A bookkeeper posts stationery to office equipment instead of the stationery account.

In this example, revenue expenditure has been incorrectly posted to equity expenditure, so:

- profit for the year will be overstated
- the statement of financial position values will be overvalued.

If the expenditure affects items in the trading account, the gross profit figure will also be incorrect.

> **EXAM HINT**
>
> Many students struggle to understand the difference between capital and revenue expenditure. Questions on this topic frequently appear and in multi-part or long-answer questions, not just in multiple-choice questions. If you are in doubt, think about in which financial statement a transaction will appear: capital expenditure is always on the statement of financial position, and revenue expenditure always appears on the income statement. Both appear as debit entries in the accounting system.

CASE STUDY: EXPENDITURE, PROFIT AND ASSETS

Dawson owns several hairdressing salons in Hanoi. He has recently purchased some equipment for his salons. However, he has not accounted for some of the purchases in his accounts. These include:

- chairs costing $3000
- shampoo costing $200
- mirrors costing $500
- hairdryers costing $300.

▲ Dawson employs more than 20 employees in his salons.

His profit for the year is $10 800. His non-current assets are $72 345.

Calculate the new profit for the year.

Calculate the new non-current assets.

END OF CHAPTER QUESTIONS

1 Give **three** examples of capital expenditure.
2 Give **three** examples of revenue expenditure.
3 Give **one** example of a revenue receipt.
4 Give **one** example of a capital receipt.
5 Why is it important to distinguish between capital and revenue expenditure?

END OF CHAPTER CHECKLIST

- Capital expenditure includes buying non-current assets or adding value to non-current assets.
- Revenue expenditure includes the day-to-day running expenses of the business and does not add value to non-current assets. For example, making repairs to a vehicle.
- If capital receipts are included in revenue, profit for the year will be overstated.
- It is important to distinguish between capital and revenue expenditure as this can affect the overall profitability of a business.

EXAM PRACTICE

A01 **A02** **A03** Answer ALL questions in this section. Questions 1–8 must be answered with a cross in the box ☒. If you change your mind about an answer, put a line through the box ☒ and then mark your new answer with a cross ☒.

1 The following is a list of a builder's expenditure for the year.

	$
motor vehicle	10 000
purchases	25 000
wages	20 000
rent of offices	6 000
machinery	7 000
petrol	3 000

What is the amount of capital expenditure?
- ☐ A $10 000
- ☐ B $17 000
- ☐ C $54 000
- ☐ D $71 000 **(1 mark)**

2 Which of the following are capital expenditure?
a the cost of a motor vehicle
b the petrol for a motor vehicle
c shop fixtures
d the wages of a shop assistant
- ☐ A a and c
- ☐ B a, b and c
- ☐ C b and d
- ☐ D b, c and d **(1 mark)**

3 Nicholas is a baker. Which item would be a capital receipt?
- ☐ A cash received from the sale of bread
- ☐ B a cheque received from the sale of an oven
- ☐ C a discount received from a creditor
- ☐ D rent received from a tenant in cash **(1 mark)**

4 What is classed as revenue expenditure?
- ☐ A the cost of maintaining a non-current asset
- ☐ B the cost of installing a new non-current asset
- ☐ C the purchase cost of a non-current asset
- ☐ D legal costs for the purchase of a non-current asset **(1 mark)**

5 Which is revenue expenditure?
- ☐ A the cost of building an extension to factory premises
- ☐ B the legal costs of buying factory premises
- ☐ C the cost of the purchase of factory premises
- ☐ D redecorating factory premises **(1 mark)**

6 What is the effect if capital expenditure is treated as revenue expenditure?
- ☐ A gross profit is understated
- ☐ B profit for the year is understated
- ☐ C total assets are overstated
- ☐ D working capital is understated **(1 mark)**

7 Which of the following is a capital receipt?
- ☐ A discount received
- ☐ B interest received from bank account
- ☐ C proceeds from sale of a non-current asset
- ☐ D sales income **(1 mark)**

8 A trader made the following payments.

	$
building repairs	1 000
carriage on office equipment	200
extension to building	2 000
new tyre for van	100
office equipment	4 000

What is the total capital expenditure?
- ☐ A $4 300
- ☐ B $6 200
- ☐ C $6 300
- ☐ D $7 000 **(1 mark)**

(Total 8 marks)

13 ACCOUNTING CONCEPTS

Accounts must be a fair and true representation of the business.

LEARNING OBJECTIVES

Understand the significance of the following accounting concepts:
- consistency
- prudence
- accruals
- materiality
- money measurement
- business entity

HINT
Accounting concepts are sometimes called accounting principles.

GENERAL VOCABULARY
bias an opinion about whether a person, group, or idea is good or bad that influences how you deal with it

mislead make someone believe something that is not true by giving them information that is false or not complete

GETTING STARTED

Accounting concepts are the basic rules that all accountants must follow when they produce a set of financial statements. All accounting and international standards are based on these concepts.

These concepts ensure the accounts are a true and fair reflection of the business. They also ensure that the accounts drawn up are free from bias and do not mislead. Finally, they standardise the accounting process so that different businesses' accounts can be compared. This helps owners (who are not involved in the day-to-day running of the business) to know that the accounts are accurate. It also allows potential investors to have faith in the figures.

Most Public Limited Companies share their annual report on the company website. When you look at these documents, you can compare the layout of the financial statements. They should all be very similar because they all follow the same accounting concepts. If you look closely at the notes at the back of the accounts, you might see some mention of the accounting concepts.

DID YOU KNOW?
The IASB (International Accounting Standards Board) was formed in 2001. It was created to ensure that accounting scandals, such as the high-profile cases at Enron, Arthur Anderson and Worldcom, would not happen again.

ACTIVITY

Over the years, many companies have made the mistake of not using the key accounting concepts.

Research these companies:
- Enron: this company did not follow the prudence concept throughout the 1990s.
- Under Armour: this company has to follow the accrual concept.

UNIT 4 — 13 ACCOUNTING CONCEPTS

13.1 DEFINITION OF ACCOUNTING CONCEPTS

At the end of each financial year, organisations prepare their financial statements. These statements include the income statement and the statement of financial position (see Chapter 14). When preparing these statements, organisations must adhere to the 'accounting concepts' or 'rules of accounting'. These concepts or rules have evolved over the years for practical and theoretical reasons. They make the preparation of financial statements more standardised. This ensures the information in the statements is easy to understand and reliable. It also makes it easier to compare different businesses' accounts.

> **KEY POINT**
> Accounting concepts are rules that need to be followed when preparing financial accounts. A concept may be defined as an idea. An accounting concept is an idea that underlies how the financial statements of an organisation should be prepared. Accounting concepts are procedures that have developed over the years to form the basic rules of accounting.

13.2 FUNDAMENTAL ACCOUNTING CONCEPTS

CONSISTENCY

The **consistency concept** requires that similar items are treated in the same way, not only in one period but in all subsequent periods. The concept states that when a business has adopted a method for the accounting treatment of an item, it should treat all similar items in the same way when preparing the financial statements. Examples of when the consistency concept is used include:

- methods of depreciation – either straight line or reducing balance (see Chapter 9, pages 88–89)
- **inventory** valuation (see Chapter 6).

The **consistency** concept is important because it makes it easier to analyse financial information and helps with decision-making. It is vital that an organisation uses the same accounting principles each year: if it was constantly changing its methods, the profits calculated would be misleading and financial analyses would be inaccurate. Owners and/or potential investors would not be able to compare the business's accounts with previous years so they would not be able to judge how successful the business was.

For example, if a business chooses to depreciate a non-current asset using the straight line method, it must continue to use this method for the useful life of that asset. However, this does not mean that the business must always use a particular method: the business may make changes if it has good reason to do so. Each change must be declared in the notes accompanying the financial statements. This allows stakeholders, such as owners, managers and suppliers, to know that the accounts over the previous years are consistent and reliable, so they can make accurate judgements and decisions.

> **SUBJECT VOCABULARY**
> **consistency concept** one of the basic principles of accounting, which says that there should be consistency in accounting methods
> **inventory** the value or quantity of raw materials, components and finished products that a business has.

> **GENERAL VOCABULARY**
> **consistency** the quality of always being the same, doing things in the same way, or having the same standards

> **SUBJECT VOCABULARY**
> **prudence concept** accountants should have use a conservative approach when preparing financial statements and should not overstate revenue/assets and not understate losses and liabilities

PRUDENCE

The **prudence concept** acknowledges that accountants often have to use their judgement when preparing financial statements. For example, they may have to determine the value of a particular asset (such as premises or machinery) or decide whether an outstanding debt will ever be paid. It is the accountant's duty and responsibility to ensure that the financial statements disclose the appropriate facts about the business and are prepared as accurately as possible. Therefore the accountant must ensure that assets are not overvalued and that all liabilities are identified. In other words, the accountant should show caution when forecasting a business's profit for the year and when valuing assets for the statement of financial position. This is particularly important for inventories, which must be valued at the lowest **cost or net realisable value**.

> **KEY POINT**
> The prudence concept means that accountants will take a conservative figure that understates rather than overstates the profit. They must ensure that all losses are recorded in the books and must also ensure that profits are not anticipated by being recorded before they have been gained.

ACCRUALS

KEY POINT
Revenue expenditure is spending on everyday normal activities of the business. Capital expenditure is spending on non-currents assets or improvements to non-current assets.

SUBJECT VOCABULARY
accruals adjustments made to accounts to record expenses that the company has not yet paid for. Examples of accrued expenses are salaries payable and interest payable. Salaries payable are wages earned by employees in one period but not paid until the next, while interest payable is interest expense that has been incurred but not paid.

non-current assets an asset that is assumed to be kept in the business for more than one year and will not be turned into cash within that year

accruals concept the practice of recognising revenues and their related expenses in the same accounting period in order to avoid misstating earnings for a period.

The **accruals concept** states that profit for the year is the difference between revenues and expenses rather than the difference between cash received and cash paid. These figures are linked to the accounting period. The accounting period refers to when the book of prime entry is prepared; this is normally a period of twelve months. The accruals concept means that all revenues and expenses must be relevant to that period.

Revenue is counted when the goods or services are sold. Revenue is not counted when the money is received, which can be later in the accounting period. Similarly, any purchases are expenses when the goods are bought, not when they are paid for. In Chapter 6 page 72, you will see items such as rent, insurance and motor expenses are treated as expenses when they are incurred, not when they are paid. When financial statements are prepared, adjustments are made: for expenses owing and those paid in advance (other receivables); for depreciation of non-current assets; and for allowance for irrecoverable debts.

The identification of expenses used to obtain revenues is referred to as matching expenses against revenues. In order to show a correct figure of profit for the year in the income statement, an accountant must match the actual expenses incurred in a period against revenues earned in the same period. A period could be one month or one year, but must be relevant to the transactions that have taken place in that period. This is particularly important when it comes to receiving cash.

MATERIALITY

SUBJECT VOCABULARY
materiality concept this concept applies when the value of an item is relatively small and does not warrant separate recording

The **materiality concept** applies when the value of an item is relatively insignificant and does not warrant separate recording – for example, the purchase of a box of paper clips, a calculator or a small clock for the office. Small expenditures like this are regarded as 'not material' and their purchase is not recorded in separate expense accounts. Instead they are grouped together in a sundry or general expense account. Materiality also relates to the classification of some items. A stapler or a hole-punch could last longer than one year, but to class it as a non-current asset would be misleading. It should, therefore, be recorded in expenses. It should not be included in the statement of financial position because it has no resale value.

▲ Low-cost items with no resale value are often grouped together in company accounts.

EXAMPLE

A business buys a stapler. The stapler cost $5 and should last for 2 years. Technically, the stapler is a non-current asset (something the business owns that lasts more than 1 year). However, because it is low value you should follow the concept of materiality and include the stapler as an expense to the business.

MONEY MEASUREMENT

SUBJECT VOCABULARY

money measurement concept the fact that every transaction is measured using monetary measures, i.e., the local currency

The **money measurement concept** states that only transactions and activities that can be measured in terms of money, and whose monetary value can be assessed with reasonable objectivity (without bias), should be entered into the accounting records.

BUSINESS ENTITY

SUBJECT VOCABULARY

business entity concept the principle that transactions associated with a business must be separately recorded from those of its owners or other businesses

The **business entity concept** ensures that the affairs of a business are treated as being quite separate from the personal activities of the owner(s) of the business. In other words, only the activities of the business are recorded and reported in the business's financial statements. Any transactions involving the owner(s) are kept separate and are excluded. For example, the owner's personal car must not be included in the financial statements.

The personal resources of the owner(s) will only affect the business's accounting records if they introduce new equity into the business or take drawings.

▲ Jasdeep prepares his own accounts but needs advice and guidance from his accountant.

CASE STUDY: ACCOUNTING CONCEPTS

Jasdeep owns a garage in Mumbai. Jasdeep prepares his own accounts and then gives them to his accountant to check. His profit for the year is 13 000 000 rupees. Jasdeep's accountant is away on holiday and Jasdeep needs some advice about how to treat the following transactions:

- Jasdeep has added his private electricity bill of 13 000 rupees to the expenses of his business.
- Jasdeep is certain one of his customers will buy a car from him for 1 000 000 rupees next month. He has included the sale in this year's accounts.
- Jasdeep chose to value some of his inventory at net realisable value of 32 500 rupees. The cost of the inventory is only 17 500 rupees.

Advise Jasdeep on the concepts involved and how they could affect his profit.

END OF CHAPTER QUESTIONS

1. Why do we need accounting concepts?
2. Explain the concept of money measurement.
3. What are the benefits of being consistent in your accounting techniques?

> **HINT**
> Use the acronym **BMCAMP** to help you remember the different accounting concepts: Business entity, Materiality, Consistency, Accruals, Money measurement, Prudence.

4 If there is any doubt about the value of a transaction, a conservative approach should be adopted. Which accounting concept is being followed here?

5 Inventory costing £250 has been damaged in a shop. Its net realisable value is now £180. Explain how much the inventory should be valued at and which concept is being used.

END OF CHAPTER CHECKLIST

- An 'accounting concept' is an accounting procedure developed over the years to form the basic rules of accounting.
- The main accounting concepts that you need to learn are: business entity, materiality, accruals, consistency, money measurement and prudence.
- Financial accounts are produced using the accounting concepts.

EXAM PRACTICE

A01 **A02** **A03** Answer ALL questions in this section. Questions 1–7 must be answered with a cross in the box ☒. If you change your mind about an answer, put a line through the box ☒ and then mark your new answer with a cross ☒.

1 Which accounting concept is the basis for the idea that the business unit is distinct from all other units?
- ☐ **A** prudence
- ☐ **B** business entity
- ☐ **C** money measurement
- ☐ **D** materiality (1 mark)

2 Which accounting concept is exemplified by recording revenues and costs when they are incurred, not when cash is received or paid?
- ☐ **A** business entity
- ☐ **B** money measurement
- ☐ **C** accruals
- ☐ **D** prudence (1 mark)

3 Which accounting concept suggests that all financial transactions should be shown separately if a user of the accounts could be misled?
- ☐ **A** prudence
- ☐ **B** business entity
- ☐ **C** money measurement
- ☐ **D** materiality (1 mark)

4 When does a business recognise the income from a sale of goods on credit?
- ☐ **A** when it sends a statement to the customer
- ☐ **B** when the customer pays for the goods
- ☐ **C** when the goods are delivered to the customer
- ☐ **D** when the customer orders the goods (1 mark)

5 Which of the following could be recorded in an organisation's accounting records?
- ☐ **A** the benefits of staff training
- ☐ **B** the cost of property owned
- ☐ **C** the effect of new laws
- ☐ **D** the value of the skills of its managers (1 mark)

6 Which of the following describes the principle of consistency?
- ☐ **A** Accounts should include all probable losses and should not anticipate profits.
- ☐ **B** Accounts should only include items with a monetary value.
- ☐ **C** Accounts should treat the owner and the business separately.
- ☐ **D** Accounts should use the same methods from year to year. (1 mark)

7 A trader reduced the telephone expenses in the financial statements by the amount of his personal telephone bill, which had been included in the telephone expenses account. Which accounting principle is the trader using?
- ☐ **A** business entity
- ☐ **B** going concern
- ☐ **C** accruals
- ☐ **D** prudence (1 mark)

8 Give an example of the business entity concept. (1 mark)

9 What is a disadvantage of not using the prudence concept? (1 mark)

10 Which accounting concept is being used when a business uses the same method of depreciation? (1 mark)

(Total 10 marks)

14 FINANCIAL STATEMENTS OF A SOLE TRADER

▲ Accountants may be able to help sole traders save money, even when they charge for their services.

LEARNING OBJECTIVES

- Prepare income statements to show gross profit and profit for the year
- Prepare statements of financial position to show assets, liabilities and equity

GETTING STARTED

In this chapter, we will learn about the financial statements of a sole trader, which include both the income statement and the statement of financial position.

EXAM HINT

You need to know the layout for both the income statement and the statement of financial position as they will not be provided for you in the exam.

ACTIVITY

Look online at some company accounts and look at the layout of their financial statements.

14.1 INTRODUCTION TO THE INCOME STATEMENT

The main purpose of an income statement is to allow the owners to see how profitably the business is operating. Chapter 1 page 8 discusses other groups that are interested in the financial results of a business, such as banks (if the business require a loan) and the tax authorities.

14.2 USES OF THE INCOME STATEMENT

A trading organisation pays a lot of attention to how much profit is made before deducting expenses (i.e. the gross profit). This appears in the first section of the income statement. The profit for the year is shown in the next section of the account. This yearly profit is equally important to the owners and other groups.

SUBJECT VOCABULARY

cost of sales the direct costs, which are usually material and labour, to make or to buy a product

GROSS PROFIT	This is the excess of revenue over the cost of sales in the period.
PROFIT FOR THE YEAR	What remains of the gross profit after all other expenses have been deducted.

14.3 PREPARATION OF AN INCOME STATEMENT

A trial balance must be drawn up for the double entry system before an income statement can be prepared. A trial balance contains nearly all the information required.

Example 1: The trial balance for Jasdeep Sarha is shown in **Figure 14.1**. Look out for the closing inventories, which usually appear at the bottom of the trial balance in the notes section.

- **Revenue returns** are goods that have been returned by the customer; sometimes called Returns inwards.
- **Purchase returns** are goods that the business sends back to the supplier; sometimes called Returns outward.
- **Carriage inwards** is a cost incurred when a supplier charges for delivery on goods purchased.

Jasdeep Sarha
Trial Balance at 31/12/2016

	Dr	Cr
Sales Revenue		80 000
Revenue Returns	5000	
Inventories at 1.1.16	7000	
Purchases	34 000	
Purchase Returns		3000
Rent	6000	
Wages	8000	
Electricity	2000	
Administration	3000	
Fuel	2500	
Carriage Inwards	300	
Insurance	1500	
Buildings	50 000	
Motor Vehicles	25 000	
Trade Receivables	6000	
Bank	4000	
Cash	400	
Trade Payables		3700
Bank Loan		20 000
Equity		60 000
Drawings	12 000	
	166 700	166 700

Notes

| Inventories 31.12.16 | | 3300 |

▲ Figure 14.1 A trial balance for Jasdeep Sarha.

EXAM HINT

Always check the dates for inventories. There will be an opening inventory and a closing inventory.

EXAM HINT

Note that accounts in the trial balance may appear in order of financial statement, as in Figure 14.1, or alphabetically (see the trial balance in the case study on page 163).

The first section of the income statement is sometimes referred to as the trading account. It is used to calculate gross profit.

All you do is transfer the figures from the trial balance into the income statement. The income statement for Jasdeep Sarha is shown in **Figure 14.2**.

Jasdeep Sarha
Income Statement for year ended 31/12/2016

		£	£
	Sales revenue		80 000
Less	Revenue Returns		5000
Equals	Net Revenue		75 000
	Cost of Sales		
	Opening Inventories	7000	
Add	Purchases	34 000	
Add	Carriage In	300	
Less	Purchase Returns	38 300	
Equals	Net Purchases	38 300	
Less	Closing Inventories	3300	
Equals	Cost of Sales		35 000
	Gross Profit		40 000
Less Expenses			
	Rent	6000	
	Wages	8000	
	Electricity	2000	
	Administration	3000	
	Fuel	2500	
	Insurance	1500	23 000
	Profit for the Year		17 000

▲ **Figure 14.2** An income statement for Jasdeep Sarha.

HINT

You should only use each figure from the trial balance once, so tick off the figures as you go so you don't miss anything out. This will make it easier when preparing the statement of financial position.

CASE STUDY: TRIAL BALANCE PART 1

Jasraj owns a restaurant in Dubai. He has provided the following figures in his trial balance.

	Dr	Cr
Sales Revenue		150 000
Administration	10 000	
Bank		13 000
Bank Loan		29 500
Buildings	100 000	
Equity		100 000
Carriage Inwards	500	
Cash	25 000	
Drawings	12 000	
Electricity	7000	
Fuel	5000	
Insurance	6000	
Inventories at 1.1.16	12 000	
Motor Vehicles	30 000	
Purchase Returns		6000
Purchases	45 000	
Rent	30 000	
Revenue Returns	6000	
Trade Payables		18 000
Trade Receivables	3000	
Wages	25 000	
	316 500	316 500

Notes

Inventories 31.12.16		8000

Prepare an income statement for Jasraj.

14.4 DEFINITION AND CONTENT OF A STATEMENT OF FINANCIAL POSITION

A **statement of financial position** is a financial statement that sets out the book values of assets, liabilities and equity at a particular point in time. In simple terms, a statement of financial position shows what a business 'owns' and what it 'owes' on a specific date.

First, we find the details of the assets, liabilities and equity in the records of the business. Then we write them out as a statement of financial position. These details are readily available since they consist of all the balances remaining in the records once the income statement for the period has been completed. All balances remaining have to be assets, liabilities or equity: the other balances should have been closed off when the income statement was completed.

14.5 LAYOUT OF THE STATEMENT OF FINANCIAL POSITION

The statement of financial position is one of the most important financial statements and it must be easy to follow and understand. Over the years, the presentation of financial information has evolved. The present format of the statement of financial position is shown in **Figure 14.4**.

The statement of financial position starts by listing all the assets that the business 'owns' at the date of the statement. The assets are split into two categories: non-current assets and current assets. This is followed by details of the funds acquired to finance the business.

ASSETS

Assets are shown under two headings: non-current assets and current assets.

NON-CURRENT ASSETS

Non-current assets are assets that:
- are expected to be of use to the business for more than one year
- are to be used in the business
- were not bought only for the purpose of resale.

Examples are buildings, machinery, motor vehicles, fixtures and fittings. Non-current assets are listed first in the statement of financial position. The list starts with the assets that the business will keep the longest, and goes down to assets with the shortest life expectancy. For example:
1. Property
2. Fixtures and fittings
3. Machinery
4. Motor vehicles

Non-current assets can also be categorised as tangible (physical assets) and intangible (non-physical assets). Tangible assets include motor vehicles and buildings whereas intangible assets include items such as **patents**.

> **SUBJECT VOCABULARY**
>
> **patent** buying the right to use another company's invention

CURRENT ASSETS

Current assets are assets that are likely to change in the near future – within 12 months of the statement of financial position date. They include inventory of goods for resale at a profit (always the closing figure), amounts owed by trade receivables, cash in the bank, and any cash in hand. Current assets are listed starting with the assets that are least likely to be turned into cash and finishing with cash itself, i.e:
1. Inventory
2. Trade receivables
3. Cash at bank
4. Cash in hand

LIABILITIES

There are two categories of liability: current liabilities and non-current liabilities.

CURRENT LIABILITIES

Current liabilities are liabilities due for repayment in the short term, usually within one year. Examples are bank overdrafts and amounts due to trade payables for the supply of goods for resale.

Current liabilities can be deducted from the current assets. This gives the net current assets or working equity. This figure is very important in accounting since it shows the amount of resources the business has in the form of readily available cash to meet everyday running expenses.

UNIT 4
14 FINANCIAL STATEMENTS OF A SOLE TRADER

NON-CURRENT LIABILITIES

Non-current liabilities are liabilities not due for repayment in the near future. Examples are bank loans, loans from others such as friends or relatives, and mortgages. Non-current liabilities are added to the current liabilities and equity in **Figure 14.4**.

EQUITY ACCOUNT

This is the proprietor's or partners' account with the business. It starts with the balance brought forward from the previous accounting period. Any personal cash introduced into the business is also added, as well as the profit made by the business in this accounting period. Amounts drawn from the business are deducted (this is called 'drawings') and any loss made by the business is also deducted.

Look again at the trial balance for Jasdeep Sarha, shown in **Figure 14.3**. The figures that have been used in the income statement (**Figure 14.2**) are marked by an asterisk(*).

Jasdeep Sarha
Trial Balance at 31/12/2016

	Dr	Cr	
Sales Revenue		80 000	*
Sales Returns	5000		*
Inventories at 1.1.16	7000		*
Purchases	34 000		*
Purchase Returns		3000	*
Rent	6000		*
Wages	8000		*
Electricity	2000		*
Administration	3000		*
Fuel	2500		*
Carriage Inwards	300		*
Insurance	1500		*
Buildings	50 000		
Motor Vehicles	25 000		
Trade Receivables	6000		
Bank	4000		
Cash	400		
Trade Payables		3700	
Bank Loan		20 000	
Capital		60 000	
Drawings	12 000		
	166 700	166 700	

Notes

Inventories 31.12.16   3300

▲ Figure 14.3 Trial balance for Jasdeep Sarha, with figures used in the income statement marked.

The statement of financial position (**Figure 14.4**) is drawn up using the remaining balances and the profit from the year calculated in the income statement. Only one figure is used in both the income statement and the statement of financial position – the closing inventories.

Jasdeep Sarha
Statement of Financial Position at 31/12/2016

		£	£
	Assets		
	Non-current Assets		
Add	Buildings		50 000
Add	Motor Vehicles		25 000
Equals			75 000
	Current Assets		
	Inventories	3300	
Add	Trade Receivables	6000	
Add	Bank	4000	
Add	Cash	400	
Equals			13 700
	Net Assets (NCA + CA)		88 700
	Capital and Liabilities		
	Capital		
	Opening Capital		60 000
Add	Profit for the Year		17 000
Less	Drawings		12 000
Equals	Closing Capital		65 000
	Liabilities		
	Non-current Liabilities		
Add	Bank Loan		20 000
	Current Liabilities		
Add	Trade Payables		3700
Equals	**Total Capital and Liabilities**		88 700

▲ **Figure 14.4** Statement of financial position for Jasdeep Sarha.

It is important to note that the statement of financial position shows the position of the business at one point in time, for example, 'as at 31 December 2016'. It is like taking a snapshot of the business at a single moment in time. The income statement, on the other hand, shows the profit/loss of the business for a period of time (normally a year), for example, 'for the year ended 31 December 2016'.

KEY POINT

Working capital = current assets – current liabilities

Net assets = non-current assets + current assets

Closing capital should equal net assets

EXAM HINT

Always check your bank figure in the trial balance. If it is a debit it is a current asset. If it is a credit, the bank is overdrawn and it is a current liability.

CASE STUDY: TRIAL BALANCE PART 2

Jasraj would now like to complete the statement of financial position for his trial balance. Remember to transfer the profit for the year from the income statement.

	Dr	Cr
Sales Revenue		150 000
Sales Returns	6000	
Inventories at 1.1.16	12 000	
Purchases	45 000	
Purchase Returns		6000
Rent	30 000	
Wages	25 000	
Electricity	7000	
Administration	10 000	
Fuel	5000	
Carriage Inwards	500	
Insurance	6000	
Buildings	100 000	
Motor Vehicles	30 000	
Trade Receivables	3000	
Bank		13 000
Cash	25 000	
Trade Payables		18 000
Bank Loan		29 500
Capital		100 000
Drawings	12 000	
	316 500	316 500

Notes

Inventories 31.12.16   8000

END OF CHAPTER QUESTIONS

1. What does an income statement show?
2. What does a statement of financial position show?
3. What is a non-current asset?
4. What is meant by the term 'cost of sales'?
5. What is capital?

END OF CHAPTER CHECKLIST

- The trading account is used to calculate gross profit.
- The income statement lists revenue expenditure for a business.
- The statement of financial position lists capital expenditure for a business.
- Carriage inwards affects gross profit, whereas carriage outwards affects profit for the year.

EXAM PRACTICE

Answer ALL questions in this section. Questions 1–10 must be answered with a cross in the box ☒. If you change your mind about an answer, put a line through the box ☒ and then mark your new answer with a cross ☒.

1 Which of the following is a current liability?
- ☐ A capital
- ☐ B trade payables
- ☐ C trade receivables
- ☐ D inventory (1 mark)

2 Which of the following would appear in a statement of financial position?
- ☐ A closing inventory
- ☐ B cost of sales
- ☐ C opening inventory
- ☐ D interest paid (1 mark)

3 A business provides the following information:

Revenue	$10 000
Purchases	$8000
Opening inventory	$1000
Closing inventory	$1500
Sales returns	$200
Purchase returns	$300

What is the cost of sales?
- ☐ A $2000
- ☐ B $2100
- ☐ C $7200
- ☐ D $8200 (1 mark)

4 A sole trader has omitted depreciation from his financial statements.
What are the effects on the financial statements?

	non-current assets	profit for the year
☐ A	overstated	overstated
☐ B	overstated	understated
☐ C	understated	overstated
☐ D	understated	understated

(1 mark)

5 Why should a sole trader record all the financial information about her business?
- ☐ A because she is required to do so by law
- ☐ B because she needs to pay her trade payables on time
- ☐ C so that she can prepare financial statements
- ☐ D so that she knows how much her trade receivables owe her (1 mark)

6 Amina lists her current assets in order of liquidity. In which order will the current assets appear?
- ☐ A bank, cash, inventory, trade receivables
- ☐ B cash, bank, trade receivables, inventory
- ☐ C inventory, trade receivables, bank, cash
- ☐ D trade receivables, inventory, bank, cash (1 mark)

7 A trader provided the following information for the year ended 31 August 2016.

Sales	$80 000
Cost of sales	$50 000
Profit for the year	$14 000

What were the expenses for the year ended 31 August 2016?
- ☐ A $16 000
- ☐ B $30 000
- ☐ C $36 000
- ☐ D $66 000 (1 mark)

8 A business provides the following information.

capital 1 January 2016	$60 000
drawings during the year	$40 000
capital introduced during the year	$10 000
capital 31 December 2016	$80 000

What is the profit for the year?
- ☐ A $10 000
- ☐ B $20 000
- ☐ C $50 000
- ☐ D $70 000 (1 mark)

UNIT 4 — 14 FINANCIAL STATEMENTS OF A SOLE TRADER

9 A trader has 1500 units of inventory, of which 50 units can only be sold for $10 per unit.

Each unit costs $15 and the unit sale price is $20.

What is the value of the inventory?

- A $22 250
- B $22 500
- C $29 000
- D $30 000

(1 mark)

10 What is an example of an intangible asset?

- A trade payable
- B a patent
- C prepayment
- D motor vehicle

(1 mark)

11 Bonnie makes parts for cars and her financial year ends on 31 March. After preparing her income statement for the year ended 31 March 2016, her trial balance shows the following items.

31 March 2016	
Bank	500 Dr
Bank loan repayable 2019	2800
Trade payables	700
Trade receivables	1000
Machinery	20 000
Provision for depreciation on machinery	12 000
Inventories	3000
Drawings	4500
Capital account at 1 April 2015	6000
Profit for the year	7500

a Prepare Bonnie's statement of financial position at 31 March 2016.

b i Define working capital.

   ii From your answer to (a) above, calculate Bonnie's working capital at 31 March 2016.

(5 marks)

12 The following trial balance was extracted from the books of Amir Sadiq as at 31 March 2016.

	Dr	Cr
Sales revenue		200 000
Revenue returns	12 000	
Inventories at 1.1.16	18 000	
Purchases	99 000	
Purchase returns		8000
Rent	40 000	
Wages	25 000	
Electricity	7000	
Administration	10 000	
Fuel	21 000	
Carriage inwards	4000	
Insurance	6000	
Buildings	140 000	
Motor vehicles	37 000	
Trade receivables	3000	
Bank		13 000
Cash	15 000	
Trade payables		18 000
Bank loan		40 000
Capital		180 000
Drawings	22 000	
	459 000	459 000

Notes

Inventories 31.12.16   17 000

Prepare an income statement and statement of financial position for Amir Sadiq.   **(20 marks)**

13 Rajit has a business making furniture. After preparing his income statement for the year ended 31 December 2015, a summary of his trial balance shows the following items:

	$
Non-current assets at cost	50 500
Current assets	47 000
Current liabilities	19 000
Capital account at 1 January 2015	74 000
Drawings	9000
Profit for the year 1	3000

Prepare Rajit's statement of financial position at 31 December 2015.   **(20 marks)**

14 Solomon is a sole trader and his trial balance at 31 March 2017 was as follows:

Solomon
Trial Balance at 31 March 2017

	$ Dr	$ Cr
Sales revenue		500 000
Administration	11 111	
Bank		54 321
Bank loan		44 444
Buildings	250 000	
Capital		123 456
Carriage inwards	4 321	
Cash	34 567	
Drawings	20 483	
Electricity	7 777	
Fuel	21 211	
Insurance	6 789	
Inventories at 1.1.16	12 345	
Motor vehicles	55 555	
Purchase returns		8 888
Purchases	237 899	
Rent	44 444	
Revenue returns	17 500	
Trade payables		18 901
Trade receivables	3 456	
Wages	22 552	
	750 010	750 010

Notes
Inventories 31.12.16   17 000

Prepare an income statement and statement of financial position for Solomon. **(20 marks)**

(Total 75 marks)

15 OTHER RECEIVABLES AND PAYABLES

▲ Understanding the different types of payables and receivables will help you manage your business cash flow more efficiently.

LEARNING OBJECTIVES

- Explain why it is necessary to account for other trade receivables and trade payables
- Distinguish between other receivables and payables
- Calculate and record other receivables and payables in the books of account

HINT
Other payables may also referred to as accruals, and other receivables may also be referred to as prepayments.

GETTING STARTED

So far, the focus has been on revenue and expenses that are paid on time and are relevant to the period in question. For example, wages paid in September are for work done in September, or electricity paid for in March is used in March. In the real world, however, not all transactions will match the period in question. For example, rent may be paid in advance (a prepayment) while bills may be paid after the commodity (e.g. electricity) has been used (an accrual). In this chapter, we will learn how to deal with other receivables and payables for both income and expenses.

ACTIVITY

Do you always pay your bills on time? Or do you pay them early? What do you think happens to income and expenses if they are paid in advance or are paid later at the end of the financial year?

15.1 ADJUSTMENTS NEEDED FOR EXPENSES OWING AND EXPENSES PAID IN ADVANCE

Not all businesses pay their electricity bills on time. In fact, some prefer to pay their bills in advance. Example 1 looks at how two businesses each pay €600 per year for their electricity. The amount they use must be matched to the accounting period (1 April 2016 to 31 March 2017). This is an example of the accruals concept.

Example 1: Business A pays for €450 of electricity during the accounting period. However, the business has used €600 of electricity. €600 is included in expenses because this is the actual cost to the business. €150 (the amount not paid) must be added as an other payable under current liabilities.

Business B pays €675 for electricity during the accounting period. However, the business has only used €600 of electricity. In this case, only €600 is put in expenses as this is the actual cost in this accounting period. €75 is added for other receivables under current assets.

15.2 OTHER PAYABLES

Example 2: Rent of €1000 per year is payable at the end of every three months but it is not always paid on time. Details of the payments are shown below:

Amount	Rent due	Rent paid
€250	31 March 2016	31 March 2016
€250	30 June 2016	2 July 2016
€250	30 September 2016	4 October 2016
€250	31 December 2016	5 January 2017

The rent account is as follows:

Dr		Rent Account	Cr
2016		€	
Mar 31	Cash	250	
Jul 2	Cash	250	
Oct 4	Cash	250	

The rent paid on 5 January 2017 appears in the books for the year 2016 as part of the double entry bookkeeping.

The expense for 2016 is €1000 because that is the year's rent. This is the amount we need to be transfer from the income statement at the end of the period. But if €1000 was put on the credit side of the rent account, the account would not balance. We would have €1000 on the credit side of the account and only €750 on the debit side.

To make the account balance, the €250 rent owing for 2016, but paid in 2017, must be carried down to 2017 as a credit balance. It is a liability on 31 December 2016. Instead of rent owing, it would be called Other payables. The completed account is as follows:

Dr		Rent Account			Cr
2016		€	2016		€
Mar 31	Cash	250	Dec 31	Income statement	1000
Jul 2	Cash	250			
Oct 4	Cash	250			
Dec 31	Balance c/d	250			
		1000			1000
			2017		
			Jan 1	Balance b/d	250

15.3 OTHER RECEIVABLES

Example 3: Insurance for a business costs €840 a year, starting from 1 January 2016. The business agreed to pay this at a rate of €210 every three months. However, payments were not made at the correct times. The details are shown on the following page.

Amount	Insurance due	Insurance paid
€210	31 March 2016	€210 – 28 February 2016
€210	30 June 2016	€420 – 31 August 2016
€210	30 September 2016	
€210	31 December 2016	€420 – 18 November 2016

The insurance account for the year ended 31 December 2016 is shown as:

Dr		Insurance Account		Cr
2016		€		
Feb 28	Bank	210		
Aug 31	Bank	420		
Nov 18	Bank	420		

The last payment shown, of €420, is not just for 2016. It can be split as €210 for the three months to 31 December 2016 and €210 for the three months to 31 March 2017. For a period of 12 months, the cost of insurance is €840, so this is the figure that needs to be transferred to the income statement.

If this figure of €840 is entered in the account, then the amount needed to balance the account is €210. At 31 December 2016, the business has paid a further €210 which has not been used. This is an asset that we need to carry forward to 2017, as a debit balance. It is an other receivable or prepaid expense. The account should be completed as follows:

Dr		Insurance Account				Cr
2016		€	2016			€
Feb 28	Bank	210	Dec 31	Income statement		840
Aug 31	Bank	420				
Nov 18	Bank	420	Dec 31	Balance c/d		210
		1050				1050
2017						
Jan 1	Balance b/d	210				

15.4 ADJUSTMENT FOR INVENTORY OF STATIONERY ETC. CARRIED FORWARD

Other receivables also arise when a business buys items for use within the business and these items are not used up in the period. For instance, packing materials and stationery items may not be entirely used up during the period in which they were bought: stationery is often left over at the end of the accounting period. This stationery is a form of prepayment and needs to be carried down to the next period in which it will be used.

Example 4: A business buys stationery to the value of €2200 in 2016. At the end of the year, they still have €400 of this stationery in hand.

The stationery used up is (€2200 – €400) = €1800. The remaining stationery needs to be carried forward to 2017 as an asset balance (debit balance), as shown on the following page.

GENERAL VOCABULARY

in hand acquired and available

Dr			Stationery Account		Cr
2016		€	2016		€
Dec 31	Bank	2200	Dec 31	Income statement	1800
			Dec 31	Balance c/d	400
		2200			2200
2017					
Jan 1	Balance b/d	400			

The stationery is added to the other prepaid expenses in the statement of financial position.

15.5 REVENUE OWING AT THE END OF PERIOD

A business may have some other kinds of revenue, such as rent receivable, that have not been received by the end of the accounting period. In this case, the business needs to make adjustments.

Example 5: A company's warehouse is larger than they need, so they rent part of the warehouse to another business for €800 per annum. Here are the details for the year ended 31 December 2016:

Amount	Rent due	Rent received
€200	31 March 2016	4 April 2016
€200	30 June 2016	6 July 2016
€200	30 September 2016	9 October 2016
€200	31 December 2016	7 January 2017

The account for 2016 appears as shown below:

Dr		Rent Receivable Account			Cr
			2016		€
			Apr 4	Bank	200
			Jul 6	Bank	200
			Oct 9	Bank	200

The rent of €200 received on 7 January 2017 is entered in the books in 2017 (not shown).

Any rent paid by the business is charged as a debit to the income statement. Rent received is transferred to the credit of the income statement, since it is revenue/income.

The amount the company needs to transfer to the income statement for 2016 is that owed to them for the 12 months, i.e. €800. The company completes the rent received account by carrying down the balance owing as a debit balance to 2017. The €200 owing is an asset on 31 December 2016. The rent receivable account can now be completed, as shown on the next page.

Dr		Rent Receivable Account				Cr
2016			€	2016		€
Dec 31	Income statement		800	Apr 4	Bank	200
				Jul 6	Bank	200
				Oct 9	Bank	200
				Dec 31	Balance c/d	200
			800			800
2017						
Jan 1	Balance b/d		200			

15.6 EXPENSES AND REVENUE ACCOUNT BALANCES AND THE STATEMENT OF FINANCIAL POSITION

In all the examples so far – dealing with adjustments in the financial statements – there has been a balance on each account after the trading and income statements have been prepared. All balances remaining should appear in the statement of financial position. So where and how should we record them?

Usually, all the amounts owing for expenses are added together and shown as one figure. They are called 'other payables' or 'expenses owing'. These items are normally recorded in the statement of financial position under current liabilities because they are expenses that have to be discharged in the near future.

All prepaid items are also added together. They are called 'other receivables', or 'payments in advance'. They are recorded in the statement of financial position under current assets after the trade receivables. Amounts owing are usually added for rents receivable or other revenue owing to trade receivables.

The statement of financial position for the accounts in Examples 2–5 would look like this:

Statement of Financial Positions as at 31 December 2016			
	€	€	€
Current assets			
Inventories		xxx	
Receivables		200	
Other receivables (210 + 400)		610	
Bank		xxx	
Cash		xxx	
		xxxx	
Current liabilities			
Payables	xxx		
Other payables	250	xxx	

> **HINT**
> An expense paid in advance should be deducted from the expense. Rent €800 including €50 paid in advance should be €750 in expenses plus a prepayment of €50 in current assets.

> **HINT**
> An owed or outstanding expense is added to expenses in the income statement and added to current liabilities in the statement of financial position.

CASE STUDY: OTHER RECEIVABLES AND PAYABLES

Garrick owns a warehouse in Beijing. At the moment, he only uses 60% of the building. He rents the other part of the building to Elsa, and charges her RMB 68 000 per annum. At the financial year end, Elsa has only paid RMB 62 000 towards the rent.

State the amount that should be entered in Garrick's income statement.

State the amount that should be entered in Garrick's statement of financial position.

SUBJECT VOCABULARY

depreciation a reduction in the value of an asset over time, due in particular to wear and tear, e.g. the reduction in the value of a machine

irrecoverable debts debts that are not expected to be paid, for example if a customer is in financial difficulty

15.7 WORKED EXAMPLE: FINANCIAL STATEMENTS FOR A SOLE TRADER

You should now understand the adjustments you need to make before preparing the financial statements for a business. These include adjustments for **depreciation** (see Chapter 7), writing off **irrecoverable debts**, and the allowance for irrecoverable debts (see Chapter 16). You also need to consider other payables, other receivables, and discounts allowed and received. Chapter 6 discussed closing inventory, revenue returns, purchase returns, and carriage inwards and outwards.

Example 6 is a fully worked example that includes all the items mentioned above. There is also a step-by-step guide that explains the adjustments made.

Example 6: Xi Fin Lu, a sole trader, extracted the following trial balance from his books for the year ended 31 March 2017.

Xi Fin Lu
Trial Balance as at 31 March 2017

	Dr £	Cr £
Purchases and revenue	224 000	419 700
Inventory 1 April 2016	51 600	
Equity 1 April 2016		72 000
Bank		43 500
Cash	900	
Carriage inwards	4600	
Discounts	14 400	9300
Revenue returns	8100	
Purchase returns		5700
Carriage outwards	21 600	
Rent and insurance	17 400	
Allowance for irrecoverable debts		6600
Office equipment	20 000	
Delivery vans	27 000	
Trade receivables and trade payables	119 100	61 200
Drawings	28 800	
Irrecoverable debts	400	
Wages and salaries	89 000	
General office expenses	4500	
Provision for depreciation		
Office equipment		8000
Delivery vans		5400
	631 400	631 400

Notes:
1. Inventory 31 March 2017 was valued at £42 900.
2. Wages and salaries owing £2100 and office expenses owing £200 at 31 March 2017.
3. Rent prepaid 31 March 2017 was £1800.
4. Increase the allowance for an irrecoverable debt to £8100.
5. Provide for depreciation on the office equipment at 20% per annum using the straight line method.
6. Provide for depreciation on the delivery vans at 20% per annum using the reducing balance method.

▲ **Figure 15.1** Xi Fin Lu's trial balance.

The income statement for the year ended 31 March 2017 is shown in **Figure 15.2**.

Xi Fin Lu
Income Statement for the year ended 31 March 2017

	£	£	£
Revenue			419 700
Less Revenue returns			8 100
			411 600
Less Cost of sales			
Opening inventory		51 600	
Add Purchases	224 000		
Add Carriage inwards	4 600		
	228 600		
Less Purchase returns	5 700	222 900	
		274 500	
Less Closing inventory		42 900	231 600
Gross Profit			180 000
Add Discounts received	(G)		9 300
			189 300
Less Expenses			
Wages and salaries (89 000 + 2100)	(C)	91 100	
Discounts allowed	(F)	14 400	
Carriage outwards		21 600	
Rent and insurance (17 400 – 1800)	(A)	15 600	
Irrecoverable debts	(N)	400	
General office expenses (4500 + 200)	(D)	4 700	
Increase in allowance for an irrecoverable debt (8100 – 6600)	(L)	1 500	
Depreciation:			
Office equipment	(H)	4 000	
Delivery vans	(J)	4 320	157 620
Profit for the year			31 680

▲ Figure 15.2 Xi Fin Lu's income statement.

The statement of financial position as at 31 March 2017 is shown in **Figure 15.3**.

176 UNIT 4

15 OTHER RECEIVABLES AND PAYABLES

Xi Fin Lu
Statement of financial position as at 31 March 2017

		£	£	£
Assets				
Non-current Assets				
Office equipment	(I)	20 000	12 000	8000
Delivery vans	(K)	27 000	9720	17 280
		47 000	21 720	25 280
Current Assets				
Inventories			42 900	
Trade receivables		119 100		
Less Allowance for an irrecoverable debt	(M)	8100	111 000	
Other receivables	(B)		1800	
Cash in hand			900	156 600
Net Assets (NCA + CA)				181 880
Current Liabilities				
Capital				
Opening Capital				72 000
Profit for the Year				31 680
Drawings				28 800
Closing Capital				74 880
Liabilities				
Non-current Liabilities				
Current Liabilities				
Trade payables			61 200	
Bank overdraft			43 500	
Other payables	(E)		2300	107 000
Total Capital and Liabilities				181 800

▲ Figure 15.3 Xi Fin Lu's statement of financial position.

15.8 STEP-BY-STEP GUIDE: DEALING WITH FURTHER ADJUSTMENTS TO FINANCIAL STATEMENTS

The letters (A) to (N) shown after each adjustment can be **cross referenced** to the income statement (**Figure 15.2**) and statement of financial position (**Figure 15.3**) of Xi Fin Lu.

1 **Other receivables (amounts paid in advance)**

In the financial statements

a If a trial balance is provided in a question, you must deduct the amount of the other receivables from the appropriate expense account and put the resulting figure in the income statement. Ensure that only the expenses incurred for a particular period are charged against the profits for that period. In the worked example above (**Figure 15.1**), note (3) states that rent prepaid was £1800. This amount should be deducted from the rent

> **HINT**
> Use the step-by-step guides below when working on exercises involving adjustments to financial statements.

> **SUBJECT VOCABULARY**
> **cross reference** in accounting, this refers to the practice of adding to the related accounting information in another location

in the trial balance, i.e. £17 400 − £1800 = £15 600. You should enter this figure as an expense in the income statement (A).

b In the statement of financial position, show the amount of the prepayment in the current assets section directly under the trade receivables, i.e. prepaid expenses £1800 (B).

2 Other payables (amounts owing)

In the financial statements

a If a trial balance is provided in a question, you must add the amount of the other payables to the appropriate expense account. Put this figure in the income statement. In the worked example, note (2) states wages and salaries owed £2100 and office expenses owing £200. You should add these figures as follows:

Wages and salaries	£89 000 + £2100 = £91 100
General office expenses	£4500 + £200 = £4700

The amounts to be charged as expenses to the income statement are: wages and salaries £91 100 (C) and general office expenses £4700 (D).

b In the statement of financial position, show the amount of the other payables in the current liabilities section directly under the trade payables, i.e. expenses owing £2100 + £200 = £2300 (E).

3 Discounts allowed and received

Discounts allowed

Charge discounts allowed as an expense in the income statement. In the worked example, the discount allowed, £14 400, is charged as an expense (F).

Discounts received

Add discounts received as income in the income statement directly underneath the gross profit figure. In the worked example, the discount received of £9300 has been added as income (G).

4 Depreciation

Straight line method

Figure 15.1, note (5), states that depreciation on office equipment should be provided for at 20% per annum, using the straight line method.

a Find the cost price of the office equipment   £20 000
b Find the percentage given   20%
c Calculate 20% of £20 000   = £4000
d Charge £4000 as an expense in the income statement (H).
e In the statement of financial position, deduct depreciation £4000 from this year, plus depreciation deducted in previous years £8000* = £12 000 from the cost price of the asset, to give you the carrying value of the asset £20 000 − £12 000 = £8000. Enter these figures in the appropriate columns in the statement of financial position (I). (*See trial balance credit side.)

Reducing balance method

Figure 15.1, note (6), states that depreciation on delivery vans should be provided for at 20% per annum, using the reducing balance method.

a Find the cost price of the delivery vans   £27 000
b Find the total amount of depreciation to date
   (refer to trial balance credit side)   £5400
c Find the difference (£27 000 − £5400)   £21 600
d Find the percentage given   20%
e Calculate 20% of £21 600   = £4320

f Charge £4320 as an expense in the income statement (J).

g In the statement of financial position, deduct depreciation £4320 from this year, plus depreciation deducted in previous years £5400* = £9720 from the cost price of the asset to give you the carrying value of the asset £27000 – £9720 = £17280. Enter these figures in the appropriate columns in the statement of financial position (K). (*See trial balance credit side.)

5 **Allowance for irrecoverable debts**

Creating an allowance

a If you have to create an allowance for the first time, refer to the question for details of the amount to be set aside. Let's assume that, in the worked example, an allowance was created in 2016 amounting to £6600.

b The allowance for irrecoverable debts £6600 would have been charged to the income statement as an expense in 2016.

c In the statement of financial position, the allowance for irrecoverable debts £6600 would have been deducted from the trade receivables. The trade receivables can be found under the heading current assets.

Increasing the allowance

a Refer to the question to find the new allowance. In our example the new allowance for this year is £8100 (see note (4) in **Figure 15.1**).

b Find last year's allowance. In this example, the figure is £6600 (this figure can be found in the trial balance, credit side).

c Charge the difference between the new and old allowance, £8100 – £6600 = £1500 to the income statement (L).

d In the statement of financial position, deduct the new allowance £8100 from the trade receivables (M).

Reducing the allowance

a Refer to the question to find the new allowance. Using our worked example, assume that in 2018 it was decided to reduce the allowance to £5000.

b Find the old allowance. In the worked example, this would be £8100.

c Take the difference between the old and new allowance, £8100 – £5000 = £3100 and add this amount as income to the income statement.

d Deduct the new allowance for irrecoverable debts (£5000) from the trade receivables in the statement of financial position.

6 **Irrecoverable debts**

Write irrecoverable debts off as an expense in the income statement. In this example, irrecoverable debts written off are £400. This is shown as an expense in the income statement (N).

END OF CHAPTER QUESTIONS

1 A business's financial year ends on 30 September. On 1 July 2016, $200 was paid for insurance for six months to 31 December.

What is the correct entry in the statement of financial position on 30 September 2016?

a other payable of $100

b other receivable of $100

c other payable of $200

d other receivable of $200

2 The following information is extracted from the rent account of a business.

	Rials
owing at 1 January 2016	400
rent paid in year ended 31 December 2016	1700
rent paid in advance at 31 December 2016	250

How much rent was payable for the year ended 31 December 2016?

a Rials1050

b Rials1550

c Rials1850

d Rials 2350

3 Business rates paid in advance are treated as other receivables for the following accounting period.

Which accounting principle is being followed?

a consistency

b accruals

c money measurement

d realisation

4 A trader owes the following amounts for electricity.

1 January HK$2000

31 December HK$2500

The charge for electricity shown in the income statement for the year ended 31 December was HK$15 500.

What was the amount paid for electricity during the year?

a HK$15 000

b HK$15 500

c HK$16 000

d HK$20 000

5 In his income statement, Xi incorrectly included insurance paid in advance of RMB3500 as insurance outstanding.

How will this affect Xi's profit for the year?

a overstated by RMB3500

b overstated by RMB7000

c understated by RMB3500

d understated by RMB7000

6 A business made no adjustment for insurance paid in advance at the end of the financial year.

What is the effect of this?

a current liabilities are overstated

b current liabilities are understated

c profit for the year is overstated

d profit for the year is understated

7 Why should all expenses owing be shown in a business's financial statements?

a so the correct total of current assets is shown in the statement of financial position

b so the income of a period is matched against the costs of that period

c to show how much customers owe the business

d to show the amount owed to trade suppliers.

8 Susan receives a cheque from a tenant on 10 December 2016. This is rent due to the business for the period 1 January to 31 March 2017.

How is this treated in Susan's financial statements for the year ended 31 December 2016?

a expenses owing
b income owing
c expenses paid in advance
d income paid in advance

9 A trader rents a shop. On 1 January 2017, his rent payable account had a credit balance of LKR6000. During 2017, he paid LKR40 000 rent. At 31 December 2017, he owed LKR4000 rent.

What was the rent payable for the year 2017?

a LKR36 000
b LKR38 000
c LKR42 000
d LKR44 000

10 Khalid's financial year ends on 30 September. On 1 July 2016, $2000 was paid for insurance for six months to 31 December 2016.

What will be recorded in Khalid's statement of financial position on 30 September 2016?

a an other receivable of $1000
b an other payable of $1000
c an other receivable of $2000
d an other payable of $2000

11 Zafar runs a transport business and has a fleet of motor vehicles.

Which is a liability to Zafar?

a depreciation of motor vehicles for the year
b motor vehicle expenses outstanding
c motor vehicle insurance paid in advance
d purchase of fuel for motor vehicles

12 John's financial year ends on 31 December.

In 2016, he paid $16 500 for advertising in the local newspaper. This was for 15 months to 31 March 2017.

What will be recorded in John's statement of financial position at 31 December 2016?

a an other payable of $3300
b an other payable of $13 200
c an other receivable of $3300
d an other receivable of $13 200

13 Zara's financial year ends on 31 December. She rents premises at an annual rent of $5000. On 1 January 2016, prepaid rent of $1000 appeared as a debit balance on the rent account. During 2016, rent of $8000 was paid.

What was the balance brought down on the rent account on 1 January 2017?

a $1000 debit
b $2000 credit
c $3000 credit
d $4000 debit

14 Explain the accruals concept.

15 Explain the term Other receivables, and give an example.

16 Where should other receivables and payables appear on the statement of financial position?

END OF CHAPTER CHECKLIST

- Accounts record when resources change hands, not when the money is paid for these resources.
- The accruals concept is concerned with the differences between the actual payment of cash and the legal requirement of paying cash.
- Expenses paid in advance are a current asset.
- Expenses owed or outstanding (other payables) are a current liability.
- Income paid in advance is a current liability.
- Income owed or outstanding (other receivables) is a current asset.

EXAM PRACTICE

A01 **A02** **A03** Answer ALL questions in this section.

1 A sole trader's electricity account for the year ended 31 March 2017 showed the following.

	$
1 April 2016 Balance brought down	(Cr) 3000
April 2016–March 2017 Bank – payments made during the year	18 000
On 31 March 2017 $4000 was owing by the trader for electricity	

Calculate the amount charged for electricity in the trader's income statement for the year ended 31 March 2017. Show your workings.

(3 marks)

2 Ruth is a trader. Her financial year ends on 31 March. She provides the following information.

	$
April 1 Insurance prepaid for 3 months to 30 June 2016	60
July 1 Paid insurance premium for 12 months to 30 June 2017 by cheque	264

Prepare the insurance account as it would appear in Ruth's ledger for the year ended 31 March 2016. Show clearly the amount transferred to the income statement. **(3 marks)**

3 The trial balance for Xanadu is shown below. Use it to prepare an income statement and statement of financial position for Xanadu.

	Dr	Cr
Bank	3840	
Cash	120	
Forklift truck: cost	20 000	
Forklift truck: depreciation to 31 May 2016		4500
Motor cars: cost	18 000	
Motor cars: depreciation to 31 May 2016		6000
Sales		375 000
Purchases	195 000	
Opening inventories at 1 June 2015	62 000	
Rent	20 000	
Revenue returns	420	
Electricity	8000	
Trade receivables	16 200	
Trade payables		14 600
Discount received		180
Wages and Salaries	37 000	
Allowance for irrecoverable debts		2640
Irrecoverable debts	520	
General office expenses	18 000	
Owner's drawings	18 500	
Capital 1st June 2015		14 680
	417 600	417 600

Notes:
1. Closing inventory is $50 000.
2. Electricity of $2000 is to be owed at the year-end.
3. Rent of $4000 has been prepaid at the year-end.
4. Depreciation on the forklift is calculated over 4 years on the straight line method, assuming a residual value of $2000.
5. Depreciation on cars is calculated at 40% on the reducing balance method.

(22 marks)
(Total 28 marks)

16 IRRECOVERABLE DEBTS

▲ Irrecoverable debts can lead to closure of a business.

LEARNING OBJECTIVES

- Explain why it is necessary to provide an allowance for irrecoverable debts
- Distinguish between an irrecoverable debt and an allowance for irrecoverable debts
- Calculate and record irrecoverable debts and allowance for irrecoverable debts in the books of accounts allowance

GETTING STARTED

Customers do not always pay their debts. Therefore, should a business require all customers to pay for their goods in cash in advance? If you only accept cash payments, some customers may refuse to do business with you, so you have to trust your customers. But what happens if a customer/receivable does not pay? How long do you give them to pay? These questions are asked by businesses all the time when they sell goods on credit.

SKILLS CREATIVITY

ACTIVITY

What would you do if a customer did not pay you? Write down what you think you might do and how it would affect the accounts of your business. In this chapter, we will look at what happens when your receivables do not pay their debts.

An irrecoverable debt occurs when a trade receivable is unable to pay the amount they owe. If we know a debt will not be paid, we cannot leave this in the accounts as it would go against the concept of prudence (see chapter 13). We would be overstating our trade receivables and overstating the assets of the business.

HINT

The prudence concept is about being cautious when estimating sales and costs.

16.1 IRRECOVERABLE DEBTS

If a business finds that it is impossible to collect a debt, then it should be written off as an irrecoverable debt. This may happen if the trade receivable is suffering a loss in his or her business, or if the owner has gone bankrupt and is therefore unable to pay the debt. An irrecoverable debt is an expense on the business that is owed the money. Here is an example of debts being written off.

Example 1: Riley Products sold goods costing £50 to C West on 5 January 2016. Unfortunately, West experienced financial difficulties and was unable to pay his debt. Goods were also sold to B Fenwick for £240 on 16 February 2016. Fenwick paid £200 on account on 17 May. He was unable to pay the outstanding £40.

When drawing up the financial statements to 31 December 2016, Riley Products decided to write these off as irrecoverable debts. The accounting entries are shown in **Figure 16.1**.

Dr			C West Account			Cr
2016		£		2016		£
Jan 5	Revenue	50		Dec 31	Irrecoverable debts	50

Dr			B Fenwick Account			Cr
2016		£		2016		£
Feb 16	Revenue	240		May 17	Cash	200
				Dec 31	Irrecoverable debts	40
		240				240

Dr			Irrecoverable Debts Account			Cr
2016		£		2016		£
Dec 31	B Fenwick	50		Dec 31	Income Statement a/c	90
Dec 31	C West	40				
		90				90

Income Statement for the year ended 31 December 2016 (extract)

	£
Gross Profit	xxx
Less Expenses:	
Irrecoverable debts	90 90

▲ Figure 16.1 The accounts of Riley Products

SKILLS ANALYSIS

CASE STUDY: SOURCE DOCUMENTS

Bhagya runs a building firm in Kandy. Her business is very successful and has expanded rapidly over the last few years. However, several customers have outstanding bills of over 12 months.

Bhagya has decided to write them off as irrecoverable debts.

Rashmi LKR876 000

Chatura LKR457 000

Gayan LKR987 000

Prepare the irrecoverable debts account for year ended 31 March 2017.

16.2 ALLOWANCE FOR IRRECOVERABLE DEBTS

In most cases, customers pay their bills. However, a business may suspect that some customers will not pay. If a business is likely to have some irrecoverable debts, the auditor may ask the business to have an allowance for these debts. An allowance is a just-in-case scenario and means the business will not overstate its profits or understate its losses. This follows the rules set out by the prudence concept. It is well known that the longer a debt is owing, the more likely it is to become an irrecoverable debt. Therefore, it is important for businesses to have an effective credit control system in place: this is the purpose of the allowance for irrecoverable debts.

A business can use its accounts to estimate the allowance for irrecoverable debts by:

- looking at each debt and estimating which ones will be irrecoverable debts
- estimating, on the basis of experience, what percentage of the debts will result in irrecoverable debts. For example, 5% of the outstanding trade receivables' figure could be estimated as irrecoverable.

Example 2: In 2014, Hanifa Begum opened a new business. She has trade receivables totaling $20 000. Hanifa estimates her allowance for irrecoverable debts to be 5%.

5% of $20 000 is $1000

In the income statement, this could be recorded in two places: added underneath gross profit if it has decreased from the previous year, or put in expenses if the allowance has increased.

In Hanifa's case, this is the first time the allowance has been calculated (because it is a new business), so it will be placed in expenses. Her gross profit will reduce by $1000, as shown in **Figure 16.2**.

		$
	Gross Profit	32 000
	Expenses	
Less	Increase in allowance for irrecoverable debts	1 000
	Profit for the year	31 000

▲ Figure 16.2 Extract income statement for Hanifa Begum for year ended 31/12/2014.

We will also need to adjust the statement of financial position, as shown in **Figure 16.3**.

		$
	Current Assets	
	Trade Receivables	20 000
Less	Allowance for irrecoverable debts	1 000
		19 000

▲ Figure 16.3 An extract from Hanifa's statement of financial position at 31/12/2014.

In 2015, Hanifa Begum has trade receivables totalling $30 000. This year she has estimated her allowance for irrecoverable debts to be 2%.

2% of $30 000 is $600.

EXAM HINT

In the exam, you will be expected to calculate the allowance for irrecoverable debts and then transfer this figure to the Income Statement and Statement of Financial Position. This is not as easy as it sounds because the allowance will change from one year to the next. In **Figures 16.2–16.6**, we look at the accounts of a business over a three-year period.

In the income statement, we have to calculate whether there has been an increase or decrease in the allowance. In this case, there has been a decrease of $400 ($1000 – $600). Hanifa overestimated her allowance last year, so her profit for the year will have been lower. In 2015, we can add the difference back to the gross profit, as shown in **Figure 16.4**.

		$
	Gross Profit	45 000
Add	Decrease in allowance for irrecoverable debts	400
	Profit for the year	45 400

▲ Figure 16.4 Extract income statement for Hanifa Begum for year ended 31/12/2015.

The statement of financial position will also need to be adjusted. This time we use the percentage figure that was calculated, as shown in **Figure 16.5**.

		$
	Current Assets	
	Trade Receivables	30 000
Less	Allowance for irrecoverable debts	600
		29 400

▲ Figure 16.4 Extract statement of financial position for Hanifa Begum for year ended 31/12/2015.

For the year 2016, Hanifa had trade receivables totalling $25 000 but wants to increase her allowance for irrecoverable debts to 5% again.

5% of $25 000 equals $1250.

Again, we need to compare this with the allowance for the year before (2015). The difference this year is an increase of $650. Extracts from the financial statements are shown in **Figures 16.5** and **16.6**.

		$
	Gross Profit	50 000
	Expenses	
Less	Increase in allowance for irrecoverable debts	650
	Profit for the year	49 350

▲ Figure 16.5 Extract income statement for Hanifa Begum for year ended 31/12/2016.

		$
	Current Assets	
	Trade Receivables	25 000
Less	Allowance for irrecoverable debts	1250
		23 750

▲ Figure 16.6 Extract statement of financial position for Hanifa Begum for year ended 31/12/2016.

> **HINT**
> Remember the increase or decrease in the allowance is recorded to the income statement, while the actual allowance is recorded to the statement of financial position.

SKILLS ANALYSIS

CASE STUDY: IRRECOVERABLE DEBTS

Michael owns a sports equipment business in Jakarta. He is concerned by the number of trade receivables who do not seem to be paying their debts, so he decided to open an allowance for irrecoverable debts.

For 2015, Michael decided to create an allowance for irrecoverable debts at 4% of trade receivables. His financial year end is on 31 July each year. Trade receivables at the end of July 2015 was $42 000. His gross profit for the year was $75 320.

- Prepare an allowance for irrecoverable debts account at 31 July 2015.
- Prepare an income statement extract for the year ended 31 July 2015 to show the corrected profit for the year.
- Prepare a statement of financial position at 31 July 2015 to show current assets.

At the financial year end 2016, Michael had trade receivables of $47 000. He has changed his allowance for irrecoverable debts to 5%.

- Prepare an allowance for irrecoverable debts account at 31 July 2016.
- Prepare an income statement extract for the year ended 31 July 2016 to show the corrected profit for the year.
- Prepare a statement of financial position at 31 July 2016 to show current assets.

END OF CHAPTER QUESTIONS

1 David owes KES1000 to Parvinder. He pays 90% of the debt. Parvinder writes off the remaining debt. What entry will Parvinder make to write off the irrecoverable debt?

	account to be debited KES	account to be credited KES
a	irrecoverable debts 100	David 100
b	David 100	irrecoverable debts 100
c	irrecoverable debts 900	David 900
d	David 900	irrecoverable debts 900

2 A trader sold goods to Ana on credit. Ana failed to pay the amount owing and this was written off as an irrecoverable debt.

Which entry will the trader make to write off the irrecoverable debt?

	account to be debited	account to be credited
a	Ana	irrecoverable debts
b	Ana	income statement
c	irrecoverable debts	Ana
d	revenue	Ana

3 Zafar owed Ali $500. Zafar was only able to pay Ali $200. Ali wrote the balance off as an irrecoverable debt.

Which entries record this in Ali's ledger?

	account to be debited $	account to be credited $
a	irrecoverable debts 500 Zafar 300	bank 200
b	bank 200 Zafar 300	irrecoverable debts 500
c	irrecoverable debts 300	Zafar 500 bank 200
d	Zafar 500	irrecoverable debts 300

4 A business has made a gross profit of £345218 and a profit for the year of £23987. Trade receivables amount to £45123 before irrecoverable debts of £752 have been written off. An allowance for irrecoverable debts of 5% is required.

Which is the correct entry for the allowance for irrecoverable debt?

a £2256.16

b £2218.55

c £1199.35

d £2293.75

5 Ken Lune has an allowance for irrecoverable debts at 7% of receivables. Last year's allowance was HK$3280. His receivables this year are HK$35000.

What impact on the profit for last year would this year's allowance make?

a Increase by HK$2450

b Increase by HK$830

c Decrease by HK$830

d Decrease by HK$2450

6 Define the term receivables.

7 In which ledger would you find the irrecoverable debts account?

8 Which accounting concept is met by the use of an allowance for irrecoverable debt?

9 In which ledger would you find the allowance for irrecoverable debts account?

10 Why would a business use an allowance for irrecoverable debts?

END OF CHAPTER CHECKLIST

- Trade receivables who will definitely not pay their debts are written off and recorded in the income statement under expenses.
- A debt that has been written off and then recovered will be credited to the income statement and added under gross profit.
- An allowance for irrecoverable debts is used just in case the credit customer/receivable is unable to pay.
- An allowance for irrecoverable debts can change each year depending on the likelihood of credit customers paying their debts.
- If there is an increase in the allowance for irrecoverable debts (i.e. if the business expects more credit customers will not pay their debts), this is debited to the income statement and included in expenses.
- If there is a decrease in the allowance for irrecoverable debts (as we expect fewer credit customers will not pay their debts), this is credited to the income statement and added under gross profit.

EXAM PRACTICE

A01 **A02** **A03** Answer ALL questions in this section.

1 Emma Ball has trade receivables totalling $38 000. She wishes to make an allowance for irrecoverable debts of 4%.

   a Calculate the allowance for irrecoverable debts.

   b Prepare a Statement of Financial Position to show how the allowance is treated. **(8 marks)**

2 Judith Curtis has a financial year-end on 31 January 2017. She provides the following information:

   Trade Receivables 31 January 2015   £14 200
   Trade Receivables 31 January 2016   £18 000
   Trade Receivables 31 January 2017   £19 000

   - £1200 is to be written off as an irrecoverable debt in the year ended 31 January 2015
   - £400 is to be written off as an irrecoverable debt in the year ended 31 January 2017

   Prepare for each year:

   a An irrecoverable debt account

   b An allowance for irrecoverable debt account

   c An extract for the Statement of Financial Position **(12 marks)**

3 The Little Teapot maintains a trade receivables ledger control account and an allowance for irrecoverable debts account. On 1 April 2017 the balances were:

   Trade receivables ledger control account €42 640

   Allowance for irrecoverable debts account €2132

   a Calculate the percentage rate used for the allowance for irrecoverable debts.

   b On 31 March 2018, the balance on the allowance for irrecoverable debts had increased to €2560. Suggest one reason for the increase.

   c Prepare the journal entry to record the change in the allowance for irrecoverable debts. Present your answer as a narrative account.

   (12 marks)
   (Total 32 marks)

17 INCOMPLETE RECORDS

LEARNING OBJECTIVES

- Calculate the profit for the year by comparing the open and closing equity figures
- Calculate revenue and purchases using appropriate accounting techniques, to include control accounts
- Prepare income statements and statements of financial position from incomplete records and information

▲ Business owners do not always record every transaction. This results in incomplete accounting records.

GETTING STARTED

In this chapter, we will learn about what happens when a business does not keep a full set of accounting records. Many small businesses will not keep a full set of ledgers as most of their transactions will be for cash. The main book used to record transactions will be the cash book. Any missing information can be found in bank statements. These businesses do not need to open ledgers as they have no credit customers.

SKILLS CRITICAL THINKING

ACTIVITY

Name three businesses that use cash for most of their transactions. Why do they mainly use cash? How might this affect the reliability of their financial statements?

17.1 PREPARING FINANCIAL STATEMENTS FROM INCOMPLETE RECORDS

A business may not keep full accounting records, but it is still necessary to prepare financial statements at the end of the business's financial year. The method used to prepare the accounts in these circumstances is to compare the capital or equity at the beginning and end of the accounting period.

Capital or equity in the business can only increase if the owner provides additional funds or if the business makes a profit.

Example 1: A business has capital or equity at the end of 2015 of £20 000. During 2016, no drawings or extra cash were brought in by the owner. At the end of 2016, the capital or equity is £30 000. The profits of the business for the year are:

                    this year's capital   last year's capital
profit for the year = £30 000   −   £20 000   =   £10 000

If the drawings were £7000, the profits must have been £17 000:

last year's capital + profits − drawings = this year's capital
£20 000 + ? − £7000 = £30 000

A profit of £17 000 completes the formula. This is worked out by normal arithmetical deduction:

£20 000 + £17 000 − £7000 = £30 000

If, during the second year of trading, the owner contributes additional capital or equity, the calculation is:

last year's capital + capital introduced + profits − drawings = closing capital

Example 2: Figure 17.1 shows the calculation of profit when there is not enough information to draft an income statement. There is only information about assets and liabilities.

H Ahmad has not kept proper bookkeeping records. She does, however, have notes of the transactions of her business in diary form. Here are the details of her assets and liabilities as at 31 December 2015 and at 31 December 2016:

			€
At 31 December 2015	Assets:	Motor van	10 000
		Fixtures	7000
		Inventory	8500
		Trade receivables	9500
		Bank	11 100
		Cash	100
	Liabilities:	Trade payables	8000
		Loan from J Singh	6000
At 31 December 2016	Assets:	Motor van (after depreciation)	8000
		Fixtures (after depreciation)	6300
		Inventory	9900
		Trade receivables	11 240
		Bank	11 700
		Cash	200
	Liabilities:	Trade payables	8700
		Loan from J Singh	4000
	Drawings are €9000		

▲ Figure 17.1 H Ahmad's assets and liabilities in 2015 and 2016.

First, we need to draw up a **statement of affairs** as at 31 December 2015 (**Figure 17.2**). This would be called a statement of financial position if it was drawn up from a set of records. The capital or equity is the difference between the assets and liabilities.

EXAM HINT

We can summarise this as:
- *closing* capital
- *minus* opening capital
- *equals* retained profit
- *add* drawings
- *minus* capital introduced
- *equals* profit for the year

HINT

Remember the accounting equations: assets *minus* liabilities *equals* capital.

SUBJECT VOCABULARY

statement of affairs a document showing a company's assets and liabilities at a certain date, usually prepared when a company is about to go bankrupt

H Ahmad		
Statement of Affairs as at 31 December 2015		
Assets		
Non-current Assets	€	€
Motor van		10 000
Fixtures		7 000
		17 000
Current assets		
Inventory	8 500	
Trade receivables	9 500	
Bank	11 100	
Cash in hand	100	29 200
Net Assets (NCA + CA)		46 200
Capital and Liabilities		
Capital (Difference)		32 200
Liabilities		
Non-current Liabilities		
Loan from J Singh		6 000
Current Liabilities		
Trade Payables		8 000
Total Capital and Liabilities		46 200

▲ Figure 17.2 H Ahmad's statement of affairs as at 31 December 2015.

H Ahmad's statement of affairs at the end of 2016 is shown in **Figure 17.3**.

H Ahmad			
Statement of Affairs as at 31 December 2016			
Assets			
Non-current Assets		€	€
Motor van			8 000
Fixtures			6 300
			14 300
Current assets			
Inventory		9 900	
Trade receivables		11 240	
Bank		11 700	
Cash in hand		200	33 040
Net Assets (NCA + CA)			47 340
Capital and Liabilities			
Capital			
Opening Capital			32 200
Add Profit for the year	C		?
	B		?
Less Drawings	A		9 000
Liabilities			?
Non-current Liabilities			
Loan from J Singh			4 000
Current Liabilities			
Trade Payables			8 700
Total Capital and Liabilities			?

▲ Figure 17.3 H Ahmad's statement of affairs as at 31 December 2016.

The following formula can be used to calculate the figure of profit:

opening equity + profit for the year − drawings = closing equity

You can then find the missing figures in **Figure 17.3** − (A), (B) and (C) − by deduction:

(A) is the figure we need to make the statement of affairs totals equal, i.e. €34 640

(B) is therefore €34 640 + €9 000 = €43 640

(C) is therefore €43 640 − €32 200 = €11 440

To check:

			€
Equity			32 200
Add Profit for the year	(C)		11 440
	(B)		43 640
Less Drawings			9 000
	(A)		34 640

Obviously, this method of calculating profit is not very satisfactory. A full statement of profit or loss, is much more informative. For this reason, you should try to avoid the 'comparison of equity' method of ascertaining profit whenever possible. Instead, always draw up financial statements from the available bookkeeping records, where possible.

CASE STUDY: INCOMPLETE RECORDS

Jonno is a mobile hairdresser in Hong Kong. He visits customers regularly. He has provided the following information:

	01-Feb-16	31-Jan-17
	HK$	HK$
Vehicle	25 000	25 000
Equipment	4 000	3 500
Inventory	800	1 100
Trade Receivables	2 500	2 100
Trade Payables	1 000	700
Bank	300	250

During the year ended 31 January 2017, Jonno made drawings of HK$18 000.

Calculate the business profit or loss for the year ended 31 January 2017.

17.2 STEP-BY-STEP GUIDE: INCOMPLETE RECORDS

A formal approach should be followed when preparing financial statements from incomplete records. The following 'step-by-step guide', together with the example of M Cole, shows the stages involved in preparing the financial statements.

M Cole requires his financial statements to be drawn up for the year ended 31 December 2016. He has not kept full accounting records. He has, however, provided the following information:

a) The revenue is mostly on a credit basis. No record of revenue has been kept, but £100 000 has been received from persons he sold goods to. £95 000 was by cheque, and £5000 was by cash.
b) He paid suppliers £72 000 by cheque during the year.
c) He paid the following expenses during the year: by cheque, rent £2000 and general expenses £1800; by cash, rent £500.
d) He took £100 cash per week (for 52 weeks) as drawings.
e) Other information is available:

	At 31.12.2015 £	At 31.12.2016 £
Trade receivables	11 000	13 200
Trade payables for goods	4000	6500
Rent owing	–	500
Bank balance	11 300	30 500
Cash balance	800	100
Inventory	15 900	17 000

f) The only non-current asset consists of fixtures that were valued at 31 December 2015 at £8000. These are to be depreciated at 10% per annum.

▲ Figure 17.4 Financial information for M Cole.

HINT

Follow the step-by-step guide when tackling an exam question involving incomplete records.

STEP-BY-STEP GUIDE

HINT

When preparing the cash and bank summary, remember to include the opening and closing balances of cash and bank, if they are given in the question.

STEP 1

Draw up a statement of affairs. Take into account all the opening figures on the closing day of the last accounting period. M Cole's statement of affairs is shown in **Figure 17.5**.

M Cole
Statement of Affairs as at 31 December 2015

	£	£
Assets		
Non-current Assets		
Fixtures		8000
Current Assets		
Inventories	15 900	
Trade receivables	11 000	
Bank	11 300	
Cash in hand	800	39 000
Net Assets (NCA + CA)		47 000
Capital and Liabilities		
Capital (Difference)		43 000
Liabilities		
Non-current Liabilities		
Current Liabilities		
Trade Payables		4000
Total Capital and Liabilities		47 000

▲ Figure 17.5 M Cole's statement of affairs.

17 INCOMPLETE RECORDS

STEP 2

Draw up a cash and bank summary. It should show the totals of each separate item plus opening and closing balances, as shown in **Figure 17.6**.

Dr	Cash	Bank		Cash	Bank	Cr
	£	£		£	£	
Balances 31.12.2015	800	11 300	Suppliers		72 000	
Receipts from trade receivables	5000	95 000	Rent	500	2000	
			General expenses		1800	
			Drawings	5200		
			Balances 31.12.2016	100	30 500	
	5800	106 300		5800	106 300	

▲ Figure 17.6 A cash and bank summary for M Cole.

STEP 3

Calculate the figures for purchases and revenue to be shown in the trading account. Remember that the figures you need for this are the same as those for keeping double entry records.

Purchases

In double entry, purchases means goods that have been bought in the period. It does not matter if they have not been paid for during the period. The figure of payments to suppliers must therefore be adjusted to calculate the figure for purchases. In our example, this is shown in **Figure 17.7**.

	£
Paid during the year	72 000
Less Payments made for goods which were purchased in a previous year (trade payables 31.12.2015)	4000
	68 000
Add Purchases in this year where payment has not yet been made (trade payables 31.12.2016)	6500
Goods bought in this year, i.e. purchases	74 500

▲ Figure 17.7 Calculation of purchases.

The same answer is obtained if the information is shown in the form of a total trade payables account. The figure for purchases is the amount required to make the account totals agree (marked with an asterisk* in **Figure 17.8**).

Dr	Total Trade Payables' Account			Cr
	£			£
Cash paid to suppliers	72 000	Balances b/f		4000
Balances c/d	6500	*Purchases (missing figure)		74 500
	78 500			78 500

▲ Figure 17.8 Total trade payables' account.

Discounts received and purchase returns

- **Discounts received.** The total discount a business receives when paying its trade payables must be entered in the total trade payables' account on the debit side. This therefore affects the balancing figure of purchases.
- **Purchase returns.** The total of purchase returns for the period must be included on the debit side of the total trade payables account. This, again, will affect the balancing figure of purchases.

These items are covered fully in Chapter 6.

Revenue

The revenue figure only equals receipts when all the revenue is for cash. Therefore, the receipt figures must be adjusted to find revenue. This can be done as shown in **Figure 17.9**.

	£
Amount received during the year:	
Bank	95 000
Cash	5 000
	100 000
Less Receipts for goods sold in a previous year	
(trade receivables 31.12.2015)	11 000
	89 000
Add Revenue made this year but payment not yet received	
(trade receivables 31.12.2016)	13 200
Goods sold this year, i.e. revenue	102 200

▲ Figure 17.9 Calculation of revenue.

The same answer is obtained if the information is shown in a total trade receivables account. The figure for revenue is the amount required to make the account totals agree (marked with an asterisk* in **Figure 17.10**).

Dr	Total Trade receivables Account		Cr
	£		£
Balances b/f	11 000	Receipts: Cash	5 000
		Cheque	95 000
*Revenue (missing figure)	102 200	Balances c/d	13 200
	113 200		113 200

▲ Figure 17.10 Total trade receivables account.

Irrecoverable debts, discounts allowed and revenue returns

- **Irrecoverable debts.** If a debt is written off as bad during the year, this figure is included in the total trade receivables account on the credit side. It therefore affects the balancing figure of revenue.
- **Discounts allowed.** The total of any discounts given to a business's customers (trade receivables) must be included in the total trade receivables account. The total discount allowed is entered on the credit side and, therefore, affects the balancing figure of revenue.
- **Revenue returns.** If there are any revenue returns, the total for the period is entered on the credit side in the total trade receivables account.

These items are covered fully in Chapter 6.

17 INCOMPLETE RECORDS

STEP 4

If there are no other payables or other receivables, either at the beginning or at the end of the accounting period, then expenses paid are equal to the expenses used up during the period. These figures are charged to the income statement.

If other receivables or other payables exist, an expense account is drawn up for these items. After we have entered all known items, the missing figure is the expenses to be charged for the accounting period. In this example, only the rent account needs to be drawn up, as shown in **Figure 17.11**.

Dr	Rent Account		Cr
	£		£
Cheques	2000	*Rent (missing figure)	3000
Cash	500		
Accrued c/d	500		
	3000		3000

▲ Figure 17.11 M Cole's rent account.

Alternatively, rent for the year can be found using the following calculation:

Other receivables – Rent	
	£
Paid: Bank	2000
Cash	500
	2500
Add: Owing 31.12.16	500
Rent for the year	3000

STEP 5

Check to see if any depreciation needs to be charged to the income statement. Note (f) in **Figure 17.4** states that the fixtures are valued at £8000, and should be depreciated at 10% per annum. Therefore, the depreciation charge for the year is 10% of £8000 = £800. This amount is charged to the income statement. Remember to deduct the depreciation from the fixtures in the statement of financial position to calculate the carrying value of the asset. This is £8000 – £800 = £7200.

Figures 17.12 and **17.13** show the financial statements using all the information given and the figures you have calculated in steps 1–5.

M Cole		
Income Statement for the year ended 31 December 2016		
	£	£
Revenue (Step 3)		102 200
Less Cost of sales		
Inventory at 1.1.2016	15 900	
Add Purchases (Step 3)	74 500	
	90 400	
Less Inventory at 31.12.2016	17 000	
Gross profit		28 800
Less Expenses		
Rent (Step 4)	3000	
General expenses	1800	
Depreciation: Fixtures	800	5600
Profit for the year		23 200

▲ Figure 17.12 M Cole's income statement for the year ended 31 December 2016.

Statement of financial position at 31 December 2016

	£ Cost	£ Dep	£ Carrying Value
Assets			
Non-current Assets			
Fixtures (Step 5)	8000	800	7200
Current Assets			
Inventories		17000	
Trade receivables		13200	
Bank (Step 2)		30500	
Cash in hand (Step 2)		800	60800
Net Assets (NCA + CA)			60800
Capital and Liabilities			
Capital			
Opening Capital		43000	
Add Profit for the year		23200	
		66200	
Less Drawings		5200	
Closing Capital			61000
Liabilities			
Non-current Liabilities			
Current Liabilities			
Trade Payables		6500	
Other payables		500	7000
Total Capital and Liabilities			68000

▲ Figure 17.13 M Cole's statement of financial position as at 31 December 2016.

17.3 INCOMPLETE RECORDS AND MISSING FIGURES

In practice, you will often find that some of the information relating to cash receipts or payments is missing. If the missing information relates to type of payment only, it is normal to assume that the missing figure is the amount required to make both totals agree in the cash column of the cash and bank summary. If the missing information relates to bank items, however, you would obtain another copy of the bank statement from the bank so you have all the information you need.

Example 3: Figure 17.14 shows a cash and bank summary where the drawings figure is unknown.

You have been given following information about these accounts.

UNIT 4   17 INCOMPLETE RECORDS

Dr	Cash	Bank		Cash	Bank	Cr
	£	£		£	£	
Balances 1.1.2016	35	1200	Bankings C	5500		
Received from trade receivables	7250	800	Suppliers	320	4930	
Bankings C		5500	Expenses	150	900	
			*Drawings	?		
			Balances 31.12.2016	50	1670	
	7285	7500		7285	7500	
Balances at 31.12.2016	50	1670				

▲ **Figure 17.14** A cash and bank summary where the drawings figure is unknown.

	Cash	Bank
	£	£
Cash paid into the bank during the year	5500	
Receipts from trade receivables	7250	800
Paid to suppliers	320	4930
Drawings during the year	?	–
Expenses paid	150	900
Balances at 1.1.2016	35	1200
Balances at 31.12.2016	50	1670

▲ **Figure 17.15** Additional information about the business's cash and bank receipts and payments.

The amount needed to make the two sides of the cash column agree is £1265. This is taken as the figure of drawings.

Example 4: Figure 17.16 shows a cash and bank summary with missing receipts from trade receivables.

You have been given the following additional information about the business's accounts.

Dr	Cash	Bank		Cash	Bank	Cr
	£	£		£	£	
Balances 1.1.2016	40	1560	Suppliers		5800	
Received from trade receivables	*?	6080	Expenses	640	230	
Withdrawn from Bank C	920		Withdrawn from Bank C		920	
			Drawings	1180	315	
			Balances 31.12.2016	70	375	
	1890	7640		1890	7640	

▲ **Figure 17.16** A cash and bank summary with missing receipts from trade receivables.

	Cash £	Bank £
Receipts from trade receivables	?	6080
Cash withdrawn from the bank for business use (this is the amount that is used besides cash receipts from trade receivables to pay drawings and expenses)		920
Paid to suppliers		5800
Expenses paid	640	230
Drawings	1180	315
Balances at 1.1.2016	40	1560
Balances at 31.12.2016	70	375

▲ Figure 17.17 Additional information about the business's cash and bank transactions.

The amount needed to make the two sides of the cash column agree is £930. This is the value of the receipts from trade receivables.

It is important to note that balancing figures is only acceptable when all the other figures have been verified. For example, if a cash expense is omitted when calculating cash received from trade receivables, this will cause an understatement of expenses and also, ultimately, of revenue.

THE T ACCOUNT METHOD

Example 5: Hazeem does not keep a full set of accounting records, but he has provided following information:

Summarised bank account			
Balance b/d	18000	Cash to payables	32000
Cash from receivables	48000	General Expenses	7000
		Balance c/d	27000
	66000		66000

	1 March 2016	28 February 2017
Trade Receivables	750	930
Trade Payables	1000	800
Inventory	800	400

▲ Figure 17.18 Information about Hazeem's accounts.

You have been asked to prepare the accounts to calculate gross profit.

To calculate gross profit, you need an income statement. Before you can prepare the income statement, you need to decide what figures may be missing – in this case, sales revenue and credit purchases. You need to set up control accounts for trade receivables and trade payables.

> **HINT**
>
> Although these are just workings, they can be worth marks, so make them as neat and as clear as possible.

Trade Receivables			
Balance b/d	750	Cash received	48000
(A) Sales Revenue	?	Balance c/d	930
	48930		48930
Balance b/d	930		

▲ Figure 17.19 A trade receivables control account for Hazeem.

UNIT 4
17 INCOMPLETE RECORDS
201

NOTE

In an exam, you may be asked to use a full control account to find sales revenue. In this case, you may need to include discount allowed, irrecoverable debts and contra items

HINT

Always bring your balance b/d at the end as it may be worth a mark in the exam.

The sales revenue figure is 48 180 (the missing figure in **Figure 17.19**).

Trade Payables			
Payments to receivables	32 000	Balance b/d	1 000
Balance c/d	800	(B) Credit Purchases	?
	32 800		32 800
		Balance b/d	800

▲ Figure 17.20 A trade payables control account for Hazeem.

The credit purchases figure is 31 800 (the missing figure in **Figure 17.20**).

Now you can draw up an income statement for Hazeem, as shown in **Figure 17.21**.

Sales Revenue		48 180
Cost of Sales		
Opening Inventory	800	
Credit Purchases	31 800	
	32 600	
Closing Inventory	400	
Cost of Sales		32 200
Gross Profit		15 980

▲ Figure 17.21 Hazeem's income statement for the year ended 28 February 2017.

SKILLS ANALYSIS

CASE STUDY: INCOMPLETE RECORDS

Izmela does not keep a full set of accounting records, but she has provided the following information:

Summarised bank account			
Balance b/d	25 000	Payments to payables	18 000
Cash from receivables	32 000	Balance c/d	39 000
	57 000		57 000
Balance b/d	39 000		

	1 April 2016	31 March 2017
Trade Receivables	1500	1100
Trade Payables	2200	1300
Inventory	1200	1600

Prepare Izmela's accounts to calculate gross profit.

USING THE T ACCOUNT METHOD TO CALCULATE EXPENSES

You can use the T account method to work out expenses, in just the same way as you worked out revenue and purchases in Example 5. However, you need to be careful with the opening and closing balances as they may be accrued or prepaid. **Figure 17.22** shows an example template.

HINT

Use the acronym PAPA to help, as follows.
PAPA refers to the Balance b/d and c/d when working out the missing figures. If you look at the 'Any Expense' T account you can see:
Prepaid Balance b/d and/or Accrued Balance b/d
then:
Accrued Balance c/d and /or Prepaid Balance c/d
Therefore, if you go in a clockwise manner, you get PAPA.

Any Expense	
Prepaid Balance b/d	Accrued Balance b/d
Cash Paid	income statement
Accrued Balance c/d	Prepaid Balance c/d

▲ **Figure 17.22** Example template to use when calculating expenses.

WORKED EXAMPLE

Azam Kahn does not keep a full set of accounting records but he has provided the following information for the year ended 30 April 2017.

Amounts paid in wages:	17 000	
Amounts paid in rent:	35 000	
	1 May 2016	30 April 2017
Wages paid in advance	850	1020
Rent owed	600	2000

▲ **Figure 17.23** Information about Azam Kahn's accounts.

Set up **T accounts** for wages and rent, but be careful with the opening and closing balances.

Wages			
Prepaid Balance b/d	850	Income Statement	16 830
Cash Paid	17 000	Prepaid Balance c/d	1 020
	17 850		17 850
Balance b/d	1 020		

Rent			
Cash Paid	35 000	Accrued Balance b/d	600
Accrued Balance c/d	2 000	Income Statement	36 400
	37 000		37 000
		Balance b/d	2 000

▲ **Figure 17.24** T accounts for wages and rent for Azam Kahn.

UNIT 4　　17 INCOMPLETE RECORDS　　203

SKILLS ANALYSIS

CASE STUDY: CALCULATING PROFITS

Ronaldo owns a take-away business in Macau. He does not keep a full set of accounting records but he is able to provide the following information for the year ended 30 April 2017.

Amounts paid in motor expenses:	12 500	
Amounts paid for advertising:	17 230	
Amount paid for rent	16 330	
	1 May 2016	30 April 2017
Motor Expenses paid in advance	900	1410
Advertising owed	350	217
Rent owed	2000	
Rent paid in advance		1120
Other information:		
Gross Profit for the year: 97 000		

Calculate Ronaldo's profit for the year ended 30 April 2017.

END OF CHAPTER QUESTIONS

1. Why do sole traders not have to keep a full set of accounting records?
2. What is a statement of affairs?
3. What do you get if you subtract total liabilities from total assets?
4. How do you calculate gross profit?
5. How do you calculate profit for the year?

END OF CHAPTER CHECKLIST

- Remember to complete the statement of affairs, calculate missing figures and the prepare the financial statements.
- Use T accounts or calculations to work out any missing figures. Choose the method that you prefer.
- If using Expense T accounts, remember to use PAPA if opening or closing balances are prepaid or accrued.
- Always show your workings clearly so you do not lose marks.

EXAM PRACTICE

A01 A02 A03 Answer ALL questions in this section. Questions 1–8 must be answered with a cross in the box ☒. If you change your mind about an answer, put a line through the box ☒ and then mark your new answer with a cross ☒.

1 A trader does not keep proper accounting records. Her capital at the end of the financial year is higher than at the start. She has not introduced any further capital during the year.

What does this show?

☐ A a net loss has been made during the year

☐ B annual drawings are greater than the profit for the year

☐ C assets less liabilities have reduced during the year

☐ D profit for the year is greater than annual drawings **(1 mark)**

2 The following figures are extracted from Xi's statement of financial position.

	$
non-current assets	60 000
current assets	20 000
current liabilities	15 000
profit for the year	12 000

What is Xi's opening capital?

☐ A $37 000
☐ B $53 000
☐ C $65 000
☐ D $77 000 **(1 mark)**

3 A trader does not keep complete accounting records but provides the following information at the end of her first year of trading.

	$
cheques received from customers	628
cash received from customers	149
amount owed by customers at the end of the year	73
discounts allowed	25

What is the revenue for the year?

☐ A $726   ☐ B $825
☐ C $850   ☐ D $875 **(1 mark)**

4 A business provides the following information.

	€
capital 1 January 2016	60 000
drawings during the year	40 000
capital introduced during the year	10 000
capital 31 December 2016	80 000

What is the profit for the year?

☐ A €10 000
☐ B €20 000
☐ C €50 000
☐ D €70 000 **(1 mark)**

5 A business has not kept full accounting records.

Which formula is used to calculate the sales revenue?

☐ A amounts received + closing receivables + discounts allowed − opening receivables

☐ B closing receivables − amounts received + opening receivables + discounts allowed

☐ C amounts received + closing receivables − opening receivables

☐ D closing receivables − amounts received + opening receivables **(1 mark)**

6 A business provides the following information.

	at 1 April 2016	at 31 March 2017
trade payables	8000	10 000

Payments to payables in the year ended 31 March 2017 were $70 000.

What were the credit purchases for the year ended 31 March 2017?

☐ A $60 000
☐ B $62 000
☐ C $6000
☐ D $72 000 **(1 mark)**

7 A sole trader's accounts showed the following details at the year end.

Closing capital was S$20 000 after drawings of S$5000, profit for the year was S$8000, and capital introduced during the year was S$3000.

What was the trader's opening capital?

☐ A S$10 000
☐ B S$14 000
☐ C S$30 000
☐ D S$31 000 **(1 mark)**

8 How can credit purchases be calculated?

☐ A closing payables + payments to payables − opening payables
☐ B closing payables + payments to payables + opening payables
☐ C closing payables − payments to payables − opening payables
☐ D closing payables − payments to payables + opening payables **(1 mark)**

9 Peter Mpho started business on 1 February 2016. He prepared his trading and income statement for his first year of trading. The following balances remained on his books at 31 January 2017:

	$
Capital	145 000
Inventory	17 500
Trade receivables	19 200
Trade payables	29 000
Premises at cost	90 000
Equipment at cost	50 000
Bank	300 debit
Petty cash	100
Drawings	10 400
Profit for the year	13 500

The following matters were then discovered:

- No adjustment had been made for wages owing at 31 January 2017 amounting to $200.
- During the year Peter Mpho had taken goods costing $600 for his own use. This transaction had not been recorded in the accounting records. This does not affect the closing inventory on 31 January 2017.
- Equipment should have been revalued on 31 January 2017. The estimated value at that date was $47 000.
- The bank statement received on 31 January showed that the bank had debited the business's bank account with charges of $1050. This had not been recorded in the accounting records.
- The cost of delivering goods to a customer, $150, was debited to the carriage outwards account. The customer had agreed to pay the delivery cost and this amount should have been debited to his account.

Prepare a statement of financial position for Peter Mpho at 31 January 2017 taking the above matters into account. **(20 marks)**

(Total 28 marks)

18 THE CALCULATION AND INTERPRETATION OF ACCOUNTING RATIOS

▲ It is important to understand the difference between profitability and liquidity.

LEARNING OBJECTIVES

- Explain the difference between profitability and liquidity
- Calculate and interpret the following profitability ratios:
  - gross profit percentage
  - profit for the year as a percentage of revenue
  - return on capital employed
- Calculate and interpret the following liquidity ratios:
  - current ratio (working capital ratio)
  - liquid ratio (acid test ratio)

GETTING STARTED

In this chapter, we will examine different ways of measuring financial performance using profitability and liquidity ratios. Up to now, we have only considered the profit and assets of a business. Using ratios allows a better understanding of how the business is doing, for example, it allows us to make year-on-year comparisons. It also allows for comparisons with other businesses, although these comparisons may not be relevant depending on the accounting methods used.

ACTIVITY

Look at some company accounts (sometimes called 'financial statements') on the internet. If possible, try to find examples from the same sector or industry. For example, compare different supermarkets or fast food outlets. This will make it easier for you to compare and make judgements.

18.1 PROFITABILITY AND LIQUIDITY

There are two basic but essential factors in the operation of a business:

1. To maintain, and if possible, increase profit. The ability to make profit is known as **profitability**.

SUBJECT VOCABULARY

profitability the ability to make profit

UNIT 4   18 THE CALCULATION AND INTERPRETATION OF ACCOUNTING RATIOS

SUBJECT VOCABULARY

liquidity the level of funds available to pay trade payables

2 For the business to have sufficient funds at all times so it can pay its debts as they become due. The level of funds available to pay trade payables is known as **liquidity**.

The importance of these two factors cannot be stressed too highly. A business that operates with a good profits record and sound liquidity will be well regarded by both customers and suppliers. If a business is consistently unable to generate profits it will fail. Weak liquidity – even if a business is making a profit – demonstrates a failure to control cash flow. Late or slow payments to trade payables could lead to suppliers not wishing to deal with the company. If a business gains a poor financial reputation, this will affect its trading performance, which will further weaken it and may cause it to fail. A good way of looking at liquidity and profitability is to find some examples that affect one but not the other. For example, credit revenue (sales) will increase profitability but have no effect on liquidity as no cash is transferred. The purchase of a non-current asset will affect liquidity but have no immediate impact on profitability.

18.2 PROFITABILITY RATIOS

Profitability ratios measure the success (or otherwise) of a business's trading activities in relation to the profit generated during an accounting period. The main ratios used to examine profitability are:

- gross profit percentage
- profit for the year as a percentage of revenue
- return on Capital employed (ROCE).

Gross profit percentage

The basic formula is:

$$\frac{\text{gross profit}}{\text{revenue}} \times 100 = \text{gross profit as percentage of revenue}$$

This is the amount of gross profit for every $100 of revenue and is known as the gross profit percentage. If the gross profit percentage is 15%, this means that for every $100 of revenue, $15 gross profit is made before any expenses are paid. This ratio is used as a test of the profitability of the revenue: the gross profit percentage does not necessarily increase as revenue increases, as shown below.

Example 1: D Clive's trading accounts are shown in **Figure 18.1**.

EXAM HINT

Always show the formula you are using in the exam. You can get a mark for this.

EXAM HINT

Make sure you learn the formulae for the ratios as they will not be given in the exam.

EXAM HINT

Profitability ratios are always measured as a percentage (%).

D Clive				
Income Statements for the years ended 31 December 2015 and 2016				
	2015		2016	
	£	£	£	£
Revenue		70 000		80 000
Less Cost of sales				
Opening inventory	5000		9000	
Add Purchases	60 000		72 000	
	65 000		81 000	
Less Closing inventory	9000	56 000	11 000	70 000
Gross profit		14 000		10 000

▲ Figure 18.1 D Clive's income statements for 2015 and 2016.

In 2015, the gross profit percentage was:

$$\frac{14\,000}{70\,000} \times 100 = 20\%$$

In 2016, the gross profit percentage was:

$$\frac{10\,000}{80\,000} \times 100 = 12.5\%$$

Although revenue increased from £70 000 to £80 000, gross profit fell from £14 000 to £10 000, a decrease of 7.5% (20% – 12.5%). There can be many reasons for such a fall in the gross profit percentage, for example:

- the purchase price of goods from suppliers may have increased more than the selling price to customers
- a business may have reduced the selling price of goods to increase revenue
- the revenue mix (the proportion of sales of different types of goods) may have changed – different kinds of goods carry different rates of gross profit per $100 of revenue
- wastage or theft of goods might have increased.

These are only some of the possible reasons for the decrease in gross profit percentage. The point of calculating the ratio is to find out why and how such a change has taken place.

Profit for the year as a percentage of revenue

The formula is:

$$\frac{\text{profit for the year}}{\text{sales revenue}} \times 100 = \text{profit for the year as a percentage of revenue}$$

This calculation will show how much profit has been made for every £100 of revenue. It considers the expenses (or overheads), unlike the gross profit percentage (which ignores expenses other than cost of sales). Changes in the ratio will be due to either:

- changes in the gross profit percentage ratio, and/or
- changes in the expenses per £100 of revenue.

When changes are due to expenses, the business will investigate to see if anything can be done in future to minimise expenses and ensure that a reasonable profit for the year is made.

Return on capital employed ratio (ROCE)

This ratio is usually presented as a percentage and is calculated as follows:

$$\text{return on capital employed} = \frac{\text{profit for the year}}{\text{capital employed}} \times 100$$

This figure shows the profit made for the year as a percentage for each $100 of capital employed. The higher the ratio, the more profitable the business. Capital employed is calculated by adding non-current liabilities to closing Capital.

STATEMENT OF FINANCIAL POSITION

This example will show you how to work out the return on capital employed. **Figure 18.2** shows some information about a business, Company A.

EXAM HINT

Accounts that show the income statement and the statement of financial position may show the accounts with the earlier year first, e.g. 2017 and 2016, rather than 2016 and 2017. Be careful in the exam – this may occur in the exam and your comparison and judgements will be wrong if you do not notice.

Company A		
	£	£
Non-current Assets		50 000
Current Assets		8 000
Net Assets		58 000
Capital Liabilities		
Opening Capital	33 000	
Add Profit for the year	10 000	
Less Drawings	8 000	
Closing Capital		35 000
Non-current Liabilities		12 000
Current Liabilities		11 000
Total Capital and Liabilities		58 000

▲ Figure 18.2 Information about Company A.

Company A's profit for the year = £10 000

Capital employed = closing capital + non-current liabilities
= £35 000 + £12 000 = £47 000

Therefore, the return on capital employed is:

$$\frac{£10\,000}{£47\,000} \times 100 = 21.28\%$$

18.3 LIQUIDITY RATIOS

> **HINT**
> Remember, liquidity ratios are always measured using : 1.

A business that has satisfactory liquidity (see Section 18.1) will have sufficient funds – normally referred to as 'working capital' – to pay trade payables at the required time. A business must be able to pay trade payables on time to ensure that good business relationships are maintained. The ratios used to examine liquidity, i.e. the liquidity ratios, are:

1 current ratio (working capital ratio)
2 liquid ratio (acid test ratio).

Liquidity ratios can be compared from one period to the next to see if that particular aspect of liquidity is getting better or worse. In the past, it was thought that a current ratio around 2:1 and a liquid ratio around 1–1.5:1 were ideal. However, it is now recognised that businesses vary widely and different types of business will have different ideal ratios.

Current ratio (working capital ratio)

The current ratio measures current assets (assets that will be turned into cash within the next 12 months) against current liabilities (liabilities that will have to be paid within the next 12 months). The current ratio is stated as:

$$\frac{\text{current assets}}{\text{current liabilities}}$$

If the current assets are £125 000 and the current liabilities are £50 000, the current ratio is:

$$\frac{£125\,000}{£50\,000} = 2.5:1, \text{ or } 2.5 \text{ times}$$

If the ratio increases by a large amount, the business may have more current assets than it needs. If the ratio falls by a large amount, then perhaps too little is being kept as current assets.

Liquid ratio (acid test ratio)

The liquid ratio only takes into account those current assets that are cash or that can be changed very quickly into cash. This normally means cash + bank + trade receivables. This is the same as current assets less inventory. The acid test ratio is, therefore, stated as:

$$\frac{\text{current assets less inventory}}{\text{current liabilities}}$$

If the total of current assets is £40 000, inventory is £10 000, and the total of current liabilities is £20 000, the liquid ratio will be:

$$\frac{£40\,000 - £10\,000}{£20\,000} = 1.5:1, \text{ or } 1.5 \text{ times}$$

This ratio shows whether the business has enough liquid assets to pay current liabilities quickly. It is dangerous to allow this ratio to fall to a very low figure. If suppliers cannot be paid on time, supplies to the business may be reduced or even stopped completely. If the business does not have enough inventory to sell, it may have to close down. A supplier who has not been paid may also sue the company and force it into liquidation.

18.4 DEFINITION OF WORKING CAPITAL

Working capital is the amount by which current assets exceed current liabilities.

It is vital for businesses to have sufficient working capital so they have funds available to pay everyday running expenses. Working capital tends to circulate through a business, as shown in **Figure 18.3**. As it flows, profits are made as inventory is sold to trade receivables; the quicker it is sold, the quicker the business makes profits.

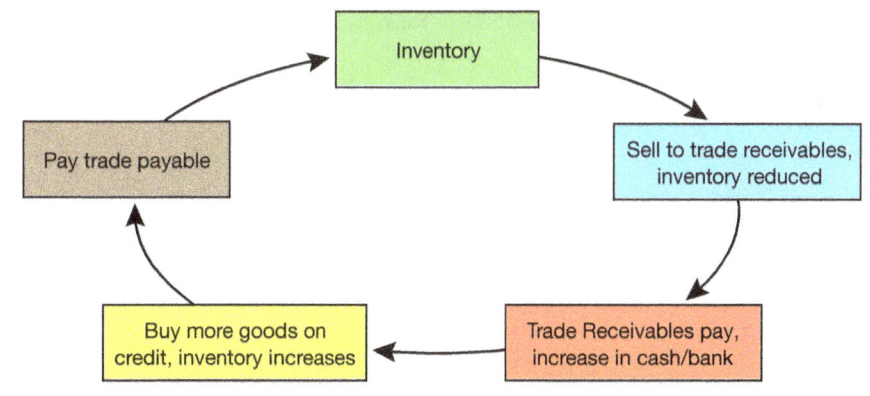

▲ Figure 18.3 The flow of capital through a business.

18.5 WORKED EXAMPLE: CALCULATING RATIOS

A fully worked example showing how to calculate ratios and interpret accounts is shown here. Check all the calculations yourself and see whether your conclusions about the changes in the ratios agree with what has been written.

Figures 18.4 and **18.5** show the financial statements for two similar retail stores, J and K.

Income statement

	J £	J £	K £	K £
Revenue		80000		120000
Less Cost of sales:				
Opening inventory	25000		22500	
Add Purchases	50000		91000	
	75000		113500	
Less Closing inventory	15000	60000	17500	96000
Gross profit		20000		24000
Less Depreciation	1000		3000	
Other expenses	9000	10000	6000	9000
Profit for the year		10000		15000

▲ Figure 18.4 Income statement for stores J and K.

Statement of financial positions

	J £	J £	K £	K £
Non Current Assets				
Equipment at cost	10000		20000	
Less Depreciation to date	8000	2000	6000	14000
Current Assets				
Inventory	15000		17500	
Trade receivables	25000		20000	
Bank	5000		2500	
	45000		40000	
Net assets		47000		54000
Financed by:				
Capital				
Less Current liabilities				
Trade payables	5000		10000	
Balance at start of year		38000		36000
Add Profit for the year		10000		15000
		48000		51000
Less Drawings		6000		7000
		47000		54000

▲ Figure 18.5 Statement of financial position for stores J and K.

The margins for these two companies are shown in the table below.

	J	K
Gross profit as a % of revenue	$\dfrac{£20\,000}{£80\,000} \times 100\% = 25\%$	$\dfrac{£24\,000}{£120\,000} \times 100\% = 20\%$
Profit for the year as a % of revenue	$\dfrac{£10\,000}{£80\,000} \times 100\% = 12.5\%$	$\dfrac{£15\,000}{£120\,000} \times 100\% = 12.5\%$
Rate of return on capital employed	$\dfrac{£10\,000}{£42\,000} \times 100\% = 23.81\%$	$\dfrac{£15\,000}{£44\,000} \times 100\% = 34.9\%$
Current ratio	$\dfrac{£45\,000}{£5000} = 9:1$	$\dfrac{£40\,000}{£10\,000} = 4:1$
Liquid ratio	$\dfrac{£45\,000 - £15\,000}{£5000} = 6:1$	$\dfrac{£40\,000 - £17\,500}{£10\,000} = 2.25:1$

A brief analysis of the findings

Having calculated the ratios, you can analyse the findings. In an exam, it will not be sufficient to say that the ratios differ: you should give an explanation of why they are different, relating your answer to the businesses in question.

Business K is more profitable, both in terms of actual profit for the year (£15 000 compared with £10 000) and in terms of capital employed. K has managed to achieve a return of £34.09 for every £100 invested, i.e. 34.09%, whereas J return is lower at 23.81% or £23.81 for every £100 invested. This difference could be because:

- K managed to sell more merchandise because of lower prices, i.e. it took only 20% margin compared with J's 25% margin
- K made more efficient use of mechanical equipment. Note that it has more equipment (£20 000, compared with J's £10 000) and perhaps as a consequence it kept other expenses down to £6000, compared with J's £9000
- J's current ratio of 9:1 is far greater than a business would normally need. In contrast, K's current ratio is only 4:1. J, therefore, has too much money lying idle
- J's liquid ratio is higher than necessary and follows a similar trend to that shown by the current ratio
- J also paid trade payables more quickly than K – but only slightly.

When all these factors are considered, it is clear that business K is being run more efficiently and, consequently, more profitably.

18.6 LIMITATIONS OF RATIOS

- Ratios are based on historic data and are focused on what has taken place, not on what is going to happen.
- Companies use different methods to value their assets, for example depreciation and inventory. This means objective comparison can be difficult.
- Published accounts only focus on the financial aspects of the business. They do not take into account non-financial information such as staff, reputation, marketing and the state of the economy.
- It can be difficult to find two companies of similar status to compare.
- Ratios only show a year end figure, which could be adjusted to show a favourable position.

HINT

Profitability ratios are a percentage (%) while liquidity ratios are a ratio (:1). Don't lose marks in the exam by missing out this information. For example, return on capital employed is X% and current ratio is X : 1.

UNIT 4 | 18 THE CALCULATION AND INTERPRETATION OF ACCOUNTING RATIOS | 213

SKILLS ANALYSIS

CASE STUDY: ACCOUNTING RATIOS

Caterpillar Inc is a world leading manufacturer of construction and mining equipment. The company sells over 400 different types of product and has factories worldwide including in Russia, Brazil and China. Their most famous products are their excavators, but they also sell clothes.

Below are extracts from the financial statement for Caterpillar Inc for the 3 months ended 31 March. All figures are in $millions.

	2017	2016
Sales revenue	9822	9461
Cost of sales	6758	6822
Profit for the year	192	271
Current assets (including inventories)	35 548	31 967
Inventories	9082	8614
Current liabilities	27 635	26 132

Calculate the following ratios for both years:
- gross profit percentage
- profit for the year as a percentage of revenue
- current ratio
- liquid ratio.

Comment on Caterpillar Inc's performance over the two years.

EXAM HINT

In the exam, make sure you show the formula being used and all the calculations. State whether the ratio you have calculated is better or worse, quantify your answer and give reasons why it has changed. For example: (gross profit/ revenue) × 100 = (8000/ 32 000) × 100 = 25%. Compared with last year's figure of 21%, the business has improved its gross profit percentage by 4%. This shows that for every £1 of revenue the business makes 25p gross profit. The improved profitability could be due to higher selling prices or cheaper cost of sales.

END OF CHAPTER QUESTIONS

1 Xi provides the following information:

	$
revenue	150 000
cost of sales	90 000
closing inventory	15 000

What is the gross profit percentage?

a 30%
b 40%
c 50%
d 60%

2 Which of the following is a measure of profitability?

a current ratio
b liquid ratio
c cash ratio
d return on capital employed

3 The statement of financial position of a business includes the following information.

	$
Trade receivables	10 000
Trade payables	14 000
Bank overdraft	6000
Inventory	15 000

What is the liquid ratio?

a 0.50 : 1
b 0.71 : 1
c 1.14 : 1
d 1.25 : 1

4 Eric's liquid ratio is 1.3 : 1, while Ken's liquid ratio is 0.4 : 1.
   What does a comparison of these ratios show?

   a Eric controls his overhead expenses better than Ken.
   b Eric's cost of sales is lower than Ken's.
   c Ken has a lower return on capital employed than Eric.
   d Ken has less liquidity than Eric.

5 A business has the following assets and liabilities.

	$
Non-current assets	30 000
Current assets	4000
Current liabilities	2000
Non-current liabilities	12 000

   What is the current ratio?

   a 2.0 : 1   b 2.4 : 1
   c 3.0 : 1   d 5.0 : 1

6 A business has calculated the following ratios.

	Gross profit percentage	Profit for the year percentage
Year 1	40%	19%
Year 2	40%	25%

   Why did the profit for the year percentage increase in Year 2?

   a cost of sales decreased
   b cost of sales increased
   c expenses decreased
   d expenses increased

7 The profit for the year of a business was $15 000. Balances in the business's books include the following:

	$
Premises	80 000
Trade receivables	12 000
Trade payables	7000
Inventory	2000
Cash	1000
Long term loan	20 000

   What is the return on capital employed (ROCE) %?

   a 15.79%   b 17.05%
   c 19.23%   d 22.06%

8 A business provides the following information for the year ended 30 April 2017.

	$
Revenue	90 000
Cost of sales	55 000
Expenses	15 000

   What is the gross profit percentage?

   a 22.22%   b 38.89%
   c 61.11%   d 77.78%

9 The table shows information about Ahmed's business for the last two years.

	2015	2016
Revenue	$40 000	$50 000
Gross profit percentage	35%	28%
Profit for the year percentage	15%	14%

What does a comparison of these results show about Ahmed's business?

a Expenses were controlled better in 2015 than in 2016.

b Expenses were controlled better in 2016 than in 2015.

c The value of gross profit was greater in 2015 than in 2016.

d The value of gross profit was greater in 2016 than in 2015.

10 A business provides the following information.

	$
Non current assets	55 000
Current assets	15 000
Current liabilities	10 000
Profit for the year	7500

What is the return on capital employed (ROCE)?

a 10.71%   b 12.50%

c 13.64%   d 15.00%

11 A business provides the following information.

	$
Trade payables	28 000
Trade receivables	45 000
Five year bank loan	20 000
Inventory	10 000
Bank overdraft	7000

What is the liquid ratio?

a 0.82 : 1   b 1.29 : 1

c 1.57 : 1   d 1.86 : 1

12 A trader wants to improve his gross profit percentage.

How can this be done?

a reduce administration costs

b reduce depreciation of equipment

c reduce rate of cash discount allowed

d reduce rate of trade discount allowed

END OF CHAPTER CHECKLIST

- Ratio analysis is a very good way of measuring and analysing the performance of a business.
- Ratios must be compared with previous years to determine any trends in performance. On their own, ratios are good, but they do not necessarily provide any analysis.
- Ratios can be used to compare businesses in the same industry, but can be impractical if comparing different businesses, such as a supermarket and a fast food company.
- Comparisons are likely to be unhelpful unless the businesses are of a similar size.
- Ratios can act as a guide to predict how the business may perform in the future.

EXAM PRACTICE

A01 **A02** **A03** Answer ALL questions in this section.

1 Zakari is a trader. He provides the following information for the year ended 31 January 2017.

	$
Revenue – cash	24 000
Revenue – credit	66 000
Cost of sales	
Opening inventory	25 000
Purchases – cash	18 000
Credit	52 000
Closing inventory	30 200
Running expenses	14 400
Trade receivables at 31 January 2017	6300
Trade payables at 31 January 2017	5700

Zakari decides to compare his results with those for the previous financial year.

a Calculate the missing figures in the following table to show the ratios for Zakari's business for the year ended 31 January 2017.

Ratio year ended 31 January	2016	2017
Gross profit percentage	25%	?
Profit for the year as a percentage of revenue	10%	?

b For **each** ratio, suggest **two** possible reasons for the change in the ratio between 31 January 2016 and 31 January 2017.

(6 marks)

2 David Hoon is a sole trader. He prepared the following statement of financial position at 28 February 2015.

David Hoon
Statement of Financial Position at 28 February 2015

	$
Non-current assets at carrying value	45 000
Current assets	
Inventory	12 000
Trade receivables	9500
Cash	500
Current liabilities	
Trade payables	6300
Bank overdraft	8200
Capital	52 500

a i Calculate, correct to **two** decimal places, David's current ratio and liquid ratio at 28 February 2015. Show your workings.

ii State and explain which of the above ratios gives a better indication of the liquidity position of David's business.

David Hoon's profit for the year ended 28 February 2015 was $4950.

b Calculate, correct to **two** decimal places, David's return on capital employed (ROCE).

Base your calculation on the capital at 28 February 2015. Show your workings.

(10 marks)

(Total 16 marks)

19 FINANCIAL STATEMENTS OF A PARTNERSHIP

▲ Business people who enter partnerships need to understand the requirements of financial statements for partnerships.

LEARNING OBJECTIVES

- Understand the nature of a partnership and the reasons for forming one
- Understand the nature and structure of a limited liability partnership (LLP)
- Apply provisions of Section 24 of the Partnership Act 1890 in relation to partners' salaries, division of profit and loss, interest on loans, capital and drawings
- Understand the nature and purpose of an appropriation account
- Prepare income and appropriation accounts
- Prepare partners' current accounts and capital accounts
- Prepare statements of financial position to include partners' capital balances and current account balances

GETTING STARTED

So far, we have learned about the accounts of sole traders. In this chapter, we will look at partnerships and how their accounts differ from those of a sole trader.

ACTIVITY

Recap the differences between a sole tradership and a partnership (Chapter 1, pages 4–7). This will help you to understand why the accounts are different.

Then research the UK's Partnership Act 1890 using the internet. Make notes on the main points of this act.

19.1 THE NEED FOR PARTNERSHIPS

Up to now, we have mainly focused on businesses owned by only one person. However, businesses that are set up to make a profit can often have more than one owner. There are various reasons for multiple ownership and there are two types: partnerships and limited companies.

The advantages and disadvantages of partnerships are summarised in the table below.

▼ Advantages	▼ Disadvantages
Easier and cheaper to set up than limited companies.	The partners have unlimited liability (except limited partners, see Section 19.2) and may be responsible for the debts of other partners.
A business can raise more Capital with additional partners.	A partnership is dissolved on the death of a partner.
Additional partners bring in a variety of skills and expertise that benefit the partnership.	A partnership may have difficulty in raising sufficient capital for large-scale operations. Increased unlimited liability could also be a deterrent to expanding the business.
The experience or ability required to manage the business cannot always be provided by one person working alone.	There may be delays and conflicts in decision-making when several partners are involved.
The responsibility of management can be shared by additional partners.	
A partnership of family members can bring a stronger desire to succeed within a dependable environment.	
Partnerships are ideal organisations for professional practices such as medicine, law and accounting.	
Profits from partnerships are taxed as the personal income of the partnership.	

19.2 LIMITED PARTNERS

A partnership may be **unlimited** or **limited** (see Chapter 1, pages 5–6).

In an unlimited partnership, all partners are accountable for the debts of the business. In a limited partnership, there must be at least one partner who is not limited. All limited partnerships in the UK must be registered with the Registrar of Companies. Limited partners are not liable for the debts of the business. The following characteristics are found in limited partnerships:

1 A limited partner's liability for the debts of the partnership is limited to the capital or equity they have invested in the partnership. They can lose that capital, but they cannot be asked for any more money to pay the debts unless they break the regulations relating to their involvement in the partnership (see points 2 and 3 below).

2 The partners are not allowed to take out or receive back any part of their contribution to the partnership during its lifetime.

3 The partners are not allowed to take part in the management of the partnership business.

4 The partners cannot all be limited: as mentioned above, there must be at least one partner with unlimited liability.

19.3 NATURE OF A PARTNERSHIP

A partnership has the following characteristics:

1 It is formed to make profits.

2 In the UK, it must obey the law as set out in the UK's Partnership Act 1890. Limited partnerships must comply with the Limited Liability Partnership Act 2000.

3 Normally, there can be a minimum of two and a maximum of 20 partners. Each partner (except for limited partners, described in Section 19.2) must pay his or her share of any debts that the partnership is unable to pay. Each partner is personally liable. If necessary, partners can be forced to sell their private possessions to pay their share of any debts. This is what is meant by 'unlimited' liability.

In the UK, the Partnership Act 1890 was drawn up by Parliament to settle any issues within a partnership. It is only used if there is no partnership agreement in place. The act states that each partner is entitled to participate in management. It also states that each partner gets an equal share of profit, an indemnity in respect of liabilities assumed in the course of business and the right to not be expelled by other partners. A partnership ends on the death of a partner, unless an agreement is made prior to the death. If no partnership agreement is in place, then all profits and losses are shared equally among the partners.

In the exam you may be asked two types of question:

1 What the Partnership Act entails; for example, that if there is no partnership agreement, all profits and losses are shared equally.

2 To prepare the appropriation account according to the partnership agreement; again, profit and losses should be shared equally.

> **EXAM TIP**
> You will always have to calculate the share of profit or losses. Be careful with your ratio when calculating this as it is easy to make mistakes and lose marks.

> **KEY POINT**
> Where no partnership agreement exists, the accounting section of the Partnership Act 1890 applies, so all profits and losses are shared equally.

19.4 WHERE NO PARTNERSHIP AGREEMENT EXISTS

Sometimes, no formal partnership agreement exists, either express or implied. In the UK in these circumstances, Section 24 of the Partnership Act 1890 governs the situation. The accounting content of this section is as follows.

- Profits and losses are to be shared equally.
- There is to be no interest allowed on equity.
- No interest is to be charged on drawings.
- Salaries are not allowed.
- If a partner puts a sum of money into the business in excess of the capital he or she has agreed to subscribe, that partner is entitled to interest on this advance at the rate of 5% per annum.

19.5 THE FINANCIAL STATEMENTS

If the revenue, inventory and expenses of a partnership are exactly the same as those of a sole trader, the income statements for the partnership and sole trader will be identical. However, the income statement for a partnership usually has an extra section called the profit and loss **appropriation account**. The distribution of profits is shown in this account. The heading to the income statement does not include the words 'appropriation account'; this is purely an accounting custom.

> **KEY POINT**
> The income statement for a sole trader uses the same layout as for a partnership. However, with a partnership there is an appropriation account at the bottom. This account shows how the profit is shared between the partners.

19.6 WORKED EXAMPLE: APPROPRIATION ACCOUNT

Here is an example showing the accounts for two partners: Riley and Connor. Their profit for the year is £80 000.

Interest on drawings: Some partnership agreements state that partners should be charged interest on any money taken out of the business during the year. This is to deter partners from taking too much cash out of the business.

In this example, Riley takes drawings of £2000 and Connor withdraws £3000 from the business. Interest is charged at 10%.

Riley: £2000 @ 10% = **£200**

Connor: £3000 @ 10% = **£300**

Partnership salaries: Some partners may work in the business, whereas other partners may simply invest in the business without being involved in the running of the business. Partners who work in the business may be entitled to a salary. In this example, Riley is paid an annual salary of £8000.

Interest on capital: This is paid on the individual capital invested in the business by each partner. In the exam, you will normally be expected to calculate this. Riley and Connor have capital of £20 000 and £30 000 respectively. Interest on capital is 5%.

Riley: £20 000 @ 5% = **£1000**

Connor: £30 000 @ 5% = **£1500**

Share of profits: This will involve another calculation and the ratio will be given in the exam. The ratio will normally reflect the workload of the partners or the amount of capital that has been invested. Riley and Connor share profits on a 7:3 ratio.

£70 000 / 10 (7 + 3) = £7000

Riley: 7 × £7000 = £49 000

Connor: 3 × £7000 = £21 000

The appropriation account for Riley and Connor's partnership is shown in **Figure 19.1**.

> **EXAM HINT**
>
> Normally in the exam the salary figure will be given, but remember a salary is paid for the year, so check to make sure that the examiner has not asked for a different period such as a six-month appropriation account.

		£	£
Profit for the year			80 000
Add Interest on drawings	Riley	200	
	Connor	300	500
Less salary	Riley		8000
Less Interest on capital	Riley	1000	
	Connor	1500	2500
			70 000
Share of Profit or Loss	Riley		49 000
	Connor		21 000
			70 000

▲ **Figure 19.1** The appropriation account for Riley and Connor.

19 FINANCIAL STATEMENTS OF A PARTNERSHIP

CASE STUDY: SOURCE DOCUMENTS

Aran and Newine are accountants. They work in a partnership, sharing profit and losses in the ratio 2:1. They maintain capital at £12 000 and £15 000 respectively. Their partnership agreement means that Newine is credited with a salary of £9380 and partners are credited with 6% interest on capital. The profit for the year is £44 000.

Complete an appropriation account for Aran and Newine.

19.7 CURRENT ACCOUNTS

The current account will show the profits, interest on capital, and salaries to which the partner may be entitled. These figures are credited to a separate current account for the partner. The drawings and any interest on drawings are debited to this account. The balance of the current account at the end of each financial year represents the amount of undrawn (or withdrawn) profits. A credit balance will be undrawn profits, while a debit balance will be drawings in excess of the profits to which the partner is entitled.

The current account for Riley and Connor (see the Worked example in Section 19.6) is shown in **Figure 19.2**.

Current Account

	Riley	Connor		Riley	Connor
Drawings	2000	3000	Balance b/d	20 000	30 000
Interest on Drawings	200	300	Salary	8000	
			Interest on capital	1000	1500
Balance c/d	75 800	49 200	Share of profits	49 000	21 000
	78 000	52 500		78 000	
			Balance b/d	75 800	

▲ Figure 19.2 Current account for Riley and Connor.

EXAM HINT

The amount of interest on drawings will usually be given in the exam, so you will not have to calculate it.

Example 1: **Figure 19.3** shows the appropriation account, capital account and current account of Taylor and Cheung.

Taylor and Cheung
Appropriation Account

	HK$	HK$	HK$
Profit for the year			50 000
Interest on drawings:			
Taylor		500	
Cheung		1 000	1 500
			51 500
Less:			
Interest on capital:			
Taylor	1 000		
Cheung	3 000	4 000	
Salary		20 000	24 000
			27 500
Balance of profits shared:			
Taylor (three-fifths)		16 500	
Cheung (two-fifths)		11 000	27 500
			27 500

Taylor
Capital Account

Dr				Cr
	2016			HK$
	Jan 1	Bank		20 000

Cheung
Capital Account

Dr				Cr
	2016			HK$
	Jan 1	Bank		60 000

Taylor
Current Account

Dr						Cr
2016		HK$	2016			HK$
Dec 31	Drawings	12 000	Dec 31			
Dec 31	Appropriation account			Appropriation account		
	Interest on drawings	500		Interest on capital		1 000
Dec 31	Balance c/d	5 000		Share of profits		16 500
		17 500				17 500
			2017			
			Jan 1	Balance b/d		5 000

UNIT 4 — 19 FINANCIAL STATEMENTS OF A PARTNERSHIP

Dr		**Cheung** **Current Account**			Cr
2016		HK$	2016		HK$
Dec 31	Drawings	20 000	Dec 31		
Dec 31	Appropriation account			Appropriation account	
	Interest on drawings	1000		Interest on equity	3000
				Share of profits	11 000
Dec 31	Balance c/d	13 000		Salary	20 000
		34 000	2017		34 000
			Jan 1	Balance b/d	13 000

▲ **Figure 19.3** Appropriation account, capital account and current account of Taylor and Cheung.

Notice that Cheung's salary was not paid to him. It was merely credited to his account. If it had been paid in addition to his drawings, the HK$20 000 cash paid would have been debited to the current account. This would have changed the HK$13 000 credit balance into a HK$7000 debit balance.

EXAM HINT

If your calculations do not divide exactly, quickly check that you have not missed something. If they still do not divide exactly, check how you need to round off the figures.

SKILLS INTERPRETATION

CASE STUDY: SOURCE DOCUMENTS

Gembira and Vanna are doctors who have formed a partnership together. Their profit for the year was £46 784. The partnership agreement provides:

- Vanna to be paid a salary of £8000 per annum
- interest on capital to be provided at 10% per annum
- profit to be shared 3:2 respectively.

▲ Gembira and Vanna work in a surgery in Cardiff.

Interest on drawings is calculated at £480 and £106 respectively, and the capital accounts are: Gembira £23 000 and Vanna £27 000.

Complete an appropriation account and current accounts for Gembira and Vanna.

END OF CHAPTER QUESTIONS

1 What is unlimited liability?

2 Why might some partners not receive a salary?

3 Why is interest on capital charged by the business?

4 Why might partners have different ratios for sharing profit?

5 Reza and Vasudha are in partnership sharing profits and losses in the proportions Reza 2/3 and Vasudha 1/3.
   They have agreed that Reza will receive an annual salary of $9000.
   Profit for the year was $24 000.
   What is Vasudha's share of the profit for the year?

   a $5000   b $8000

   c $10 000   d $16 000

6 In partnership accounts, which item appears in both the profit and loss appropriation account and in the partners' current accounts?

a current account balances

b drawings

c interest on drawings

d interest on loans

7 Anna and Margarita are partners. They share profits equally. The profit for the year before appropriation is €43 000.

Anna receives a salary of $10 000. She also receives interest on capital of €1000. Margarita receives interest on capital of €2000.

What is Anna's total income from the business?

a €15 000

b €21 500

c €26 000

d €32 500

8 Azizi and Halisi are in partnership. They share profits and losses in the ratio 2 : 1.

The following is extracted from their financial statements for the year ended 30 April 2016.

	$
Profit for the year	56 000
Partners' salaries – Azizi	8 000
Halisi	12 000
Profit available for distribution	36 000

How much in total will be recorded in Halisi's current account on 30 April 2016?

a $18 667

b $24 000

c $30 667

d $32 000

9 A partnership makes a loss during the financial year.

How is this shown in the accounts?

	account to be debited	account to be credited
a	appropriation account	partners' capital accounts
b	appropriation account	partners' current accounts
c	partners' capital accounts	appropriation account
d	partners' current accounts	appropriation account

10 Which of the following is not entered in a partnership profit and loss appropriation account?

a drawings

b interest on capital

c interest on drawings

d partners' salaries

11 Amy and Beth are in partnership, sharing profits equally. No salaries are paid to the partners.

The following information is available for the financial year ended 31 December 2016:

	$
Profit for the year	100 000
Interest charged on partners' drawings	
Amy	6000
Beth	4000

How much is credited to Beth's current account for the year ended 31 December 2016?

a $50 000

b $51 000

c $55 000

d $59 000

12 In which section of a statement of financial position would a credit balance on a partner's current account appear?

a capital

b current assets

c current liabilities

d non-current liabilities

13 Jamal and Omar are in partnership. Jamal is credited with an annual salary of $20 000. The balance of the partnership's profit for the year is shared equally between the partners. The profit for the year was $100 000.

What is the total amount credited to Jamal's current account for the year?

a $40 000

b $50 000

c $60 000

d $70 000

END OF CHAPTER CHECKLIST

- A partnership exists when two or more people are engaged in business with the aim of making a profit.
- There should be a partnership agreement.
- The appropriation account shows how the profit and losses are shared between the partners.

EXAM PRACTICE

A01 A02 A03 Answer ALL questions in this section.

1 John Faha and May Ishima are business partners.
- They each receive interest on partners' capital payable at 10% per annum.
- Ishima receives a salary of $15 000 per annum.
- profits and losses are to be shared: Faha 2/5, Ishima 3/5.

Balances for the year ended 30 April 2017 included the following:

	Dr	Cr
		$
Capital accounts 1 May 2016		
John Faha		100 000
May Ishima		40 000
Non-current assets at cost	50 000	
Gross profit		72 000
Discounts	3000	1000
Heating and lighting	6500	
Rent and Rates	15 000	
Wages	6500	

The following information is also available:

At 30 April 2017:	$
General expenses accrued	800
Rent prepaid	2000
Wages due but unpaid	1700

Depreciation on non-current assets is to be provided at 20% using the straight line method.

a Draw up the income statement and appropriation account starting from gross profit.

Faha and Ishima are considering whether or not they should pay interest on their cash drawings.

b Explain **two** reasons why charging interest on drawings could be an advantage to the partnership. **(12 marks)**

2 Kidd and Mellor are in partnership. They share profits in the ratio: Kidd three-fifths to Mellor two-fifths. The following trial balance is extracted as at 31 March 2017:

Trial balance as at 31 March 2017

	Dr	Cr
	£	£
Equipment at cost	26 000	
Motor vehicles at cost	36 800	
Allowance for depreciation at 31.3.2017:		
Equipment		7800
Motor vehicles		14 720
Inventory at 31 March 2017	99 880	
Trade receivables and trade payables	83 840	65 100
Cash at bank	2460	
Cash in hand	560	
Revenue		361 480
Purchases	256 520	
Salaries	45 668	
Office expenses	1480	
Motor expenses	2252	
Heating and lighting	2000	
Current accounts at 31.3.2017:		
Kidd		5516
Mellor		4844
Equity accounts:		
Kidd		86 000
Mellor		50 000
Drawings:		
Kidd	16 000	
Mellor	22 000	
	595 460	595 460

For the year ended 31 March 2017, complete:

a an income statement and appropriation account
b a statement of financial position
c a capital account.

Take into consideration the following notes:

- inventory at 31 March 2017 was valued at £109 360
- office expenses owing were £440
- allowance for depreciation: motor vehicles 20% of cost, equipment 10% of cost
- charge interest on equity at 6%
- charge interest on drawings: Kidd £628, Mellor £892
- charge £15 000 for salary for Mellor.

(12 marks)
(Total 24 marks)

20 FINANCIAL STATEMENTS OF A MANUFACTURER

▲ Manufacturers' accounts and traders' accounts have different requirements.

SUBJECT VOCABULARY

manufacturing account accounts that deal with making products rather than buying and selling them

GENERAL VOCABULARY

essential extremely important

LEARNING OBJECTIVES

- Understand the difference between the inventories of raw materials, work-in-progress and finished goods
- Prepare manufacturing accounts to show prime cost, production cost and total cost

GETTING STARTED

So far, we have learned about businesses involved only in trading. There are additional accounting requirements for businesses with manufacturing activities. They need to prepare a **manufacturing account** to determine the cost of producing goods. This account, which is normally for internal management purposes, shows the production cost. This figure is transferred to the trading account.

Cost records are essential to allow an accurate assessment of the production cost. Management must review production costs regularly (for example, on a monthly basis). If there are increases in costs of materials, or if production targets are not met, suitable action can then be taken.

ACTIVITY — SKILLS: CRITICAL THINKING

1 There are three types of manufacturing inventory. Can you guess what the three categories might be? Do research on the internet or in your local area. You could, for example, try to take photographs of types of inventory.

2 What would a car manufacturer class as raw material, **work-in-progress** and finished goods?

3 List five different types of manufacturing business and give examples of their three types of inventory.

SUBJECT VOCABULARY

work-in-progress items or goods that the business has not yet completed

▲ Explain the three types of inventory for a furniture manufacturer in these photos.

UNIT 4   20 FINANCIAL STATEMENTS OF A MANUFACTURER

20.1 DIRECT AND INDIRECT COSTS

> **HINT**
> Direct costs can be directly linked to the item being manufactured. This includes raw materials and direct labour.

A manufacturing business **accumulates** production costs in stages. Direct costs are costs that can be directly identified with specific products or individual contracts. These costs should be calculated first. They include:

- **direct materials.** Raw materials required for the manufacture of a product
- **direct labour.** Wages of the machine operators who make the product
- **direct expenses.** Expenses that can be identified to each unit of production, for example, the hire of a special machine.

The total of all the direct costs is known as the prime cost – see **Figure 20.1**.

> **SUBJECT VOCABULARY**
> **accumulate** gradually increase in numbers or amount

Indirect costs occur in the factory or other places where production happens, but cannot be easily linked to the items being manufactured. They are fixed for a period of time and do not change with the output / units being produced from the factory. Examples of indirect costs include:

- rent of factory premises and factory business rates
- insurance of factory premises
- depreciation of factory equipment
- factory heating and lighting
- wages of supervisors.

Indirect costs can also be referred to as indirect manufacturing costs, production overheads or factory overhead costs (see **Figure 20.1**).

> **KEY POINT**
> Prime cost is direct material + direct labour + direct expenses.
> Indirect costs are factory costs that cannot be easily linked to items being made.
> Indirect manufacturing costs or production overheads are also called factory overhead costs.

```
Direct materials        ⎫
Direct labour           ⎬ Prime cost    ⎫
Direct expenses         ⎭               ⎪
                                        ⎬ Production cost    ⎫
Add                                     ⎪  (transfer to      ⎪
Indirect manufacturing costs            ⎭   trading account) ⎬ Total cost
(or production overheads)                                    ⎪
                                                             ⎪
Add                                                          ⎪
Administrative expenses                                      ⎪
Selling and distribution                                     ⎪
expenses                                                     ⎪
Finance charges                                              ⎭
```

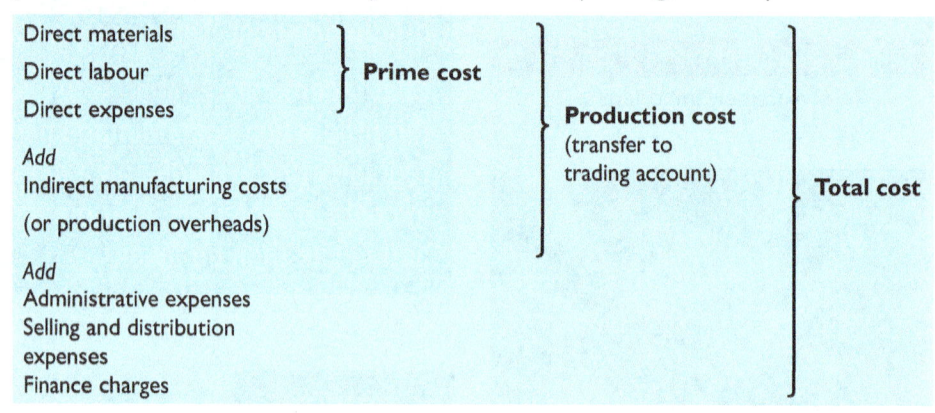

▲ **Figure 20.1** Total cost calculation

20.2 FORMAT OF FINANCIAL STATEMENTS

> **KEY POINT**
> All expenses are added into a manufacturing account. This is not the case in an income statement.

If a company manufactures its own products, it will need to prepare a manufacturing account before preparing the income statement. The financial statements required are the:

- manufacturing account
- income statement
- statement of financial position.

An example of a manufacturing account is shown in **Figure 20.2**.

	Raw materials	$	$
	Opening inventory of raw materials		12 000
Add	Purchases of raw materials		56 000
Add	Carriage inwards		2 300
Less	Return of raw materials purchased		5 000
			65 300
Less	Closing inventory of raw materials		18 000

continued overleaf

			$	$
Equals	**Raw materials consumed**			47 300
Add	Direct labour			22 000
Add	Other direct expenses			10 000
Equals	**Prime cost**			79 300
	Indirect costs			
Add	Factory fuel		7000	
Add	Indirect wages		12 000	
Add	Factory insurance		9000	
Add	Supervisor's wages		22 200	
Add	Depreciation: machinery		3000	
Add	Depreciation: factory		5000	58 200
				137 500
Add	Opening inventory of work in progress			34 000
				171 500
Less	Closing inventory of work in progress			29 500
Equals	**Production cost**			142 000

▲ Figure 20.2 An example of a manufacturing account.

When completed, the manufacturing account shows the total production costs relating to the goods manufactured and available for sale during the accounting period. This figure is then transferred to the income statement. It replaces the cost of goods purchased.

Figure 20.3 shows an extract from the income statement of the business whose manufacturing account is shown in **Figure 20.2**.

Income Statement extract

	$	$
Revenue		
Cost of manufacturing		480 200
Opening inventory of finished goods	12 000	
Production cost	142 000	
	154 000	
Closing inventory of finished goods	17 000	137 000
Gross Profit		343 200

▲ Figure 20.3 An extract from the income statement of a manufacturing business.

NOTE
Many students are so used to deducting expenses (such as wages, rent, depreciation, etc.) in the income statement that they fall into the trap of deducting these instead of adding them in the manufacturing account. Remember, we are building up the cost of manufacture so all costs are added.

EXAM HINT
In the manufacturing account, we add everything together except the closing inventories for:
- raw materials
- work in progress
- finished goods
- any raw materials returns.

CASE STUDY: MANUFACTURING ACCOUNTS

Jolah owns a small scooter manufacturing business in Dhaka. He has managed to produce the following balances:

	Taka
Direct Labour	52 330
Indirect Labour	13 200
Raw Materials 01.01.17	6000
Raw Materials 31.12.17	17 366
Purchases of Raw materials	82 494
Patents	3456

Calculate the Prime Cost for Jolah.

INCOME STATEMENT

HINT

Administration expenses, office workers' wages, selling and distribution expenses and advertising and marketing may be provided in the exam. These expenses DO NOT go in the manufacturing account. They go in expenses, in the income statement.

HINT

The production cost of goods manufactured is transferred to the income statement.

This account includes:
- the production cost brought down from the manufacturing account
- opening and closing inventories of finished goods
- revenue.

When completed, this account will disclose the gross profit. This figure will then be carried down to the income statement section of the financial statements.

The manufacturing account and the income statement should be set out as shown in **Figure 20.4**.

Manufacturing Account

	£
Production costs for the period:	
Direct labour	xxx
Direct materials	xxx
Direct expenses	xxx
Prime cost	**xxx**
Indirect manufacturing costs (or production overheads)	xxx
***Production cost of goods completed c/d to trading account**	xxx

Income Statement extract

		£	£
Sales			xxx
Less **Production cost of sales:**			
Opening inventory of finished goods	(A)	xxx	
Add: ***Production costs of goods completed b/d**		xxx	
		xxx	
Less Closing inventory of finished goods	(B)	xxx	xxx
Gross profit			xxx

(A) is production costs of goods unsold in previous period

(B) is production costs of goods unsold at end of current period

▲ Figure 20.4 How to set out a manufacturing account and a trading account.

This income statement includes:
- gross profit brought down from the trading account
- all administration expenses – e.g. managers' salaries, legal and accountancy fees, secretarial salaries and expenses etc.
- all selling and distribution expenses – e.g. staff salaries and commission, carriage outwards, advertising etc.
- all finance charges – interest charged on loans, bank charges, discounts allowed etc.

Some of the charges usually found in the income statement will have already been included in the manufacturing account. Only the remaining charges need to be charged to the income statement.

When complete, the income statement will show the profit for the year.

STATEMENT OF FINANCIAL POSITION

The statement of financial position of a manufacturing company is virtually the same as a statement of financial position prepared for another organisation. There is one key difference, however. In the current assets section, all three closing inventories must be included, that is:
- inventory of raw materials
- inventory of work in progress
- inventory of finished goods.

20.3 WORKED EXAMPLE: A MANUFACTURING ACCOUNT

Figure 20.5 shows a list of balances as at 31 December 2016 for a lawnmower manufacturer. The steps to determine the prime cost and the production cost of goods completed are shown in **Figure 20.4**.

	£
1 January 2016, Inventory of raw materials	7200
31 December 2016, Inventory of raw materials	9450
1 January 2016, Work in progress	3150
31 December 2016, Work in progress	3780
Year to 31 December 2016	
Wages: Direct	35640
Indirect	22950
Purchase of raw materials	78300
Fuel and power	8910
Direct expenses	1260
Factory wages	2700
Carriage inwards on raw materials	1800
Rent of factory	6400
Depreciation of factory plant and machinery	3780
Internal transport expenses	11620
Insurance of factory buildings and plant	11350
General factory expenses	2970

▲ **Figure 20.5** Balances of a lawnmower manufacturer as at 31 December 2016.

The manufacturing account for the lawnmower manufacturer is shown in **Figure 20.6**.

Manufacturing Account for the year ended 31 December 2016	£	£
Inventory of raw materials 1.1.2016		7200
Add Raw materials purchased		78300
Carriage inwards		1800
		87300
Less Inventory of raw materials 31.12.2016		9450
Cost of raw materials consumed		77850
Direct wages		35640
Direct expenses		1260
Prime cost		114750
Add Indirect Manufacturing Cost		
Fuel and power	8910	
Indirect wages	22950	
Factory wages	2700	
Rent	6400	
Depreciation of plant	3780	
Internal transport expenses	11620	
Insurance	11350	
General factory expenses	2970	70680
		185430
Add Work in progress 1.1.2016		3150
		188580
Less Work in progress 31.12.2016		3780
Production cost of goods completed c/d		184800

▲ **Figure 20.6** Manufacturing account for a lawnmower manufacturer as at 31 December 2016.

Unit cost of production

Once you have calculated the total cost of production, you can easily work out the production cost per unit. In this example, 2100 units were produced at the cost of £184 800 (see **Figure 20.6**). The cost per unit is as follows:

$$\text{cost per unit} = \frac{\text{cost of production}}{\text{no. of units produced}} = \frac{£184\,800}{2100 \text{ units}} = £88 \text{ per unit}$$

> **HINT**
> You might need to work out depreciation for your factory non-current assets.

INCOME STATEMENT

The income statement is concerned with finished goods. If, in **Figure 20.4**, there had been £31 500 inventory of finished goods at 1 January 2016 and £39 600 at 31 December 2016, and the revenue of finished goods amounted to £275 000, the income statement would appear as shown in **Figure 20.7**.

Income statement for the year ended 31 December 2016	£	£
Revenue		275 000
Less Cost of sales		
Inventory of finished goods 2016	31 500	
Add Production cost of goods completed b/d	184 800	
	216 300	
Less Inventory of finished goods 2016	39 600	176 700
Gross profit c/d		98 300

▲ Figure 20.7 An example income statement.

The income statement is then constructed in the normal way. In the statement of financial position, all three closing inventory figures would appear under the current assets section as shown in **Figure 20.8**.

Statement of financial position as at 31 December 2016 (extract)	
	£
Current assets	
Inventory:	
Raw materials	9450
Work in progress	3780
Finished goods	39 600

▲ Figure 20.8 An example statement of financial position (extract).

END OF CHAPTER QUESTIONS

1 What is a direct cost?

2 What is an indirect cost?

3 What is prime cost?

4 What are the two types of depreciation?

5 What are the three types of inventory?

6 Which of the following is a factory overhead?

   a carriage on finished goods

   b carriage on raw materials

   c wages of factory supervisors

   d wages of machine operators

7 Which of the following is a direct cost?

   a royalties

   b depreciation of machinery

   c selling and administration expenses

   d factory power

8 Calculate the prime cost using the following information:
   Royalties: €12 000
   Factory wages: €3400
   Raw materials consumed: €28 000
   Direct labour: €15 600
   Depreciation: €7000
   Factory rent: €12 000

   a €78 000   b €66 000

   c €59 000   d €55 600

9 Calculate the production cost using the following information:
   Prime cost: $92 000
   Selling and administration: $15 000
   Depreciation: office equipment: $6000
   Factory power: $10 000
   Factory insurance: $2000
   Closing inventory work in progress $5600
   Opening inventory work in progress: $8800

   a $107 200   b $108 800

   c $83 200   d $128 200

END OF CHAPTER CHECKLIST

- Direct costs are costs that can be traced to a specific product that is being manufactured – for example, raw materials, piece-rate wages, patents and royalties.
- Prime cost is the total marginal cost of products produced derived from the addition of the costs of raw material used, direct labour and other direct costs.
- There are three types of inventory: raw materials, work-in-progress and finished goods.
- You add everything in the manufacturing account except for closing inventory and any raw materials that have been returned.
- Only put indirect costs that relate specifically to the manufacturing process in the manufacturing account.

EXAM PRACTICE

A01 **A02** **A03** Answer ALL questions in this section.

1 The Little Teapot Company makes equipment for cafes and restaurants. It was formed on 1 January 2017 by Ismail Nasser.

The following information was extracted from the books at the end of the first financial year.

	$
Revenue	251 400
Purchases of raw materials	98 500
Direct factory wages	56 400
Indirect factory wages	22 400
Factory general expenses	7 990
Factory fuel and power	3 700

At 31 December 2017, the following additional information was provided.

	$
Fuel and power accrued amounted to	250
Direct factory wages accrued amounted to	850
Inventory was valued at – raw material	3 300
– work in progress	2 120
– finished goods	5 810

Factory machinery was valued at $19 550. It had been purchased for $24 000 on 1 January 2017. There were no other purchases or sales of machinery during the year.

a Prepare the manufacturing account of The Little Teapot Company for the year ended 31 December 2017.

b Prepare the trading account of The Little Teapot Company for the year ended 31 December 2017. **(15 marks)**

2 Gideon Fleetwood is a manufacturer of plastic parts for motor vehicles. He provided the following information.

	At 1 April 2016 $	At 31 March 2017 $
Inventory		
Raw materials	18 230	21 450
Work in progress	15 680	14 120
Finished goods	56 905	43 140

For the year ended 31 March 2017:

	$
Sales revenue of finished goods	915 000
Purchases of raw materials	285 880
Purchases of finished goods	12 555
Direct factory wages	175 054
Factory general expenses	123 725

The following additional information is available on 31 March 2017:

- Direct factory wages accrued amounted to $5 654.
- The factory general expenses include insurance on the factory, which is prepaid by $232.
- The factory machinery was valued at $78 400.
- On 1 April 2016 the factory machinery was valued at $112 000. Additional machinery costing $28 000 was purchased during the year. There were no sales of machinery during the year. Depreciation is to be provided at 15%.

a i State the basis on which Gideon Fleetwood should value his inventory.

ii Name one accounting principle Gideon Fleetwood is applying by valuing his inventory.

b Prepare the manufacturing account of Gideon Fleetwood for the year ended 31 March 2017.

c Prepare the Trading Account to gross profit of Gideon Fleetwood for the year ended 31 March 2017.

(20 marks)
(Total 35 marks)

GLOSSARY

account a record showing money coming into and going out of a business, its profits, and its financial situation

accruals adjustments made to accounts to record expenses that the company has not yet paid for. Examples of accrued expenses are salaries payable and interest payable. Salaries payable are wages earned by employees in one period but not paid until the next, while interest payable is interest expense that has been incurred but not paid.

accruals concept the practice of recognising revenues and their related expenses in the same accounting period in order to avoid misstating earnings for a period

accumulate gradually increase in numbers or amount

auditor an independent accountant who examines the accounts of a limited company on behalf of the owners to see if they show a 'true and fair' view of how the business is performing

back up to make a copy of information stored on a computer

balancing off finding the difference between the two sides of an account

bank reconciliation statement a statement comparing the cash book balance with the bank statement balance

bankruptcy when someone is judged to be unable to pay their liabilities by a court of law

bank statement a statement issued by the bank to show the balance in a bank account and the amounts that have been paid into it and withdrawn from it

book of original entry the accounting journals in which business transactions are initially recorded. The information in these books is then summarised and posted into a general ledger, from which financial statements are produced

business document documents used when processing the sale or purchase of goods and services

business entity concept the principle that transactions associated with a business must be separately recorded from those of its owners or other businesses

capital money invested in the business by the owner(s)

Capital expenditure appears on the statement of financial position. Capital expenditure tends to last longer than a year and usually involves non-current assets.

capital receipts the sale of non-current assets

claimant someone who claims something, especially money, from the government, a court, etc., because they think they have a right to it

clear a cheque or payment clears when the money is sent from one bank to another

consistency concept one of the basic principles of accounting, which says that there should be consistency in accounting methods

cost of sales the direct costs, which are usually material and labour, to make a product

countersign sign a paper that has already been signed by someone else

credit an amount of money that is put into someone's bank account or added to another amount

credit balance a balance showing that more money has been received or is owed to a company than has been paid out or is owed by the company

cross reference in accounting, this refers to the practice of adding to the related accounting information in another location

debit a record in financial accounts that shows money that has been spent or that is owed

debit balance a balance showing that more money has been paid out or is owed by a company than has been received or is owed to the company

deed of partnership a formal agreement to begin a partnership

depletion when an amount of something is greatly reduced or nearly all used up

depreciation a reduction in the value of an asset over time, due in particular to wear and tear, e.g. the reduction in the value of a machine

dishonoured cheque a cheque that the bank will not pay because there is not enough money in the account to pay it

divorce of ownership when shareholders are owners of the business, but they are not necessarily involved in the day-to-day running of the business

double entry the accounting system in which each transaction is recorded twice, as a debit in one account and as a credit in another

drawings money taken (withdrawn) from the business by the owner(s)

GLOSSARY

financial statements documents produced by an organisation to show the financial status of a business at a particular time, including the income statement and the Statement of financial position

gross profit the difference between revenue and costs of sales. It is the profit figure before operating expenses have been deducted

imprest a sum of money given to someone in an organisation to make small payments

Income Statement a statement of all income and expenses recognised during a specified period

incorporation the official listing of a company by meeting certain legal requirements that apply in a particular country or a particular state; companies that are incorporated become corporations

inventory the value or quantity of raw materials, components and finished products that a business has.

irrecoverable debts debts that are not expected to be paid, for example if a customer is in financial difficulty

limited liability the legal responsibility to pay only a limited amount of debt if something bad happens to you or your company

limited partnership a type of partnership where partners are responsible for the partnership's debts only up to the amount they originally invested

liquidity the ability of a business to pay its debts / the level of funds available to pay trade payables

lodgement a receipt that has been entered in the cash book but has not yet appeared on the bank statement

manufacturing account accounts that deal with making products rather than buying and selling them

materiality concept the principle that trivial matters can be disregarded, and important matters must be disclosed

money laundering hiding illegally obtained money in a business, e.g. exchanging good money (notes and coins) for stolen money through normal day-to-day business transactions

money measurement concept the fact that every transaction is measured using monetary measures, i.e. the local currency

non-current assets an asset that is assumed to be kept in the business for more than one year and will not be turned into cash within that year

other operating expenses the indirect costs of a business, which are not directly involved in the production process. Examples are the cost of rent, advertising, stationary and bank charges

patent buying the right to use another company's invention

payroll packages a software package that allows a firm to organise its staff wages and income tax

posting transferring balances from the accounts into the nominal ledger

profitability the ability to make profit

prudence concept accountants should use a conservative approach when preparing financial statements and should not overstate revenue/assets and not understate losses and liabilities

remittance an amount of money that you send to pay for something

revenue expenditure expenditure that does not increase the value of non-current assets but is incurred in the day-to-day running expenses of the business

revenue receipts receipts from the normal trading activities of the business

royalty an amount paid to use a patent

sole trader an individual who owns his or her own business

statement of affairs a document showing a company's assets and liabilities at a certain date, usually prepared when a company is about to go bankrupt

Statement of Financial Position shows the value of a business on a specific date, including the assets, liabilities and capital

suspense account an account in the general ledger in which amounts are temporarily recorded

trade payables suppliers who we still owe money to the business

undercast undervalue

unlimited liability full responsibility for the debts of the business

unpresented cheque a cheque that has not yet cleared through the banking system

work in progress items or goods that the business has not yet completed

whistleblower a person who exposes any kind of information or activity that is deemed illegal, dishonest, or not correct within an organisation that is either private or public

ACCOUNTING STANDARDS TERMINOLOGY

IAS / IFRS TERMINOLOGY (International Accounting Standards / International Finance Reporting Standards)	PREVIOUSLY USED UK GAAP TERMINOLOGY (Generally Accepted Accounting Practice in the UK)
Financial statements	Final accounts
Statement of profit or loss and other comprehensive income	**Trading and profit and loss account**
Revenue	Sales
Raw materials/ordinary goods purchased	Purchases
Cost of sales	Cost of goods sold
Inventory	Stock
Work in progress	Work in progress
Gross profit	Gross profit
Other operating expenses	Sundry expenses
Allowance for irrecoverable debt	Provision for doubtful debt
Other operating income	Sundry income
Investment revenues/finance income	Interest receivable
Finance costs	Interest payable
Profit for the year	Net profit
Retained earnings	Profit/loss balance
Statement of changes in equity (limited companies)	**Appropriation account**
Statement of financial position	**Balance sheet**
Non-current assets	**Fixed assets**
Property	Land and buildings
Plant and equipment	Plant and equipment
Investment property	Investments
Intangible assets	Goodwill etc
Current assets	**Current assets**
Inventory	Stock
Trade receivables	Debtors
Other receivables	Prepayments
Bank and cash	Bank and cash
Current liabilities	**Current liabilities/creditors: amounts due within 12 months**
Trade payables	Creditors
Other payables	Accruals
Bank overdraft and loans	Loans repayable within 12 months
Non-current liabilities	**Long term liabilities/creditors: amounts falling due after 12 months**
Bank (and other) loans	Loans repayable after 12 months
Capital or equity	**Capital**
Share capital	Share capital
Statement of cash flows	**Cash flow statement**
Other terms	
Inventory count	Stock take
Carrying value	Net book value

INDEX

A

accountants 5, 21, 81
   see also auditors; ethics
accounting concepts (principles) 24, 152–7
   see also accounting period concept; accruals (matching) concept; business entity concept; consistency concept; materiality concept; money measurement concept; prudence concept
accounting departments 22–3
accounting equation 61, 63
accounting period concept 121, 156, 163, 169, 171, 172, 190, 194, 197
accounting ratios 206–16
accounts 38, 61–2, 238
   see also accounts payable; accounts receivable; statements of account
   appropriation 219–23, 225, 240
   balancing off 75–80, 100–5, 238
   bank 13, 14
   capital 62–3, 64–5, 66, 67, 163–5, 221–3
   contra 127, 128, 129
   control 121–31
   current 221–3
   expense 78, 110, 154, 176, 177, 197
   manufacturing 228, 231–3, 238
   purchase returns 42, 44, 71, 82, 159, 196
   purchases 40, 82
   revenue returns 44, 45, 71–2, 74, 79, 82, 196
   sales revenue 82
   software for (computerised) 11, 12–18, 61, 87, 128
   suspense 114, 115–16, 239
   T 64, 200–1
   three-column 78
   trading 159, 165, 233–4
accounts payable 22
accounts receivable 23
accruals 169–82
accruals (matching) concept 154, 170, 181, 238
accumulation 89–90, 229, 238
acid test ratio see liquid ratio
adjustments 174–8
   bank overdrafts 137
   expenses 169
   incomplete records 195, 196
   irrecoverable debt 185–6
   revenue owing end of period 72–3
   stock carried forward 171–2
Adobe 11
Alibaba 12
Amazon 12
anti-spyware software 17
antivirus software 17
appropriation accounts 219–23, 225, 240
apps 13
assets 62–63, 69, 70, 71, 81, 87
   net 163, 164, 176, 192, 194, 198, 209, 211
   non-current 86, 89–90, 93–4, 95, 146–7, 162, 239, 240
auditors 7, 185, 238
audits 7, 23

B

back up (data) 15, 17, 18, 238
BACS 32, 139
bad debts 56–7, 178, 196
   see also irrecoverable debts
balance brought down (b/d) 76, 77, 123
balance brought forward (b/f) 76, 77
balance carried down (c/d) 76, 77, 123
balance sheets see statements of financial position
balancing off accounts 75–80, 100–5, 238
bank accounts 13, 14
bank charges 139
bank overdrafts 50–2, 137
bank reconciliation statements 132–43, 238
bank statements 131, 132, 135, 139
bank summaries 193, 197
bank transfers 132
Bankers' Automated Clearing Services 32, 137
banking transactions 130–1
bankruptcy 5, 181, 236
bookkeeping 27–97

books of original entry 36, 54, 58, 238
   see also cash books; journals; petty cash books; purchase returns day books; purchases day
      books; sales day books; sales return days books
business documentation 28–35, 36, 238
business entity concept 155, 238
business organisations 4–10
   see also limited partnerships; partnerships; private limited companies; public limited companies (plcs); sole traders
business transactions 61

C

capital 5, 6, 190–1, 220, 238, 240
   see also closing capital
capital accounts 62–3, 64–5, 66, 67, 163–5, 221–3
capital expenditure 146–7, 148–9, 150
capital receipts 147, 238
carriage inwards 159, 165
carriage outwards 165, 174, 175
cash books 37, 46, 47–55, 124, 125, 132–3, 135–6, 137
cash discounts 45–50, 68, 124
cash flow statements see statements of cash flow
cash revenue 40, 75
cash summaries 195, 199
cash transactions 62–6, 73, 80
cheques 132, 133, 134, 138–9, 238, 239
claimants 33
clearing payments 132, 238
closing capital 164, 176, 191, 193, 198, 208, 209, 211
cloud 12, 238
Companies Act (2006) 7
Companies House 9
   see also Registrar of Companies
compensating errors 81, 109, 111–12
competitors 8, 21, 22, 23
complete reversal of entries 81, 108, 112–13
computer hardware 12, 17, 18, 87

INDEX

computer security 15, 17
computer software (computerised accounts) 11, 12–18, 61, 87, 128, 239
confidentiality 21–2
consistency concept 153, 238
contra accounts 127, 128, 129
contracts 5, 29
　see also deeds of partnership
control accounts 121–31, 200–1
conveyancing 148
costs
　cost of sales (cost of goods sold) 158, 160, 201
　direct 229, 236
　fixed 234, 238
　indirect 229, 236
　manufacturing 229
　prime 229, 230, 231, 232, 233, 236
　production 229, 231
　unit cost of production 233
　variable 234, 239
countersignature 33, 238
credit (Cr) 39, 42, 62, 238
　see also 'in' and 'out' approach
credit balance 77, 238
credit notes 29, 30–1, 34, 36, 43–5
credit revenue (transactions) 40, 42, 68–75
cross referencing 178
current accounts 221–3
current assets 162, 240
current liabilities 162
current ratio 209–11, 212
customers 8, 23

D

data, protection of 15, 16–17, 18, 238
day books
　purchases 37, 38–9, 40
　purchases returns 37, 43, 124, 125
　sales 37, 40, 41, 124, 125
　sales (revenue) returns 37, 44, 45, 124, 125
debit (Dr) 39, 42, 62–3, 238
　see also 'in' and 'out' approach
debit balance 77–8, 238
debts, bad (irrecoverable) 56–7, 127, 129, 174, 178, 183–9, 196
decay 86
declining balance method see reducing balance method
deeds of partnership 5, 6, 238

depletion 87
depreciation 86–97, 174, 177–8, 197
direct costs 229, 236
direct debits 139
direct expenses 229
direct labour 229
direct materials 229
directors 7, 8
discounts, cash 45–50, 68, 124
discounts allowed 45–6, 177, 196
discounts received 45–6, 177, 196
dishonoured cheques 138–9, 238
disposal value 87, 89, 92
divorce of ownership 7, 238
documentation, business 28–35, 36, 238
double entry 11, 37, 39, 42, 50, 53–6, 57, 61–82, 91, 238
drawings 6, 163, 219, 220, 221–3, 238
　examples 164, 165, 174, 176, 198–200, 209, 211
Dyson Ltd 9

E

ebay 12
economic factors, depreciation 86–7
employees 8
equity 190–1, 210, 240
equity accounts 62–3, 64–5, 66, 67, 163–5
erosion 86
errors 81, 121, 128
　correction of 57, 104–5, 108–20
errors of commission 81, 109
errors of omission 81, 109, 111
errors of original entry 81, 108, 110–11
errors of principle 81, 108, 110
errors of transposition 81, 108
ethics 20–5
exam practice (questions)
　accounting environment 9–10, 18–19, 24–5
　bookkeeping 34–5, 57–9, 81–5, 95–7
　control processes 105–7, 117–20, 129–31, 140–3
　financial statements/ adjustments 150–1, 155–7, 165–8, 178–82, 187–9, 203–5, 213–16, 223–7, 235–7
expense accounts 78, 110, 154, 176, 177, 197
expenses 72–4, 154, 169–71, 173, 181, 229

　see also expense accounts

F

factory overhead costs 229
financial statements 23, 145–237
　see also statements of financial position
finished goods inventory 230, 231, 232, 233, 234
firewalls 17
fixed assets 81, 89, 90, 240
　see also non-current assets
fixed costs 234, 238
fixed instalment method 88
formulae (spreadsheets) 14
fraud prevention 128

G

general (nominal) ledgers 14, 37, 40–7, 60
government 8
gross profit 158, 159, 200
gross profit percentage 207–8, 212
guide for
　adjustments to financial statements 176–8
　incomplete records 194–8

H

hard drives 12, 16, 17
hardware 12, 17, 18, 87
health risks 15

I

IASB 152, 240
ICAI 81
IESBA 23
impersonal accounts 38
imprest 53
'in' and 'out' approach 63–8, 69–74
inadequacy 87
income statements 158–63, 165, 188, 219, 230–2, 233–4
　examples 91, 92, 175, 185–6, 197, 201, 207, 211
incomplete records 190–205
incorporations (Inc) 7, 9, 238
indirect costs 229, 237
information, management 128
　see also management reports; manual records
information technology 11–19
Institute of Chartered Accountants of India 81
intangible assets 162

INDEX

integrity 21
interest 23
interest (bank) 139
interest on capital 220
interest on drawings 220
internal audits 23
International Accounting Standards Board 152, 240
International Ethics Standards Board for Accountants 23
International Federation of Accountants 21
internet 12, 15, 17
inventory 68–70, 82, 153, 238
    finished goods 230, 231, 232, 233, 234
    raw materials 229, 230, 232, 234
    work-in-progress 230, 231, 232
inventory checks 13
inventory control 13, 14, 16
invoices 29, 30, 34, 38–41
irrecoverable debts 127, 129, 174, 178, 183–9
    see also bad debts
IT 11–19
IT departments 11

J
journals 37, 54–7, 114–15
    examples 109, 110, 111, 112, 113, 116

K
knowledge 21

L
labour costs 229
leases 87
ledgers 37, 60–1
    see also general (nominal) ledgers; purchases (payables) ledgers; receivables ledgers (revenue ledgers)
liabilities 62–3, 68, 69, 71, 162–3, 240
    see also limited liability; limited partnerships, unlimited liability
limited companies 7, 9, 152, 240
limited liability 7, 238
Limited Liability Partnership Act (2000) 219
limited partnerships 6, 218, 219, 238
liquid ratio 209, 210, 212
liquidity 8, 207, 238
liquidity ratios 209–10

lodgements 135, 238
long term liabilities 240
    see also non-current liabilities

M
management information (reports) 13, 14, 128
manual records 61
manufacturing accounts 228, 231–3, 238
manufacturing costs 229
manufacturing sector 228–37
matching (accruals) concept 154, 170, 181, 238
materiality concept 154, 239
memory sticks 16
missing figures 198–200
money laundering 22
money measurement concept 155, 239

N
net assets 163, 164, 176, 192, 194, 198, 209, 211
Nissan 234
nominal accounts 38
nominal (general) ledgers 14, 37, 40–7, 60
non-current assets 86, 89–90, 93–4, 95, 146–7, 162, 239, 240
non-current liabilities 163, 240

O
objectivity 21
obsolescence 87
off-the-shelf software packages 11
online banking 13
operating systems 12, 17
organisation type 4–10
    see also limited partnerships; partnerships; private limited companies; public limited companies (plcs); sole traders
overcasting 105
overdrafts 50–2, 137

P
Pacioli, Luca 57, 61
Partnership Act (1890) 5, 219
Partnership Act (1932) 5
partnerships 5–7, 9, 217–27
    see also deeds of partnership
passwords 12, 15, 16, 17
payables (purchases) 54–5, 177
    see also accounts payable

payables (purchases) control accounts 121, 122, 124, 125, 126, 128, 129
payables (purchases) ledgers 12, 14, 37, 39–40, 43, 47, 60, 125–6, 127
payroll 23
payroll packages 13, 14, 239
personal accounts 38
petty cash books 33, 37, 51–5
petty cash vouchers 51, 52
physical depreciation 86
plcs (public limited companies) 7, 9, 152
posting 37, 60, 239
prepaid expenses 169–71, 173
prepayments 169–82
prime costs 229, 230, 231, 232, 233, 236
private ledgers 61
private limited companies 7, 9
private sector organisations 7, 9
production costs 229, 231
professional behaviour 22
professional competence and due care 21
professional ethics 20–5
profit
    gross 158, 159, 200
    gross profit percentage 207–8, 212
    profit for the year 158, 191, 197, 203
    profit for the year as a percentage of revenue 208, 212
    see also share of profits
profitability 206–9, 239
profitability ratios 207–9
provision
    for depreciation accounts 89–93
    irrecoverable debts 178, 185–7, 188
prudence concept 153, 183, 185, 239
public 23
public interest 22, 23
public limited companies (plcs) 7, 9, 152
public sector organisations 7–8
purchase invoices 38–40
purchase orders 29
purchase returns (accounts) 42, 44, 71, 82, 159, 196
purchase returns day books 37, 43, 124, 125
purchases 12, 14, 82

see also purchase orders; purchase returns (accounts); purchase returns day books; purchases accounts; purchases day books; purchases (payables) ledgers
purchases accounts 40, 82
purchases day books 37, 38–9, 40
purchases (payables) ledgers 12, 14, 37, 39–40, 43, 47, 60, 125–6, 127

Q
Quickbooks 11

R
raw materials inventory 229, 230, 232, 234
raw materials/ ordinary goods purchased 74, 75, 154, 195, 229
real accounts 38
receipts 33, 147, 238, 239
   see also lodgements
receivables 176–7
   see also accounts receivable
receivables control accounts 121, 122–3, 125–8, 129, 196, 200–1
receivables ledgers (revenue ledgers) 13, 14, 37, 39, 60
   examples 39, 41, 42, 45, 47, 48–9, 126, 127
reconciliation statements 132–43, 238
reducing balance method 88–9, 177–8
Registrar of Companies 7, 218
   see also Companies House
remittance advices 12, 29, 32, 239
reports 12–14, 15, 23
   see also manual records
residual value see disposal value
'restoring' data 17
return on capital employed ratio 208, 212
returns 70–2
returns inwards see revenue returns (accounts)
returns outwards see purchase returns (accounts)
revenue 12, 74, 154, 196
   cash 40, 75
   credit 40, 42, 68–75
   see also receivables ledgers (revenue ledgers); revenue expenditure; revenue invoices; revenue returns (accounts); revenue returns day books; sales returns day books
revenue expenditure 147–50, 154, 239
revenue invoices 40–1
revenue inwards see revenue returns (accounts)
revenue owing at end of period 172–3
revenue receipts 147, 239
revenue returns (accounts) 44, 45, 71–2, 74, 79, 82, 196
revenue returns day books 45
   see also sales returns day books
ROCE (return on capital employed) 208, 212
rust 86

S
Sage 11
salaries, partnership 220
sales day books 37, 40, 41, 124, 125
sales ledgers *see* receivables ledgers (revenue ledgers)
sales returns 159
sales returns day books 37, 44, 124, 125
   see also revenue returns day books
sales revenue accounts 82
Satyam Computer Services scandal 22
scrap value see disposal value
security, computer 15, 17
share of profits 220
shareholders 7, 8, 9, 23
skills 21
software (computerised accounts) 11, 12–18, 61, 87, 128, 239
sole traders 5, 7, 9, 158–68, 174–6, 239
spreadsheets 14
SRDB see sales returns day books
stakeholders 8, 9, 24
standing orders 139
statements of account 29, 31–2, 34
statements of affairs 191–2, 194, 239
statements of cash flow 23, 240
statements of comprehensive income 8, 23, 239
statements of financial position 8, 23, 161–5, 239
   accounting ratios 208–9, 211
   depreciation 90, 91, 93
   incomplete records 198
   irrecoverable debt 185, 186
   manufacturing 232–3, 234
   prepayments and accruals 173, 176, 177, 178
   suspense accounts 114
statements of profit or loss 148, 161, 193, 197, 229, 240
stock carried forward 171–2
straight line method 87–8, 89, 177
suppliers 8
   terms and conditions 68
suspense accounts 114, 115–16, 239

T
T accounts 64, 200–2
tangible assets 162
taxpayers 23
technology 11–19
   see also cloud
Tesco 117
three-column accounts 78
three-column cash books 48
time limits, depreciation 87
total accounts see control accounts
trading 28
trading accounts 159, 165, 233–4
training 15, 18
trial balances 101–7, 114–17, 158–9, 161, 163, 165, 174

U
undercasting 105, 114–15, 239
unit cost of production 233
unlimited liability 5, 239
unlimited partnerships 5–6, 218
unpresented cheques 133, 134, 239

V
variable costs 234, 239
VisiCalc 14

W
Waste Management Inc. 86
wear and tear 86
websites 12
whistleblowers 117, 239
work-in-progress inventory 230, 231, 232
working capital/equity 164, 210
working capital ratio see current ratio
writing off bad debts 56–7

NOTES

NOTES

NOTES